Taking the University to the People

SEVENTY-FIVE YEARS OF COOPERATIVE EXTENSION

TAKING THE
UNIVERSITY
TO THE
PEOPLE

Seventy-five Years of Cooperative Extension

WAYNE D. RASMUSSEN

IS IOWA STATE UNIVERSITY PRESS / AMES

Wayne D. Rasmussen grew up on a ranch near Lavina, Montana. He worked as a ranch hand, surveyor, and country school teacher before graduating from the University of Montana in 1937 and moving to Washington, D.C., to work for the Department of Agriculture. After serving four years in the Army during World War II, he was the Historian for the Department of Agriculture until his retirement in 1986. He earned a Ph.D. degree from George Washington University in 1950 and was awarded honorary doctorates by George Washington University and the University of Montana in 1987 and 1988, respectively. He has received the Department of Agriculture's Distinguished Service Award and is a Fellow of the American Agricultural Economics Association. Past President of the Agricultural History Society, he is currently its Executive Secretary-Treasurer. He is the author of numerous books, bulletins, and articles, and the editor of the four-volume work, *Agriculture in the United States: A Documentary History* (1975).

FRONTISPIECE. The Norman Rockwell painting of a county agent demonstrating a Guernsey heifer with a 4-H member and family looking on became a famous visual for county agent work and Extension Service programs. It still hangs in many county Extension offices. (Printed by permission of the Estate of Norman Rockwell. Copyright © 1948 Estate of Norman Rockwell)

© 1989 Iowa State University Press, Ames, Iowa 50010
All rights reserved

Manufactured in the United States of America

First edition, 1989

International Standard Book Number: 0–8138–0419–1

Library of Congress Cataloging-in-Publication Data

Rasmussen, Wayne David, 1915–
    Taking the university to the people : seventy-five years of cooperative extension / Wayne D. Rasmussen. — 1st ed.
        p.   cm.
    Bibliography: p.
    Includes index.
    ISBN 0–8138–0419–1
    1. United States. Federal Extension Service — History.   2. Agricultural extension work — United States — History.   I. Title.
S544.R37   1989
630′.7′15073 — dc19   88–37672
                                                                                                     CIP

Contents

Foreword

WHEN President Woodrow Wilson signed the Smith-Lever Act on May 8, 1914, he called it "one of the most significant and far-reaching measures for the education of adults ever adopted by the government." Its purpose, clearly stated by Congress, was "to aid in diffusing among the people of the U.S. useful and practical information on subjects related to agriculture and home economics, and to encourage the application of the same."

Extension work was to "consist of giving of instruction and practical demonstrations in agriculture and home economics to persons not attending or resident in said colleges in the several communities, and imparting to such persons information on said subjects through field demonstrations, publications and otherwise."

The underlying philosophy of the system was to "help people help themselves" by "taking the university to the people." The system evolved into an institution that is responsive to priority needs and focuses its resources on providing quality information, education, and problem-solving programs on real concerns.

An early form of cost sharing, the act required matching funds from state and local sources. Thus, it ultimately became known as the Cooperative Extension System. Today, the federal partner funds approximately 30 percent of the system, state and local funds provide the remaining 70 percent, with the state usually, but not always, the dominant funding source. Each state extension service is headquartered at a land-grant university and usually is closely associated with the agricultural experiment station. This tripartite arrangement—the land-grant university, agricultural experiment station, and cooperative extension service—is a uniquely American institution. No other country has focused such attention on the practical (applied) dimension of education by extending and applying the knowledge base of our land-grant universities to the laboratories of real life where people live and work, develop and lead. Extension has been copied by many countries, but is yet to be duplicated.

The Extension Services played pivotal roles in the nation's survival through three major emergencies—World War I, the Great Depression of the 1930s, and World War II. At this writing, agriculture and rural America again are in deep economic difficulty—suffering from cash flow problems, significant asset deflation, and widespread drought. The Extension Service's ability to adapt to local, state, and/or national issues has continued to be a source of strength and resilience in times of crisis.

The staffing pattern of the Cooperative Extension System is symbolic of its educational strengths—1 percent at the federal level, approximately one-third at the land-grant university, and two-thirds located in nearly all of the nation's 3,150 counties. In addition, more than two million volunteer leaders assist in extending programs under training and direction from the professional staff—thus the origin of the term "grass-roots" organization.

As the Cooperative Extension System reaches its diamond anniversary, it is giving serious attention to restating its mission, whom it should serve, its management, and its methods of determining issues and programs (Chapter 10). A history of the evolution of Extension is of some importance at this point in its life cycle. But, more important, a modern text detailing the unique characteristics, evolution of methodologies, and current institutional changes under way in the Cooperative Extension System is the more pertinent document.

The Extension Committee on Organization and Policy (ECOP) approved proceeding with this anniversary book and the establishment of a task force to oversee its publication in 1985. The Task Force was fortunate to obtain the services of Wayne Rasmussen, former chief, Agricultural History Branch, Economic Research Service, United States Department of Agriculture to research and author this book. Iowa State University Press graciously took on publishing responsibilities.

Initial major contributions underwriting the book's publication were made by Extension Service, United States Department of Agriculture, the National 4-H Council, and the Office of the Executive Director of ECOP. Additional contributions were made by the National Association of County Agricultural Agents, National Association of Extension Home Economists, National Association of Extension 4-H Agents, and Epsilon Sigma Phi. The remainder came from partners in the Extension System who guaranteed advance orders in excess of ten thousand copies.

The Task Force was involved with all aspects of this book from beginning to end. It expresses great appreciation to the author, to those whose financial support made the undertaking possible, and to all those who supplied more information and pictures than could possibly be used. Finally, it was inspired by the magnitude of change that extension education has made in the lives of people across this country and was challenged by the possibilities for the future.

SEVENTY-FIFTH ANNIVERSARY BOOK TASK FORCE

HENRY A. WADSWORTH, *Chair,* Purdue University
JOHN S. BOTTUM, Extension Service, USDA
DANNY L. CHEATHAM, Mississippi State University
FRED HARRISON, JR., Fort Valley State College
ROGER LAWRENCE, Iowa State University
LUCINDA A. NOBLE, Cornell University
GRANT A. SHRUM, National 4-H Council
HOWARD G. DIESSLIN, National Association of State Universities
and Land-Grant Colleges
MYRON D. JOHNSRUD, Administrator, Extension Service, USDA

Acknowledgments

Without the encouragement and counsel of literally hundreds of Extension people, from administrators, directors, and university staff to regional supervisors, county agents, and volunteers, this book commemorating the seventy-fifth anniversary of the Cooperative Extension System would have been impossible. It is a pleasure to dedicate the volume to them. I owe particular thanks to the chairman and members of the Seventy-fifth Anniversary Book Task Force of the Extension Committee on Organization and Policy. Many colleagues in the Department of Agriculture, particularly John E. Lee, Jr., Administrator, Economic Research Service, and the staff of the Agriculture and Rural History Section, and Joseph H. Howard, Director, National Agricultural Library, and his staff, gave both assistance and encouragement. Staff members of the National 4-H Council helped in many ways. I was fortunate to have Ovid Bay, formerly with the Extension Service, as picture editor of the volume. Juanita Holder patiently typed and retyped each chapter. Finally, Marion F. Rasmussen spent many hours proofreading and otherwise assisting with the book.

WAYNE D. RASMUSSEN

Taking the University to the People

SEVENTY-FIVE YEARS OF COOPERATIVE EXTENSION

CHAPTER ONE

Cooperative Extension: Taking the University to the People

Introduction. It was a warm spring day in Washington on May 8, 1914, when President Woodrow Wilson signed the Smith-Lever Act, establishing the Cooperative Extension Service. The local papers reported on the weather the next day, but said nothing about the new legislation that was to bring the university to the people. And even after seventy-five years, Extension people remain among the unsung heroes of the nation.

The Cooperative Extension System today is a unique achievement in American education. It is an agency for change and for problem solving, a catalyst for individual and group action with a history of seventy-five years of public service. Extension brings the rewards of higher education into the lives of all segments of our extraordinarily diverse population. At first, higher education in America was available only to the children of the well-to-do — the elite. The land-grant universities established under the provisions of the first and second Morrill Land-Grant College Acts in 1862 and 1890 provided an opportunity for the children of the working man to secure a higher education. Then came a new concept, which Cooperative Extension embodied, that the knowledge within the land-grant institutions should be made available to those not attending those institutions and should continue to be available throughout one's life. Thus was the university brought to the people.

Cooperative Extension includes professionals in America's 1862 land-grant universities in each of the fifty states, Puerto Rico, the Virgin Islands, Guam, American Samoa, Northern Mariannas, Micronesia, and the District of Columbia, in Tuskegee University and sixteen 1890 land-grant universities in sixteen states and in the federal Extension Service. With few exceptions, at least one professional Extension staff member works in each of the nation's 3,150 counties. In addition, thousands of paraprofessional staff and about 2.9 million volunteers assist in bringing programs to the people, working under the direction of the professional staff.

Extension Is Cooperation

COOPERATION WITHIN THE SYSTEM.   Extension was designed as a partnership of the land-grant universities and the U.S. Department of Agriculture (USDA). However, the provisions of the law were broad enough that the states were able to bring their counties into the system as a third legal partner. Today, Extension is truly a cooperative undertaking, with the county, state, and federal partners interdependent, yet with each having considerable independence in funding, staffing, and programming. Each partner performs distinct functions essential to the operation of the total system. Extension's organization and division of responsibilities and authorities can be compared to the American government, with its county, state, and federal units of government, each with its own responsibilities and authorities, and each with responsibilities for the nationwide system. And, like state and county governments, state and county Extension Services vary in organization but share a common mission.

Extension's educational program makes the results of research in the land-grant universities, the state agricultural experiment stations, and USDA available to all who need them. In turn, Extension reports problems facing its clientele to researchers and administrators. This cooperative two-way communication provides direction for research and education and speeds the application of research results.

The Cooperative Extension System's statement of mission is simple and straightforward: "The Cooperative Extension System helps people improve their lives through an educational process which uses scientific knowledge focused on issues and needs."

COOPERATION WITH PEOPLE.   Cooperation is the hallmark of Extension's relations with people. Its educational programs are available to anyone who wishes to participate, but no one is forced to take part. Within this voluntary cooperative framework, Extension, drawing upon research-based knowledge, teaches people to identify problems, to analyze information, to decide among alternative courses of action for dealing with those problems, and to locate the resources to accomplish a preferred course of action. The educational programs it undertakes most often arise as a response to needs identified on the local level. In addition to basic educational programs, Extension staff members and volunteers meet local needs by organizing such activities as weed and insect identification clinics, providing materials on the conservation of natural resources, distributing information about diet and health, and encouraging participation, especially by youth, in the educational aspects of county and state fairs.

Organizing within the System

THE FEDERAL PARTNER.   The federal Extension Service is headed by an administrator, who is a member of the Senior Executive Service and is appointed by the secretary of agriculture. The administrator is usually, but not always, chosen from among state directors of Extension. The first administrator, Clyde W. Warburton, served seventeen years. No one else has approached that record. Within USDA, the administrator reports to the assistant secretary for science and education. Most of the professional staff work within such major areas of responsibility as agriculture, home economics, youth, natural resources, and rural and community development, emphasizing national concerns within these areas. Overall, the staff mutually agrees on state plans of work and directs the allocation of federal funds, coordinates national initiatives, provides program leadership, maintains contact and interaction with USDA, other federal agencies, the Congress and national organizations, and assures accountability.

In 1988 Extension Service, USDA, adopted a mission statement: "The mission of Extension Service is to assure an effective nationwide Cooperative Extension System that is responsive to priority needs and the Federal interests and policies with quality information, education, and problem-solving programs."

THE STATE PARTNER.   State Extension Services in the land-grant universities created by the 1862 legislation usually are headed by directors, appointed by the universities with the concurrence of the secretary of agriculture. The Extension Services in the 1890 institutions and Tuskegee University usually are headed by administrators. These directors and administrators normally report to the dean of the College of Agriculture, although directors in states as diverse as Maine and California report to university vice-presidents. There is no fixed pattern for the organization of state Extension offices. All have staff members assigned to the major program areas within Extension, and many have specialists assigned to specific areas of importance within the state. Most of the specialists work within academic disciplines and most are members of academic departments.

Some states have specialists assigned to regional offices. Others assign specialists to county offices but make them responsible for their specialty in two or more counties. This latter means of assigning specialists' responsibilities occurs particularly frequently in states in which problems differ greatly in different areas of the state. For example, such significant differences exist between eastern and western Massachusetts. These specialists are readily available to the county Extension staffs.

Relationships between the federal Extension Service and the state Extension Services are outlined in memorandums of understanding between USDA and each of the 1862 and 1890 institutions. These standard memorandums are in effect in all but two states. In general, they outline division of responsibilities and include two basic agreements. First, each year every state will prepare a plan of work jointly approved by the state director in the 1862 institution and the administrator in the 1890 institution in the states where that institution exists and the administrator of the Extension Service, USDA. Second, the federal government will not run a competing direct national operation unless it is jointly worked out with the states. In addition, USDA and each state agree on an annual budget. The memorandum sets up a concept of joint employment that provides the state Extension Service access to the federal structure but with insulation from the political and regulatory functions of government at both the federal and state levels. It also provides for accountability, reporting, auditing, and sanctions for those who fail.

In 1977 Congress provided that not less than 4 percent of the total amount appropriated annually under authority of the Smith-Lever Act should be assigned to the 1890 institutions and Tuskegee University. Effective in 1983, the allocation was increased to 6 percent. The memorandum of understanding between each of the 1890 universities and Tuskegee University and USDA provides that the university maintain an administrative office for the conduct of Extension work. The 1862 and the 1890 institutions in each state mutually develop a plan of work for their state. This plan is reviewed and approved by the federal administrator of Extension.

THE COUNTY PARTNER.   In 1946 B. H. Crocheron, longtime director of the California Extension Service, said to the staff: " . . . to you who have known the long dark roads, the night meetings in lonely schoolhouses, the rain, the heat, the mud, the endless round of the daily task; to you who have worked so hard, to you who have accomplished so much; to you we say 'Well done!' " It is the men and women at the county level—the local agriculturalist, home economist, 4–H leader, community and rural development specialist—who actually carry the university to the people. But they do more. Howard G. Diesslin, retired executive director for Extension, National Association of State Universities and Land-Grant Colleges (NASULGC), put it this way: "County Extension agents constantly live amid and encourage change in people and their surroundings." Director Crocheron explained earlier: " . . . when farmers testify as to the value of the Extension Service it is not the savings and increased income that they so often bring forward as that the Extension Service has been a counselor, adviser, and friend. It is the human values of Extension work that are cited more frequently than any others." Or, as historian Barbara R. Cotton commented about the work of black agents in Florida before 1965: "When progress did come . . . it illuminated, for thousands of Blacks in Florida, the path for a journey into a better quality of living."

Today, the county agent, whatever his or her speciality, must often hold evening and weekend meetings at various locations and must be available constantly for consultation on a wide variety of topics. Every agent must be a communications expert, providing the link between the university and the people. The agent, however, is well prepared. Nearly all have bachelor's degrees, many have master's degrees, and some a doctorate. Several states now require that a new agent have a master's degree before consideration for appointment.

The way appointments to county professional staffs are made varies from state to state. Some states select staff members and assign them to counties, usually subject to the approval of the county governing body. Others send lists of qualified persons to the counties, where the selection is made. In still other states, the county board recruits and hires the person, subject to the approval of the state director.

The state director is responsible for the technical supervision of the county agent; the local community, often through an advisory board, usually is responsible for advising regarding the kinds of work the agent carries out. Salaries are paid sometimes by the state and sometimes by the local government. The local government usually is responsible for providing support staff and office space. The nature of the relationship of the county agent to USDA has varied over time, but in general, communication between the two is carried out through the office of the state director.

Communication is the key to the operations of the county Extension office. More and more county Extension offices are turning to computers and other electronic technology to improve the quality of communications with the state offices and with university specialists, as well as with the people they serve. Virginia Extension, for example, is using a computerized office project to integrate the new technology into the delivery of Extension educational programs. County Extension then encourages the use of computers by farmers, rural and small-town businessmen, local governments, and others. The success of the project in the Chesterfield County Extension Office is encouraging others to adopt it.

The county agent has changed over the past seventy-five years, but the successful agent still works to meet peoples' educational needs. As Marvin Anderson, former director of the Iowa Cooperative Extension Service wrote: "The agent is not so much the subject matter specialist but now needs to know more about people's needs, their problems, not to give answers but to mobilize the staff and resources to meet them."

Financing and Extension's Staff

FINANCES.   The Cooperative Extension System is financed primarily by federal, state, and local taxes, although substantial sums are contributed to Extension—mainly to 4-H—by private individuals and institutions. Volunteer services add greatly to the effectiveness of Extension's programs. In addition, the results of research carried on by the land-grant institutions and USDA provide the foundation for Extension's educational work.

The total Cooperative Extension System receives a bit more than $1 billion each year. In 1986 32 percent of this came from federal sources, 47 percent from state funds, 18 percent from local governments, and 3 percent from private contributions. In addition, Extension estimates that the total value of "in kind" and volunteer services is the equivalent of more than $4 billion.

THE STAFF.   The funding available provides the equivalent of about 170 full-time professional and support positions at the federal level. States and counties have the equivalent of some 16,500 full-time professional Extension agents and specialists developing and delivering educational programs, approximately two-thirds of whom are located in county Extension offices. About 3,300 nutrition aides work with low-income families on programs related to nutrition, diet, and health. Volunteers contribute varying periods of time to different types of programs.

Organizations in Support of Extension.   A number of organizations support Extension in various ways. These groups include a policy development and planning body, farm and other national organizations, program-oriented clubs of users, and professional organizations of Extension staff members. Many of these groups are discussed in greater detail in subsequent chapters.

EXTENSION COMMITTEE ON ORGANIZATION AND POLICY.   The state Extension Services depend on the Extension Committee on Organization and Policy (ECOP) of the National Association of State Universities and Land-Grant Colleges (NASULGC) as their national-level policy development and planning body. An outgrowth of earlier committees, ECOP dates back to 1915. It consists of fourteen voting members, three elected from each of four regional associations and two from the 1890 institutions, and two ex-officio nonvoting members — the administrator of the Extension Service, USDA, and the executive director of ECOP. The committee operates through standing and ad hoc subcommittees and task forces, which make recommendations to the committee. The committee in turn makes recommendations to NASULGC and advises the Extension Service, USDA. ECOP is a guiding force in developing Extension policies and in providing comprehensive program leadership. The committee's stated mission "is to provide nationwide program and organization leadership and to make and communicate policy decisions."

FARM ORGANIZATIONS.   In its early days, Extension depended upon local organizations of farmers to sponsor county agents. In most states, formal relationships developed with state and local farm bureaus. However, particularly after protests from other farm organizations, these relationships came to an end. In some states local farm groups continue to advise and work with their county Extension staffs.

4-H ORGANIZATIONS.   The National 4-H Council was established in 1976 as a consolidation of the National 4-H Service Committee and the National 4-H Foundation. It operates the National 4-H Center in Chevy Chase, Maryland, as a training center for young people and for adults, both volunteers and staff. The center also serves as the site for National 4-H Conferences. The 4-H Council complements the Cooperative Extension Service, drawing upon private funding for its work.

The Extension Service carries on much of its youth activity through 4-H groups, organized and overseen by 4-H or other agents in county Extension offices. However, much of the work with 4-H'ers is carried out by adult and teen volunteer leaders. In 1987 the Cooperative Extension System reported that it had more than 600,000 volunteer 4-H leaders.

NATIONAL EXTENSION HOMEMAKERS COUNCIL. The National Extension Homemakers Council, organized in 1936, is made up of 30,000 homemakers clubs with some 500,000 members. The clubs often are organized by the home economist on the county Extension staff, but leadership and program activities are carried out in large part by volunteers, with the home economist serving as a resource person. The council, dedicated to improving the quality of family life, advises and gives support to Extension's home economics programs.

NATIONAL ASSOCIATION OF COUNTY AGRICULTURAL AGENTS. The National Association of County Agricultural Agents was organized in 1915, the first professional association in the Cooperative Extension System. It is an organization of state associations of county agricultural agents. Its primary concern is to maintain and improve professional standards, and it has had marked success in meeting this goal. The association publishes a quarterly journal, the *County Agent*. It has some 5,200 members.

NATIONAL ASSOCIATION OF EXTENSION HOME ECONO-MISTS. The National Association of Extension Home Economists, organized in 1933, was the second professional organization in the Cooperative Extension System. An important force in strengthening professionalism in the field of home economics, the association publishes a quarterly journal, the *Reporter*. Its membership totals about 3,700.

NATIONAL ASSOCIATION OF EXTENSION 4-H AGENTS. The National Association of Extension 4-H Agents was organized in 1946. It, like the other professional organizations of Extension workers, has sought to enhance the professional status of its members and to promote cooperation among all Extension personnel. The association publishes a quarterly newsletter, *News and Views*. It has about 3,000 members.

SECTIONS WITHIN PROFESSIONAL ORGANIZATIONS. Extension specialists in such fields as agricultural economics, animal husbandry, communications, community development, dairying, rural sociology, and soil conservation maintain interest groups within professional associations devoted to particular disciplines. These groups often hold sessions devoted to Extension's activities within the particular discipline.

EPSILON SIGMA PHI.   Epsilon Sigma Phi is primarily a Cooperative Extension System honor society, based on tenure and quality of service. The society was organized in 1927, after W. A. Lloyd, then of the Montana Extension Service, corresponded with a number of veteran Extension workers about motivation and found that most of these individuals were characterized by a deep idealism. He proposed to ECOP that this idealism be recognized by the creation of an honor society. ECOP endorsed the idea, which was then approved by NASULGC, and state chapters were rapidly organized. In 1934 Epsilon Sigma Phi adopted a national award program, with the highest honor being the Distinguished Service Ruby. No more than one such award is made each year. The society promotes a fraternal relationship among Extension workers as well as a highly professional attitude. It numbers 11,200 members.

Epsilon Sigma Phi commemorated the founding of Extension through the Wilson and Knapp Memorial Arches in Washington, D.C., honoring the services of James Wilson, Secretary of Agriculture 1897– 1913, and Seaman A. Knapp, key figure in the organization of the Cooperative Extension System. The arches over Independence Avenue connect the two major buildings of the USDA. When they were dedicated in 1937, Congressman A. Frank Lever, joint author of the Smith-Lever Act, said in speaking of Wilson and Knapp: "To them, the mechanics of the farm were important only as incidental in the enrichment of the lives of the men and women, boys and girls, engaged in it. Their first concern was with broad humanities – People."

Reaching Out Today
REACHING MORE AMERICANS.   County Extension staff members and others in the Cooperative Extension System are reaching more people in more ways than ever before. Extension is taking the univer-

sity to the people by conducting research-based educational programs for many of the diverse groups making up our nation. Insofar as its funding and staff permit, Extension, in addition to its traditional programs with farm families, is working with part-time farmers, rural residents, suburban dwellers, and city people in areas in which it is competent to fill demonstrated needs. However, some needs are not being met simply because funding and staff are not available. Yet Paul D. Warner and James A. Christenson, sociologists and Extension specialists at the University of Kentucky, after a nationwide survey, stated there is public consensus that future support for Extension should be at least as great as it is now. "Users," they say, "are more supportive than nonusers, support increases as the frequency of use increases, and the more satisfied people are with Extension, the more they want it supported." Warner and Christenson conclude that support can be built first by increasing the number of users and second by insuring a high level of satisfaction in users.

Within funding and staffing limitations, Extension staffs are educating city as well as rural people on the importance of diet to health and the need to conserve water and other natural resources. It is showing young people ways they can explore alternative career possibilities, teaching families how to improve their quality of life, helping communities in revitalization efforts, helping small businesses increase efficiency, and improving the competency of local government, as well as taking action to meet other needs. Today, Extension is what Extension does.

EXTENSION AROUND THE WORLD. If imitation is the sincerest form of flattery, then the Cooperative Extension System can feel proud because it is the most widely copied abroad of all American governmental institutions. In 1945 M. L. Wilson and Edmund deS. Brunner wrote: " . . . since extension work has been tried successfully in so many parts of the world thus far, it can be valuable to a high degree wherever its underlying principles are applied." Perhaps Wilson and Brunner were overly optimistic, since Extension in most nations has not been as effective as it has been in the United States. Often the problem abroad has been that Extension has simply tried to reinforce governmental policies and has operated from the top down, without the intermediate authority the United States has, in its state and county

Extension services, to modify national policies to meet local needs or to transmit the farmers' needs to higher levels of government.

Nevertheless, Extension is a force for change in many nations. Many leaders of foreign Extension services have been trained in the United States in land-grant universities and in federal, state, and county Extension offices. At the same time, many Extension people have accepted overseas assignments to help developing nations establish Extension services. Frequently other Extension specialists have worked as part of a team recruited by one of the land-grant universities and financed by the Agency for International Development, the World Bank, the Ford Foundation, the Rockefeller Foundation, the Kellogg Foundation, or another internationally oriented institution. They have helped nations improve their agriculture, diets, markets, rural infrastructures, and other aspects of life. Extension today is a force for improving the quality of life in many nations.

The International Four-H Youth Exchange (IFYE) helps young people in many nations develop an understanding of people in other parts of the world. Each year, under the sponsorship of the National 4-H Council, young Americans travel overseas and live with families in foreign countries for a month or longer. Similarly, young people from many nations live with American families for varying periods of time. Those taking part, whether from the United States or one of the more than fifty other countries participating, often become ambassadors of good will in their communities and usually maintain long-term ties with families overseas.

Seventy-five Years of Change.   Through two world wars, the most severe depression the nation has ever seen, drought that sent dust storms rolling across the entire nation, and a farm depression that seriously affected a third of the nation's farms and many rural communities, Extension has been a force for sustained, rational change that improves the quality of American life. It has taken the university to the people. Indeed, it is the university of the people. Extension has been a quiet — perhaps too quiet — influence in assuring the American people a safe, sure supply of healthful food at less cost than in any other industrial nation in the world. Today, less than 3 percent of the work force produces that food, compared with 33 percent seventy-five years ago. Today, most Americans are aware of the relationship between diet and health, something we were just beginning to understand seventy-five years ago. Today, young people have opportunities to explore alternative occupations, while seventy-five years ago most simply did what their parents had done. Today, Americans are concerned with the wise use of natural resources, while seventy-five years ago they lived in an age in which such resources were carelessly exploited. Seventy-five years ago, Extension served mainly rural people. Today, while Extension serves a larger percentage of the rural population than the urban, it serves overall more urban residents than rural. Today, Extension stands on the threshold of a new beginning. Where Extension has been, where it is now, and where it may be going as it begins its seventy-sixth year of service to the American people is the subject of this book.

CHAPTER TWO

In the Beginning

Introduction.   Extension was invented by the American people to meet a vital educational need — the need to provide an educational base for making rural life profitable, healthful, comfortable, and attractive. Early attempts to meet this concern by government, private organizations, and individuals were helpful and contributed to the eventual invention of Extension and to its success. However, it took nearly three-quarters of a century after George Washington was inaugurated as our first president to establish the land-grant university system and still another half-century to establish Extension.

   This chapter begins with a discussion of early efforts to create a system of agricultural education and continues with a description of successful actions to obtain legislation establishing the land-grant universities. It concludes with a review of early efforts to carry the results of research to farmers and the appearance of the county agent.

Early Proposals for Agricultural Education.

   FEDERAL EFFORTS.   At the time of the American Revolution, 90 percent of the population lived on farms. Indeed, English attempts to control the westward movement of Americans and to tax the major agricultural exports of the colonists had been important causes of the revolt. It was farmers who fought and won the war for independence, and the new constitution reflected some of their concerns. Apparently, though, no thought was given to special considerations for them. After all, they were the largest segment of the population and whatever helped the new nation should have been of benefit to them.

In 1796, however, George Washington in his last annual presidential message to Congress proposed that a board or office be established to promote agriculture. He commented:

> It will not be doubted that with reference either to individual or national welfare agriculture is of primary importance. In proportion as nations advance in population and other circumstances of maturity this truth becomes more apparent, and renders the cultivation of the soil more and more an object of public patronage. Institutions for promoting it grow up, supported by the public purse; and to what object can it be dedicated with greater propriety? . . . Experience accordingly has shown that they are very cheap instruments of immense national benefits.

What Washington wrote in 1796 about the costs and benefits of "collecting and diffusing information" in agriculture can well be applied to Extension today.

The first federal efforts, though, on behalf of agriculture were not collecting and distributing information. Rather, they were collecting and distributing new and valuable seeds and plants. From time to time diplomatic representatives and naval officers of the new nation collected seeds and cuttings, and even unusual breeds of animals, during their travels. These they sent to federal officials, journalists, and friends. In 1819 the secretary of the treasury sent a circular letter to all consular officials, asking them to obtain useful seeds, plants, and inventions, but no money was appropriated for this purpose and not much happened. In 1825 President John Quincy Adams urged legislation for the promotion of agriculture and directed consuls to forward rare plants and seeds for distribution.

Some of the plants and seeds sent in response to the directives were lost because there was no system for their care and distribution. Commissioner of Patents Henry L. Ellsworth determined to do something about the situation and set up a system for collecting and distributing seeds. Ellsworth advocated many other activities to benefit agriculture, including a series of lectures for farmers' sons on improving agriculture. In 1839 Congress granted one thousand dollars from the Patent Office fund for the collection of statistics and for other purposes. Because the Census of 1840 for the first time had included agricultural inquiries, Ellsworth spent little on statistics. He began emphasizing agriculture in his reports and in 1842 issued the first of what were to become annual volumes on agriculture. While of limited value, consisting as they did mainly of items reproduced from the press and letters from individuals reporting upon their experiments, these annual publications were a first major step by the federal government toward acquiring and disseminating agricultural information.

AGRICULTURAL SOCIETIES AND CLUBS.   After the Revolution groups of men, usually well-to-do gentlemen farmers, began to get together to discuss ways to improve agriculture. Eventually, they formed such agricultural societies as the South Carolina Society for Promoting and Improving Agriculture and the Philadelphia Society for Promoting Agriculture, both organized in 1785. These societies usually offered premiums for agricultural improvements, sponsored lectures, and published reports on the agricultural accomplishments of members. However, their activities simply did not reach the ordinary farmer.

The Massachusetts Society for Promoting Agriculture made attempts to reach local farmers when its trustees recommended in 1792 that members hold meetings for persons interested in improving agriculture. The society went even farther in 1812 when it sent out one thousand letters intended to interest farmers in improvements. The society asked town clerks and the clergy to assist in the movement and to organize local societies.

Meanwhile, Elkanah Watson, an ex-banker and gentleman farmer, exhibited Merino sheep in the town square in Pittsfield, Massachusetts, in 1809. In 1812 he organized the Berkshire Agricultural Society. The society was to hold an exhibition or fair each year, with prizes for the best products exhibited. The movement spread rapidly across New England, giving many farmers an opportunity to show their accomplishments and to exchange information. Sometimes lectures on agricultural subjects were given by society members or university professors. However, the movement declined in the 1820s partly, at least, because of an agricultural depression.

FARM JOURNALS.   The first farm journal in America, the *Agricultural Museum*, began publication in the District of Columbia in 1810. It survived for only two years. In 1819, John Stuart Skinner of Baltimore began the *American Farmer*, destined to be both long-lived and influential. Skinner encouraged farmers to report on their achievements and their methods of solving problems. Some worthwhile ideas, along with some utterly useless ones, appeared on the pages of the journal. On the whole, the *American Farmer* and the many other periodicals that were started before the Civil War benefitted farmers by encouraging them to exchange ideas and to adopt improved methods. Most farmers, though, did not subscribe to any farm journal.

EDUCATIONAL INSTITUTIONS.   Nearly every one of the founding fathers of the new nation, from Virginia planter Thomas Jefferson to Puritanical New Englander John Adams, insisted that education must be available to every American. One of the first basic laws passed by the Congress, the Ordinance of 1785, provided that one section in every public land township should be reserved for the support of public schools, and as new states were admitted to the Union nearly all were given land to sell or otherwise use to establish universities. While most of the private institutions and state universities ignored agriculture, some such as Columbia University and Yale College established professorships of agricultural chemistry or of botany and agriculture.

Very early, both the agricultural societies and the farm journals began calling for educational programs aimed at farmers. Many farm editors urged the establishment of agricultural schools and colleges. In 1844 the editor of the *American Agriculturist* complained: "It is painful to think of the wealth which is annually lavished on vanity and folly in this country, which might, if the owners would but will it, be devoted to the glorious cause of the advancement of the science and practice of agriculture." A few agricultural schools and academies were founded in the first half of the century; the Gardener Lyceum in Gardener, Maine, established in 1821, was one of the first. Most of them, including the Gardener institution, were short-lived.

These limited efforts led advocates of agricultural education to look to state governments for aid. State agricultural colleges were established on a permanent basis by acts of state legislatures in Pennsyl-

vania and Michigan in 1855, in Maryland by an act of 1856, and in
Iowa by an act of 1858.

Many agricultural society leaders, farm journalists, and politicians
welcomed the state efforts but also urged that aid from the federal
government was necessary if agricultural education were to be available
throughout the nation. On January 21, 1841, Alden Partridge, then
president of Norwich University, proposed to Congress that it appropriate funds from the income of sales of public lands to be distributed to
the states in proportion to their representation in Congress. These
funds were to be used for the endowment of institutions to teach the
natural and economic sciences as applied to agriculture, engineering,
manufacturing, and commerce. This appears to be the first definite
proposal to Congress of its type. While it had no immediate impact, it
was a direct forerunner of proposals that other Americans would make
in the 1850s.

Farming and Rural Life in 1850.   Who were the Americans of
the 1850s who soon were to establish a nationwide system of agricultural colleges, a national department of agriculture, and a program
for giving federal land to settlers? In 1850, 11,680,000 farm residents
made up 50 percent of the population and 64 percent of the labor
force. There were one and a half million farms, averaging 200 acres in
size. Farmers were contributing mightily to the growth of the nation,
with 80 percent of total exports coming from farms.

COMMUNICATIONS.   Farm and rural life varied from one region
to another, from settled communities to isolated frontier holdings,
from family-operated farms to slave-worked plantations, from nearly
self-sufficient subsistence to market-oriented production. Communication from one part of the country to another was slow. The post office
provided service at reasonable cost in settled areas, but when someone
left the East for the frontier, communication became almost impossible. Railroads were beginning to connect cities and towns in the East
but had not reached beyond the Mississippi. Horse-drawn wagons and
buggies traveling over rough dirt roads provided farmers with their ties
to neighbors, towns, and markets.

SELF-SUFFICIENCY. Although not even an isolated frontier farm was entirely self-sufficient, all farms were much more so than they are today. Farm families raised nearly all of the food they consumed. Vegetables and fruits raised in the summer would be stored in caves or root cellars, or would be dried, pickled, or even canned for winter use. The meat from cattle and hogs slaughtered in the winter would be salted, pickled, or smoked for summer use. Chickens and milk cows supplied the farm family with eggs, meat, milk, and butter. Farm-produced grain was ground into flour or cornmeal at a local gristmill. The housewife then baked wheat bread or corn bread as the supplies on hand dictated. In many areas, wild game contributed to the food supply.

Very few farmhouses had running water or indoor sanitary facilities. They were heated by wood-burning fireplaces or stoves. Candles provided light. The wood came from the farm and the candles often were made in the home from animal fat. Some housewives spun wool from the farm sheep or linen thread from farm-produced flax. Much of the farm family's clothing was made in the home or purchased in the local village. Some farmers even made boots and shoes.

The farm itself was about as self-sufficient as the farmhouse. Much horse-drawn machinery had been invented, but most farmers had not yet purchased it. Plows were an exception. Whether made by the local blacksmith or in a factory, plows were purchased. Most of the metal tools, such as shovels, hoes, scythes, and axes, also were purchased. But harrows, rakes — including the horse-drawn kind — handles for metal tools, churns, and other simple devices often were made by the farmer. The farmer traditionally saved seed from one year to the next for both field and garden crops. Fertilizer, except in cotton and tobacco regions, was farm-produced manure if the farmer used fertilizer at all. Some farmers raised horses, but most purchased their teams and their wagons and buggies.

Farm families usually worked hard, sometimes in what seems to have been a life of drudgery. Amenities were few. Access to physicians was limited. Farm residents, particularly on the frontier and in other sparsely settled areas, often were isolated from other people. As has been pointed out in many studies, such isolation was felt particularly by the women on these farms.

EDUCATION.   As frontier areas were settled, women took the lead in establishing schools and churches. Both were regarded as essential for a stable community, whether the community was a village or town or simply a country crossroads. The extent of interest in making at least some education available to every young person varied from one part of the nation to another. As early as 1647 the Massachusetts Bay Colony had passed a law requiring that every town with fifty families employ a teacher of reading and writing and establish one elementary school. In every town of one hundred families, the law required establishment of a grammar school. This became the pattern in New England.

Even though the nation as a whole in the ordinances of 1785 and 1787 set aside public land for schools and declared that "schools and the means of education should be forever encouraged," another century would pass before all parts of the nation adopted the goal of universal education.

Morrill Land-Grant College Act.   Many people from many states supported agricultural education, but two people, Jonathan Baldwin Turner of Illinois and Justin S. Morrill of Vermont, were key figures in securing federal legislation. Turner, a native of Massachusetts and a graduate of Yale College, was a professor at Illinois College until ill health led him to turn to farming — a decision that might seem odd to a farmer. Nevertheless, he continued to agitate for what had become dominant goals in his life — the establishment, first, of common schools, and second, of agricultural colleges.

In the early 1850s Turner proposed that Illinois establish an industrial university to meet the needs of "cultivators of the soil, artisans, mechanics and merchants." Turner followed up the publication of his plan in the *Prairie Farmer* of January 1852 with a proposal that Congress grant public lands to each state for the establishment of industrial universities. This proposal was endorsed by the Illinois legislature and was presented to Congress in 1854. Many organizations endorsed the proposal, but a bill for the purpose was not introduced into Congress until 1857.

The bill was introduced by Representative Justin S. Morrill of Vermont. The reason Morrill was inspired to introduce the bill is something of a mystery. Although he had been a delegate to an 1856 meeting of the United States Agricultural Society at which the Turner proposal was discussed, Morrill never admitted to learning of Turner's plan. He said instead that he did not know where he received "the first hint of such a measure." In any case, the bill introduced by Morrill on December 14, 1857 provided for grants of public lands to the states to establish colleges to teach subjects related to "agriculture and the mechanic arts."

The bill passed both the House of Representatives and the Senate in 1859 in spite of the opposition of Southern members. These members opposed the bill on the grounds that it was unconstitutional and would enlarge the powers of the federal government at the expense of the states. Many Southerners saw little benefit to large plantation holders in such colleges. Instead, they would encourage small, non-slaveholding farmers, whose increase in number would threaten the delicate balance in Congress between slave and nonslave states. President Buchanan took the view that the bill was unconstitutional and vetoed it.

The controversies between the North and South deepened until in 1861, after Abraham Lincoln was elected president, most of the Southern states left the Union. In 1862 Congress passed and President Lincoln signed three new laws aimed particularly at assisting the family farmer—the Homestead Act, the Morrill Land-Grant College Act, and the act establishing the United States Department of Agriculture. The dream of a nationwide system of agricultural education was about to become a reality, and with it came a means for granting land to settlers and a national headquarters for disseminating information on agriculture.

The Morrill Land-Grant College Act granted each state public land in the amount of 30,000 acres for each of its Senate and House members. Since most of the states did not have that much unsold public land within their boundaries, they were given scrip to the public domain in states and territories having excess unclaimed acres. Each state was to use its money as a trust fund to endow a college where practical education in agriculture and engineering would be emphasized. Most of the states sold their scrip to land dealers at prices of between fifty cents and one dollar an acre and used the proceeds to establish new agricultural and mechanical colleges.

Implementing the Land-Grant College Act

THE SECOND MORRILL LAND-GRANT COLLEGE ACT.   The first land-grant college act gave land but no funds to the states. In 1872, Justin Morrill introduced a bill to make direct annual appropriations to each state and territory to support its land-grant college. The Second Morrill Act, as it was known, was passed in 1890. In addition to providing continuing funding, the act prohibited racial discrimination in admissions to colleges receiving the funds. However, a state could escape this provision by establishing separate institutions for white and black students if the funds were "equitably," but not necessarily equally, divided between the institutions.

Seventeen states eventually supported institutions that became known as the 1890 colleges. Alabama, Arkansas, Florida, Texas, Kentucky, Louisiana, Virginia, Mississippi, and Missouri assigned some of their funds to already existing publicly supported black institutions. Maryland gave money to an existing private institution that subsequently became part of the state system. Delaware, Georgia, North Carolina, Oklahoma, South Carolina, Tennessee, and West Virginia created new land-grant colleges for black students. Generally, the 1890 colleges were founded on a tenuous financial base and received little consistent support until the 1960s.

Tuskegee University in Alabama became eligible for Morrill Land-Grant Act funds in 1972. It had been founded in 1881 by Booker T. Washington, with the aid of an appropriation of two thousand dollars from the Alabama legislature. It continued to receive limited state funds and some special federal funds, but it also was aided by private institutional gifts. In 1906, as discussed elsewhere, Thomas M. Campbell was appointed as a cooperative demonstration agent with financing from Tuskegee Institute, the U.S. Department of Agriculture, and the General Education Board (a philanthropic institution founded by John D. Rockefeller as noted later). A short time later, John B. Pierce was appointed to a similar post at Hampton Institute, Virginia. Hampton Institute, opened in 1868, received funds under the two land-grant acts for a number of years.

The Morrill Land-Grant College Act, which had been signed on July 2, 1862, required the states to accept its provisions before being given land scrip for the establishment of colleges teaching agriculture, the mechanic arts, and military science. Iowa accepted the act on September 11, 1862. Other states followed until by 1870 all had agreed. As new states were admitted to the Union, they were given land scrip for such colleges. In more recent years, as agricultural colleges have been established in the territories, they have been given money instead of land. The most recent such grant was to the University of the District of Columbia. The way the funds were used varied greatly from state to state. Some states gave the funds to state universities for establishing colleges of agriculture and the mechanical arts, while others established new institutions or turned the funds over to private institutions. Similarly, courses of study varied widely. Many colleges, for example, had to give preparatory classes simply because many rural youth did not have access to secondary schools.

Other problems dampened the first flush of enthusiasm. Enrollment was slow. Land was available for young people wishing to farm, and many thought they could learn better by doing than by studying. By 1872–1873, twelve of the colleges had fewer than 50 students in their agricultural and mechanical departments; six between 50 and 100; six more, between 100 and 150; and only three served more than 150 students.

MEETING NEEDS.   In the new colleges it was difficult to establish courses of study that would meet both the demands of young people and of the particular state. The South was impoverished and in the throes of reorganizing its agricultural systems after the war. Many Northern farmers were producing for a world market for the first time, while others were moving to new lands in the West. Land was plentiful and there seemed to be little or no incentive for either intensive farming or the application of scientific technologies. Still another opinion, mentioned by some of the farm journals and in letters from farmers, charged that the colleges were not training their students to go back to their home or other farms and operate them. Rather, for the most part the students left farming.

The gravest problem, though, was that the agricultural colleges had very little to teach because very little agricultural knowledge had been tested scientifically. Instead, many of the colleges relied upon teaching the practical details of farm operations mainly by having the students work on college farms. While this practice met some needs in a limited way and gave the colleges time to get organized, something more had to be done if the colleges were to survive and make a contribution to the nation. Agricultural courses on a college level were not possible until the development of experiment stations that through research would provide basic knowledge upon which the courses could be built.

HATCH EXPERIMENT STATION ACT.   The concept of a nationwide system of agricultural experiment stations was expressed in 1845 by John Pitkin Norton, a professor at Yale. One of his students, Samuel William Johnson, became an advocate of agricultural experiment stations. In 1875 Johnson's efforts led to the establishment of the Connecticut Experiment Station. The same year, under the leadership of E. W. Hilgard, the University of California established an experiment station. A number of other states followed the examples of Connecticut and California.

Meanwhile, an organized movement to secure federal and state aid for the establishment of agricultural experiment stations was under way. The idea was discussed at a convention of the land-grant colleges in 1871. In 1882 the first bills to grant federal aid were introduced in Congress by William H. Hatch of Missouri and J. Z. George of Mississippi. Finally, in 1887 the Hatch Act was approved by Congress and signed by the president.

The new law provided for a yearly grant to each state for the support of an agricultural experiment station. Within a year every state had accepted the provisions of the act, and within a decade the stations were devoting themselves to research. Nevertheless, their future was somewhat uncertain. Station directors needed to convince farmers that what was being done at the stations would be of benefit to them. But if the research were to be of benefit, its results would have to be communicated to farmers.

Reaching the Farmers.   The station directors were not alone in realizing that they needed to reach farmers if they were to have support and to survive. Both the agricultural colleges and the United States Department of Agriculture were under attack by some of the farm press and farmers organizations.

THE DEPARTMENT OF AGRICULTURE.   The department, from its days as a division of the Patent Office, had the most experience in communication, issuing an annual report including some articles on the results of research as well as individual bulletins. The farm press criticized the reports as compendiums of old, useless material; farmers said that the research reports could not be applied to meet their needs. As time went by, more research was completed and reported, and the department made a greater effort to report research results in a form that would be useful to farmers. In 1889 the department began issuing bulletins as Farmers Bulletins, a format that proved popular. The annual report publication was revised to become the *Yearbook of Agriculture,* first issued in 1894.

THE EXPERIMENT STATIONS.   The experiment stations began issuing research bulletins as their programs got under way, but many issued popular bulletins and leaflets as well. The Connecticut station at New Haven, for example, issued ninety-three bulletins in the first ten years of its existence. They were a mix of scholarly reports and farm-oriented papers. In Alabama the state commissioner of agriculture for a number of years was responsible for publishing the station reports. Some of the bulletins reported the results of experiments; others were compilations of material. The agricultural colleges for the most part concentrated then, as now, on scholarly papers intended to be read by other scholars.

Many farm journals based their articles upon material published by the USDA, the experiment stations, and the colleges. In this way, the institutions influenced some farmers they otherwise would not have reached.

One must not, however, overemphasize the importance of farm papers and institutional reports in meeting the information needs of American farmers and rural residents. The total circulation of the farm papers was small compared with the total number of farmers at the turn of the century. It took some initiative for the farmer to obtain printed information from his experiment station. Most farm people were literate, but many were not entirely comfortable with the printed word. Indeed, farmers, at least by tradition and with some reason, distrusted "book farming."

This comparative failure in communication was recognized, and proposals were made and actions taken to overcome it. Many of these proposals called for some sort of direct person-to-person contact between those who possessed information and those who needed it. Some of the early local farm organizations asked farmers with specialized experience and college professors doing work related to agriculture to speak at their meetings. Some state organizations made speakers available to local groups. This led to the organization of what became known as farmers institutes.

Farmers institutes were apparently first proposed by Edmund Hitchcock, president of Amherst College, at an 1852 meeting of the Massachusetts State Board of Agriculture. Hitchcock proposed that qualified people, including professors and farmers, go into the different districts of the state during the winter months and instruct farmers and their families in their various specialties. Some ten years later the state board began to sponsor such meetings and achieved considerable success. Beginning in 1867, similar sessions were held in Connecticut by the Connecticut Board of Agriculture.

Shortly after these efforts began, the idea of farmers institutes surfaced in the Midwest, perhaps first at the Kansas Agricultural College. Specifically, the board of regents in 1868 directed the Kansas Agricultural College to set up a series of lectures "so that the benefits of farming according to correct agricultural principles may be disseminated throughout the State." Such institutes, often conducted in cooperation with local agricultural societies, were undertaken. Similar activities took place in many other states, including Illinois, Missouri, and Iowa. By the 1880s a number of states were appropriating money to their agricultural colleges or state boards of agriculture for institutes. By 1890 farmers institutes had been established on a more or less permanent basis in twenty-six states.

The idea behind farmers institutes was to provide educational facilities locally at places farmers could reach. Transporting exhibits as well as people from the state colleges to county seats and farm centers was difficult. In 1903 two railroads in Iowa, inspired by Perry G. Holden of Iowa State University, ran trains through part of the state to promote the planting of better seed corn. The trains carried lecturers from the college, corn specimens, charts, bulletins, and demonstration materials. The trains stopped at stations where farmers could gather and hear lectures, obtain publications, and go through the train to study the exhibits. The trains solved the transportation problem and attracted so much interest that many other railroads and state colleges adopted the idea. In 1911, the high point of the effort, seventy-one trains ran in twenty-eight states, attracting an attendance of 995,220. More than fifty different railroads operated the trains.

Short courses at the colleges, which began even before the institutes, provided an alternative to institutes. They were held for a week or two and concentrated on the practical applications of improved methods in one or two subjects such as dairying, corn production, or wheat raising. While these short courses did extend the work of the colleges and experiment stations to audiences not ordinarily reached and were—and still are—popular with some farmers, they reached only a limited number of persons.

The farmers institutes had developed mainly through state programs, but by 1889 the Office of Experiment Stations of the Department of Agriculture was interested in the idea. The office had been organized in 1888 under provisions of the Hatch Experiment Station Act to function as a center for the exchange of information on research projects. It also administered the distribution of the yearly funds appropriated by Congress. Both the first director of the office, Wilbur O. Atwater, and long-term director Alfred C. True recognized the importance of education and communication. Indeed, it was Atwater who had started the publication of "Farmers Bulletins" by the Department of Agriculture.

Atwater was interested enough in farmers institutes to direct the office beginning in 1889 to collect data regarding state legislation, organization, and work of the institutes. He reported that the institutes' work was a success. Secretary of Agriculture J. M. Rusk in his report for 1889 spoke of their "extraordinary benefits" and suggested that the national government "should put it in the power of the Department of Agriculture to foster and encourage the work of the institutes in the various States and Territories." Nothing came of this recommendation at the time, but in 1902 under the leadership of Secretary James Wilson and Director True, Congress appropriated two thousand dollars for work with the institutes. In 1903 an appropriation of five thousand dollars followed. These allocations reflected national recognition of the potential importance of agricultural education to working farmers and farm families.

With the appropriation in hand, True appointed John Hamilton, director of farmers institutes in Pennsylvania, as farmers institute specialist in the Office of Experiment Stations. Hamilton was to investigate and report on the progress of various state farmers institutes so they might increase their effectiveness in disseminating the results of the work of the Department of Agriculture and the state experiment stations.

Hamilton visited many of the agricultural colleges, spoke at a number of farmers institutes, and traveled on one of the agricultural trains. He published reports on the institutes, on their programs, and on new methods of organization. The office drew up lists of available qualified lecturers and helped lecturers obtain publications and other materials. It went even further. It prepared and distributed lantern slides — precursors of today's film strips, slide shows, and videotapes — with outlines for lectures on such subjects as the care of milk, potato diseases, cattle feeding and silage, and silo construction.

Hamilton persuaded experts in a number of subjects to prepare course outlines for movable schools of from one to eight weeks' duration. Such outlines were prepared on cheese making, fruit growing, cereal foods, and other subjects.

"Movable schools" was a term sometimes used interchangeably with institutes, although the movable school idea often contemplated a more active participation by those attending than did the institutes. In 1899 George Washington Carver of Tuskegee Institute developed a plan for a mule-drawn wagon that would carry farm machinery, seeds, dairy equipment, and other material to demonstrate improved methods to farmers. The first operator of the wagon was George R. Bridgeforth. Seaman A. Knapp, who had been working in Texas for the U.S. Department of Agriculture on farm demonstration work, was so impressed with Carver's idea that in 1906 he secured funds for the appointment of Thomas C. Campbell as a cooperative demonstration agent, effective November 12, 1906. From then on, Campbell was responsible for operating or supervising the demonstration wagon, often called a "Jessup wagon" in honor of a New York philanthropist who had given the money for the first wagon. He gave practical demonstrations in the use of farm implements, taught improved methods of farming, and tried to engender in the minds of black farmers a vision of a better life.

A somewhat similar movable school, one resembling a present-day van but with a two-cycle engine, was sent out by the University of

Massachusetts in 1913. A newly graduated young man, Alister Mac-Dougall, traveled with his exhibits and held meetings throughout the state, from the Berkshire Mountains to Cape Cod. MacDougall gave considerable attention to marketing and encouraged farmers to organize cooperatives to market their fruits and vegetables in Boston and New York.

Beginnings of Extension.   Even as the farmers institutes were reaching their peak, some college, experiment station, and USDA people were beginning to talk of Extension. Sometimes they equated the idea with the institutes or short courses, but gradually they created a somewhat different concept. The institutes had proven their worth and in their different forms were opening the way for Extension. Their very success led many people to call for even greater efforts to take practical education directly to farmers and their families.

The institutes, movable schools, farm trains, and short courses had some obvious shortcomings. Because the time was short, the lecturers and demonstrators could cover only one or two subjects. Helpful as the information might be, it was still limited. The information reached only those farmers who were able to attend the institutes or short courses at specified times and who were willing to make the effort to get there. The good roads movement was just getting under way, and travel was very difficult in bad weather. It was also said, and with considerable truth, that the farmers who most needed the institutes' help were the very people who were reluctant to make an effort to acquire the essential knowledge to improve their farming or who were unable to learn very much from group lectures. The need for additional education for farm people was apparent. That need had been partly met, but the time had come for another step forward.

There were precedents other than the institutes for what became agricultural Extension. The Chautauqua system was one of the most important. It began at Lake Chautauqua, New York, in 1874, with a ten-day program for Sunday school leaders combining instruction, recreation, and entertainment. Rather quickly the program was expanded to include a four-year course of assigned home reading, with four books and twelve issues of a Chautauqua magazine to be read each year. In 1883 correspondence courses were added and continued for several years. None of these courses specifically related to agriculture, but instead dealt with such subjects as literature, music, and philosophy.

Meanwhile, a number of American universities and colleges had become interested in a system of "university extension" begun in England in 1866. The system was introduced into the United States by educational institutions working through city libraries. By 1890 extension courses were being given in many different locations. The American Society for the Extension of University Teaching was organized in that year. In 1891 New York appropriated ten thousand dollars for the organization and supervision of university extension work. In the following year the University of Chicago included university extension in its original plan of organization. The movement continued to expand, although it never reached as many people as did the Chautauqua programs.

Naturally enough, the agricultural colleges began to look at the university extension movement. In 1894 Edward B. Voorhees reported to the Association of American Colleges and Experiment Stations that Rutgers University had begun a program of agricultural extension work in New Jersey in 1891. The Rutgers program included courses of six lectures each on soils and crops, feeding plants, and animal nutrition. The courses were conducted much as they might have been at the university, except that they were held in different locations around the state. At the 1897 meeting of the association, I. P. Roberts of Cornell read a paper on how university extension work could be conducted by the college of agriculture. Roberts illustrated his presentation with projects currently being carried on in New York. Within a decade several states were carrying out projects identified as agricultural extension.

BOYS' AND GIRLS' CLUBS.   Actually, a number of different endeavors that were to contribute to the creation of the Cooperative Extension Service were under way, an indication that the time was ripe for substantial advances in education for farmers, farm housewives, and children. Work with young people was sometimes seen as a way to get their elders interested in attending farmers institutes. This was the case in 1900 in Macoupin County, Illinois, when President W. B. Otwell of the county institute distributed selected corn seed to young people and encouraged them to compete for prizes in the fall. The effort was successful and quickly grew, with both young people and farmers attending the institutes on a regular basis.

Two years later a boys' and girls' club was organized in Clark County, Ohio, by school superintendent A. B. Graham. The first year the club members grew and exhibited only corn, but within a short time other products were also being shown. Schools in the county became involved, adding increased incentive to young people's organized pursuit of agricultural knowledge. By 1904 Ohio boasted a federation of rural school agricultural clubs, which used materials issued by the state college of agriculture.

The farmers institutes in a number of states got behind the movement to organize boys' and girls' clubs by working with the schools and holding institutes for farm youth. While some of the clubs enrolled both boys and girls, the trend to establish separate clubs was apparent from the beginning. In Kansas in 1907, for example, boys were engaged in corn-growing contests, while girls had flower-growing and home-gardening projects. Such distinctions were customary. As the clubs became more common, they tended also to become more identified with the new extension programs than with the institutes.

In the South the movement was supported by the General Education Board, a philanthropic organization established by John D. Rockefeller in 1902 to promote education in the United States. The South became the board's major focus and because the South was still so predominantly agricultural the board worked with a number of farm projects, including boys' and girls' clubs.

The boys' clubs in the South, like those in the North, first centered around corn growing, usually on a competitive basis. One of the first clubs was organized in 1907 in Holmes County, Mississippi, by W. H. Smith, a local school superintendent. As the idea caught on, cotton clubs and some pig clubs were organized.

Girls' canning clubs in the South were comparable to the boys' corn clubs. They originated in Aiken County, South Carolina, in 1910. A teacher in a rural school, Marie Cromer, attended a school-improvement association meeting at which a representative of the United States Department of Agriculture talked about boys' clubs and suggested that girls' clubs also should be organized. She immediately organized a club in which each girl was to grow one-tenth of an acre of tomatoes. Representatives of both the Department of Agriculture and of the state women's college helped with the project. With this assistance, the girls canned their tomatoes, using a portable canning outfit. Some mothers and some boys helped in the canning. Similar work was undertaken by Ella G. Agnew in Virginia. The idea caught on rapidly over the next few years. With General Education Board money, a number of women trained in home economics were employed as collaborators. They became known as home demonstration agents.

These boys' and girls' clubs, which became the 4-H clubs, were significant in the development of Cooperative Extension. They proved that people from local schools, the institutes, the agricultural colleges, the Department of Agriculture, and private foundations could work together to achieve sought-for goals. The movement was powered not by a single dominating force, but by cooperation, an attribute that has been characteristic of Extension for seventy-five years.

BEGINNING OF HOME ECONOMICS IN EXTENSION.   The girls' clubs were the key to making home economics one of the basic elements of Cooperative Extension. The mothers of the girls in the early canning and gardening clubs helped their young people and became interested themselves in what the home demonstration agents, as they were called, had to offer. The way then was open for the agents to encourage the organization of home demonstration clubs, which undertook various projects. Making and using fireless cookers was popular in the South. Gardening and canning clubs were a natural outgrowth of the girls' club work. Some of the women's clubs organized themselves into egg-selling and farm-market associations, combining the educational aspects of the clubs with an economic goal.

FARMERS COOPERATIVE DEMONSTRATION WORK.   The boys' and girls' clubs first, and later the home demonstration clubs, were sponsored by or were a part of farmers cooperative demonstration work in the South. This work was started by Seaman A. Knapp, often referred to as the "father" of the Extension Service. It began as one of many efforts by federal, state, and local groups to control the boll weevil, which by the early 1900s was threatening to destroy the cotton industry. The Department of Agriculture developed a plan to control the ravages of the weevil by encouraging farmers to grow cotton in such a way that it would mature earlier. Unfortunately, not many farmers adopted the plan. Secretary of Agriculture James Wilson and his staff proposed that the plan be taken directly to cotton planters. That job was given Seaman A. Knapp of the Bureau of Plant Industry, with the title of "Special Agent for the Promotion of Agriculture in the South."

Knapp, then seventy years old, had wide experience in agriculture. He had been a farmer, a professor of agriculture, and president of Iowa Agricultural College. He subsequently developed a large tract of land in western Louisiana, where he successfully introduced the production of rice. Later he served the Department of Agriculture as a plant introduction agent in the Orient and in Puerto Rico.

Experience and observation had convinced Knapp that reading pamphlets or observing work on demonstration farms operated at government expense would not lead farmers to change their practices. Rather, they could be convinced of the value of change through demonstrations carried on by the farmers themselves on their own farms and under ordinary farm conditions. Knapp decided to apply these observations on his new job. As Knapp put it: "What a man hears, he may doubt; what he sees, he may possibly doubt; but what he does, he cannot doubt."

In 1903, before federal funds were available, Knapp obtained private financing to put his plan into effect on the Walter C. Porter farm near Terrell, Texas. A group of businessmen and farmers contributed funds to carry out the work and to reimburse Porter for any losses suffered through following the new methods. This experiment was so successful that it greatly stimulated demonstration work carried on by farmers.

A COUNTY AGENT APPOINTED.   Knapp used federal funds, private funds, and General Education Board money to employ field agents and set up farmer-operated demonstration farms. The field agents worked in districts covering 10 to 20 counties. On November 12, 1906, the first county agent as such, W. C. Stallings, was appointed in Smith County, Texas. The ravages of the boll weevil had become so severe that businessmen offered to pay most of the expense involved in employing an agent to work full time with the farmers in the one county, which led to the use of the term "county agent." The success of this experiment led to similar activities in a number of other counties.

In 1910 demonstration work was carried on in 455 counties in 12 southern states by 450 agents. Their work included boys' and girls' club and home demonstration activities.

Knapp emphasized the "grass roots" approach to his demonstration work, but he also insisted that it was a federal enterprise to be developed through a highly centralized organization. The work was planned and followed up in detail by the Washington office. Definite instructions were sent out from there to all agents. Knapp defined his work as "a system of rural education for boys and adults by which a readjustment of country life can be effected and placed upon a higher plane of profit, comfort, culture, influence, and power." Although Knapp stated that he cooperated in this educational enterprise with agricultural colleges and rural schools, it is evident from his plan of operation that the cooperation was primarily on Knapp's terms. It was not until 1912, after Knapp's death, that a comprehensive arrangement was made with Clemson College to carry out extension and demonstration work jointly. This agreement set a pattern for work with other colleges.

Even though Knapp believed that his demonstration work should be highly centralized, which was exactly opposite to what took place in Extension, Knapp still contributed greatly to the program. His major contributions were his insistence upon direct involvement by farmers in the program and his idea that there should be an agent, preferably one in each county, to work directly with farmers.

FARM MANAGEMENT EXTENSION WORK.   Demonstration or county agent work developed more slowly and somewhat differently in the northern states. Although it came under the direction of the Office of Farm Management of the Bureau of Plant Industry when that office was organized in 1905, it was the outgrowth of earlier work. The office was "to investigate and encourage the adoption of improved methods of farm management and farm practice." Unlike Knapp's program, which was started to meet a particular need, the farm management work under the leadership of W. J. Spillman reflected a new interest in economic questions related to agriculture.

Studies were made of farming conditions and practices in various sections of the country, especially among the most successful farms. Plans were then drawn up whereby farmers could put into operation more efficient systems of farm management. The office used publications to reach farmers but also had district agents, usually responsible for two or more states, who worked through farmers institutes, field meetings, or successful farmers. Spillman and other leaders of the office worked in cooperation with the agricultural colleges and experiment stations and usually hired agents trained in the agricultural colleges. In a number of states the extension movement started in the colleges, as noted previously, or in counties and was subsequently supported in part by the Office of Farm Management.

In the spring of 1910 the Office of Farm Management appointed A. B. Ross as a county agent and assigned him to Bedford County, Pennsylvania. Ross, a retired lawyer, had been working with farmers in the county without financial assistance from either the state or the United States Department of Agriculture. He obtained information from the state experiment station and the USDA and then persuaded farmers to try the new practices. Because of his success, he was hired by the Office of Farm Management.

Ross became particularly interested in restoring soil fertility by encouraging farmers to plant soybeans, then harvested as a forage crop, and alfalfa and to inoculate red clover so it would grow in Pennsylvania. He encouraged farmers to improve their orchards and to grade and pack apples before sending them to market. Ross also helped farmers to buy seeds and fertilizers cooperatively.

In 1912 the Office of Farm Management provided funding for five additional county agents in Pennsylvania. Four of the five were graduates of Pennsylvania State College; the fifth was a Cornell graduate. In 1907 Pennsylvania State had appointed a superintendent of agricultural extension who had worked mainly with institutes, farm trains, fairs, and correspondence courses. In 1912 the college agreed with the Office of Farm Management to appoint a county agent leader to supervise the work of the county agents. By the time the Smith-Lever Act was passed, the Office of Farm Management was financing agents in thirteen Pennsylvania counties, with the agents working under the supervision of Pennsylvania State College.

THE FIRST FARM BUREAU AND EXTENSION.   In 1911 another step was taken that greatly influenced the future organization of Extension. Secretary Byers H. Gitchell of the Binghamton, New York, Chamber of Commerce, influenced by the report of the Country Life Commission (the origin and role of which is detailed elsewhere), called for a department in the chamber devoted to "extending to farmers the same opportunities for cooperation now enjoyed by the business men of this city." After study of the proposal, the Binghamton Chamber of Commerce agreed to establish a "farm bureau" with a farm agent in charge. The bureau would be financed by the chamber; the Delaware, Lackawanna and Western Railroad; and the United States Department of Agriculture, with the New York State College of Agriculture contributing information and advice. Among other duties, the farm agent would "do educational work through the media of institutes, etc., advising with the farmers individually and otherwise as to the best methods, crops, cropping systems, stock, labor, tools, and other equipment."

On March 20, 1911, John H. Barron was appointed as agent. Barron had been reared on a farm and was a graduate of the New York State College of Agriculture. He was first asked to cover the countryside within a fifty-mile radius of Binghamton, but after a year his responsibilities were limited to Broome County. Barron traveled around his district in a horse and buggy, talking to farmers about their problems. He sent out circular letters to local farmers, wrote articles for the local newspapers, and attended meetings of the Grange and other farmers groups. He appointed community leaders to advise him of problems and arranged for lectures and demonstrations. Essentially, he developed a program similar to what became typical work for a county agent. Barron, though, like many county agents after him, had to convince farmers that he had something to offer that would benefit them. Some farmers felt that Barron was an outsider telling them what they should do without really understanding their problems. Others believed that Barron was attempting to encourage increased production for the benefit of the railroad and local merchants without giving any thought to what farmers believed they really needed—higher prices for what they produced. However, Barron's farm background, membership in the Grange, and practical approach to farm problems won him tolerance, if not full acceptance.

The Broome County experiment influenced the development and structure of Extension. It confirmed what Knapp had found, that in those days a county was a reasonable area of coverage for an agent. Even more important, it set a precedent for a broad cooperative project with local groups and local, state, and federal governments providing assistance, but with much of the control remaining in the local groups.

Toward a New Beginning. The first decade of the century saw the idea of an educational program for farmers and farm families becoming widely recognized, with a number of activities developing to meet various needs. Farmers organizations, agricultural journals, agricultural colleges, a federal Department of Agriculture, and a state experiment station system contributed. More specific efforts, aimed at reaching individual farmers and their families—including institutes, demonstration farms, boys' and girls' clubs, home demonstration clubs, and college extension programs—showed what could be done and what needed to be done. Two particular events, the hiring of county agents in Smith County, Texas, and Broome County, New York, gave credence to the idea that farmers needed persons working with them at the local level if an effective educational program for farmers and their families were to become a reality.

CHAPTER THREE

An Idea Becomes Reality

Introduction. The Smith-Lever Act establishing Extension on a nationwide basis became law during a period of agricultural prosperity and was the culmination of several years of effort. Some of the important forces leading to its passage included the Progressive movement and the Country Life Commission, as well as the continuation of efforts by a number of institutions to educate farmers regarding new farm technologies and ways in which farm life could be improved. The Smith-Lever Act, with its unique concept of a cooperative effort by federal, state, and local governments, required careful consideration of how the new relationships should be handled, both between the U.S. Department of Agriculture and the land-grant universities, and among the institutions within the states. However, when the new Cooperative Extension System faced its first great challenge in World War I, it was prepared.

The Progressive Movement. The many efforts in the early 1900s to develop educational programs that would reach farmers and their families was part of the Progressive movement influencing many aspects of American life. Theodore Roosevelt was its political leader and spokesman, but the movement also included Robert M. Follette, Charles Evans Hughes, and Woodrow Wilson in the political arena, economist Richard Ely, the philosopher John Dewey, the educator Kenyon L. Butterfield, and the Baptist clergyman Walter Raushenbusch.

The Progressives were never a single group seeking a single objective. Some Progressives fought corruption and inefficiency in government; others sought to regulate and control big business. Many were concerned with the plight of the urban poor. Progressive goals included establishment of the right of women to vote, the popular election of senators, and a progressive income tax; the regulation of child labor; and the protection of natural resources. Progressives generally believed in the value of education in bringing about needed changes in American life. Although farm problems were not acute in this era, which ran roughly from the end of the Spanish-American War in 1898 to the outbreak of World War I in 1914, Theodore Roosevelt appointed a Country Life Commission in 1908. The commission was to report "upon the present condition of country life, upon what means are now available for supplying the deficiencies which exist, and upon the best methods of organized permanent effort in investigation and actual work" to improve the conditions of country life.

The Golden Age of American Agriculture.   In 1910, 32 million people, one-third of the nation's total population, lived on 6 million farms averaging about 140 acres each. Farmers made up about one-third of the work force. People living on farms averaged $139 a year in income, while people not on farms averaged $482. Farm products made up just over 50 percent of the nation's exports.

The period between the Spanish-American War and World War I, besides being the Progressive Era, has been called the Golden Age of American Agriculture. Horse-powered farming was at its height and was very cost efficient. By this period some of the drudgery traditionally associated with farming was handled by machines. While many family farms were still quite self-sufficient, with diversified farming, gardens, milk cows, and poultry, the mail-order houses and rail transportation to most small towns made factory-produced goods more readily available to farm families. And those families were better able to purchase the goods pictured in the catalog. There was mild inflation in the economy, an increasing demand for farm products by growing cities and industrializing nations overseas, and a decline in the rate of increases in farm production as the opening of new land was coming to an end. Thus farm surpluses, which had overshadowed markets during the 1880s and 1890s, had disappeared. Prices for farm products had gone up, leaving farmers more money to spend, particularly since the prices of goods farmers needed for production went up at a lesser rate. Farm organizations and farm leaders were no longer emphasizing only farm prices. They were concerned with rural roads, postal services, a federally backed system of land banks, and improved educational facilities.

EDUCATION.   So far as education was concerned, most farm children attended one- or two-room country schools. Even though the level of instruction often was good, these schools lacked many of the facilities of city or consolidated schools. The problem, however, lay in access to secondary schools and, for those not in school, in access to the information and technology being developed in the state experiment stations and the Department of Agriculture. The farm journalists, the institutes, the experiment stations, the colleges, and the department—helpful as they were—were not reaching many farmers, particularly those most in need of education. The colleges, experiment stations, and institutes were understaffed in relation to the job to be done. The work was neither coordinated nor systematic. Yet it seemed to some of the leaders of the Progressive movement that the United States was in danger of being unable to supply its growing population with food and fiber at reasonable prices. This point was made by John Hamilton, contemporary farmers institute specialist in the Office of Experiment Stations, in these words: "If no better system of dissemination of agricultural information is devised than that which has existed in the past it is manifest that agriculture in this country will progress far too slowly to meet the demands for food and clothing by our rapidly growing population."

Calls for Extension.   This continuing ferment in localities, counties, and states led to calls for a more systematic organization of extension, first through the state agricultural colleges and then in cooperation with the Department of Agriculture. Kenyon L. Butterfield, president of Rhode Island State College, was one of the most influential spokesmen for this point of view. He had been superintendent of farmers institutes in Michigan from 1895 to 1900 and had recommended the creation of an extension department in the Michigan Agricultural College in 1898. In 1904 Butterfield, speaking before the Association of American Agricultural Colleges and Experiment Stations, called for "a vast enlargement of extension work among farmers." The next year, as chairman of the association's newly established Committee on Extension, he urged the "idea of systematic, long-continued and thorough instruction to the farmers the year through." As he saw it, "This work will not only be dignified by a standing in the college coordinate with research and the teaching of students, but it will rank as a distinct department with a faculty of men whose chief business is to teach people who cannot come to college." At Butterfield's urging, the association proposed appropriations for the Office of Experiment Stations to investigate agricultural extension teaching, to assist the colleges in organizing the work, and to inform those interested in new developments in this form of agricultural education.

The Country Life Commission.   In 1908 Butterfield was named a member of Roosevelt's Country Life Commission. The commission's chairman was Professor Liberty Hyde Bailey of the New York State College of Agriculture, a leading figure in the land-grant college system. Bailey was nationally recognized both for his research and for making research results available to farmers. Educated at Michigan Agricultural College and Harvard, Bailey taught at Michigan Agricultural College for a few years before going to Cornell University. At Cornell's College of Agriculture Bailey built a reputation for outstanding work in horticulture and botany. He insisted that the results of research must be communicated to farmers. He and Isaac P. Roberts, who preceded Bailey as dean of the College of Agriculture, sought to overcome the prejudice that separated the professors on the campus and the farmers in the fields.

Bailey himself lectured to farm groups throughout the state, always emphasizing the practical application of the results of research. In the 1890s the state legislature began appropriating money for "the pro-

motion of agricultural knowledge in the state." Bailey used the money
to expand demonstration programs and extension schools. He also be-
gan a program to encourage nature clubs in New York's public schools.
By the time he retired in 1913 as dean of the College of Agriculture,
Bailey had laid a firm foundation for the Extension Service in New
York and had helped bring about the adoption of the idea nationwide.

While it cannot be determined that either Bailey or Butterfield was
responsible for any particular section of the commission's report, their
interest in agricultural education might well have influenced the commission's recommendations. The commission found there was widespread recognition of the need for redirecting rural schools. The commission called not only for changes in the schools for young people,
but also for "continuation schools for adults." People must be reached
in terms of their daily lives or welfare, which, for farm people, must be
in terms of agriculture and of life on the farms. The commission recognized that the Extension work carried on by some of the colleges of
agriculture was helpful, but it was "on a pitiably small scale as compared with the needs." In every agricultural college extension work,
"without which no college of agriculture can adequately serve its
State," should be coordinated with both the academic and the experiment and research branches, the commission proposed.

RECOMMENDATIONS.   The commission specifically recommended:

> Nationalized extension work. — Each state college of agriculture
> should be empowered to organize as soon as practicable a complete
> department of college extension, so managed as to reach every person on
> the land in its State, with both information and inspiration. The work
> should include such forms of extension teaching as lectures, bulletins,
> reading courses, correspondence courses, demonstration, and other
> means of reaching the people at home and on their farms. It should be
> designed to forward not only the business of agriculture, but sanitation,
> education, home making, and all interests of country life.

The recommendations of the commission emphasized home economics, opportunities for youth, and rural and community development as well as agriculture. There was an imperative need to teach
people how to handle domestic, household, and health problems. A

general elevation of country living could come about, according to the commission, through the development of a cooperative spirit in the home; simplification of the diet; the building of convenient and sanitary houses; providing running water and more mechanical help in the house; good and convenient gardens; a less exclusive ideal of money getting on the part of the farmer; providing better means of communication such as telephones, roads, and reading circles; and developing women's organizations. Nearly every one of these objectives was to be included among the goals of Extension home economists. Similarly, the need to provide educational and social opportunities for youth found expression in 4-H, while several Extension programs provided an opportunity for young men and women to develop the leadership qualities the commission considered necessary.

Local government had to act to achieve its highest point of efficiency. Good roads, better housing, improved postal services, and better public schools were essential. At the same time the commission urged the building of rural libraries, the establishment of study clubs, and the building of recreational facilities to improve the quality of rural life. Extension was later to adopt some of these goals in its rural and community development programs.

Finally, the commission foresaw one of the most basic tenets of Extension when it stated in its report:

> Care must be taken in all the reconstructive work to see that local initiative is relied upon to the fullest extent, and that federal and even state agencies do not perform what might be done by the people in the communities. The centralized agencies should be stimulative and directive, rather than mandatory and formal. Every effort must be made to develop native resources, not only of material things, but of people.

Even as the commission was preparing its report for publication, Butterfield was reporting for the committee on Extension work of the Association of American Agricultural Colleges and Experiment Stations to the association. The committee proposed that the association endorse the idea of federal appropriations for Extension work in agriculture. The sum of ten thousand dollars a year, to be matched by an equal amount of state money, was suggested. The committee also suggested that each institution in the association draw up a plan for Extension work. The association approved the planning recommendation but not the one for funding. The next year the committee repeated its funding recommendation. This time the association approved "the general idea of a federal appropriation."

Proposed Legislation.   Butterfield and Hamilton then drafted a bill to carry out the recommendations and referred it to the association; the association's executive committee approved the bill. The draft was then given to J. C. McLaughlin, Congressman from Michigan. He introduced it in the House of Representatives on December 15, 1909, where it was referred to the Committee on Agriculture. On January 5, 1910, a similar bill was introduced in the Senate by Jonathan P. Dolliver of Iowa, where it was also referred to the Committee on Agriculture.

At hearings, the association supported the bill with arguments that the maintenance of the national food supply was becoming a serious problem, that people were leaving the farm in part because of a lack of educational and social advantages, and that the federal government was in a good position to assist the states in financing extension work. The National Grange and other farm organizations supported the legislation. However, Senator Dolliver combined the Extension bills with bills to aid secondary school vocational education and teachers' colleges. Extension became a minor part of the total bill, which never came to a vote.

In 1911 a number of bills were introduced to grant federal funds for Extension. This goal was again endorsed by the association. The National Soil Fertility League, organized in the same year by a group of bankers, railroad officials, and businessmen in the Midwest to promote the interests of agriculture, campaigned actively for federal aid to Extension. The idea was also endorsed by President William Howard Taft. Secretary of Agriculture James Wilson stated that Extension, if funded by Congress, would benefit farmers and farm families. Various bills were considered by Congress in 1911, 1912, and 1913, but all foundered on the question of combining vocational education and extension work.

NEED FOR COMPROMISE.   Meanwhile farmers cooperative demonstration work, under the direction of the Department of Agriculture, was expanding in the South. Similar work, but centered in the state colleges of agriculture, was spreading in the North and West. Supporters of such work, particularly as it was carried on in the South, questioned whether the appropriation of funds directly and only to the land-grant colleges might not bring about an end to department activities. With the national and state agencies charged with extension operating more or less independently, considerable friction already had arisen. This situation led to modification of previously introduced legislation and to the development of Extension as we know it today.

The revised bill was introduced in the House by Congressman Asbury F. Lever of South Carolina and in the Senate by Senator Hoke Smith of Georgia on September 6, 1913. Instead of providing funds to the land-grant colleges for Extension, the Smith-Lever bill was "to provide for cooperative agricultural extension work between the agricultural colleges in the several States . . . and the United States Department of Agriculture." The work was to be carried on in a manner mutually agreed upon by the USDA and the state agricultural colleges.

In hearings before the House Committee on Agriculture, it was suggested that the state departments of agriculture should share in the funding. Secretary of Agriculture David Houston opposed the idea, saying that it was the policy of the department to cooperate with the agricultural colleges in such matters. The proposal was not adopted. The Senate Committee on Agriculture increased the amounts authorized to be appropriated and to be matched by the states.

Debates on the bills brought out several points. The principle of cooperation was opposed by some legislators on the ground it could lead to control of the work by the department. However, an amendment to strike the cooperative provision was defeated. The method of distributing the federal funds to be matched by the states was debated. The view prevailed that since the work was educational, the funds should be allotted in accordance with the number of people to be reached. An attempt was made to provide specifically for extension work for blacks, but the proposal was defeated, as were amendments providing that the work be carried on without racial discrimination and that in states with two or more land-grant colleges, the secretary of agriculture should determine which institution would receive the Extension funds. It was left to the legislature of each state to determine which college or colleges should administer the fund.

In general terms the legislators, at least many of them, saw Extension as bringing about more efficient farm production. This, in turn, would assure the nation a plentiful supply of low-cost food. But more efficient production not only would help consumers, it also would give farmers a bigger margin of profit. Some congressmen, however, stated that increased production could lead only to lower prices and falling profits. This argument is still being waged, seventy-five years after the bill was passed.

Congressman Lever, when he reported the bill to the House, pointed out that education through demonstration would not be limited to production agriculture. The county agent would provide leadership along all lines of rural activity—social, economic, and financial. The Extension Service would teach the principles of distribution, it would provide agricultural education work for boys and girls, and it would give particular attention to home demonstration. In other words, the basic idea of the bill was agricultural education.

The reports and debates on the bill indicated no strong opposition to it as a whole. Compromises were reached on some points of disagreement, others were settled by a majority vote, and the bill passed both houses of Congress on a voice vote. It was signed into law on May 8, 1914, by President Woodrow Wilson, who called it "one of the most significant and far-reaching measures for the education of adults ever adopted by the government." Its purpose, he commented, was to "insure the retention in rural districts of an efficient and contented population."

The Smith-Lever Act.   Secretary of Agriculture David F. Houston regarded the Smith-Lever Act as "one of the most striking educational measures ever adopted by any Government." As he saw it, nothing short of a comprehensive attempt to make rural life profitable, healthful, comfortable, and attractive would solve the problems of agriculture and of rural life. Material things were important but the higher things, the intellectual and social sides of rural life, could not be neglected.

PROVISIONS.   The act itself was distinguished from earlier grant-in-aid laws by its provision for state matching of federal funds and by the number of limitations and safeguards to insure that these funds would be spent for the purposes Congress intended. Its purpose was quite clearly stated by Congress: "To aid in diffusing among the people of the United States useful and practical information on subjects relating to agriculture and home economics and to encourage the application of the same." Agricultural Extension work was to "consist of the giving of instruction and practical demonstrations in agriculture and home economics to persons not attending or resident in said colleges in the several communities, and imparting to such persons information on said subjects through field demonstrations, publications, and otherwise."

Each state was to receive $10,000 of federal funds annually, and additional amounts determined on the basis of its rural population, from an initial fund of $600,000, which was to increase by $500,000 annually for seven years and thereafter continue at a total of $4,100,000. These additional amounts of federal funds had to be offset or matched by appropriations by the state legislature or by contributions "provided by State, county, college, local authority, or individual contributions from within the State."

PLANS OF WORK.   Before the federal funds authorized by the act could be paid to any college, plans for implementing the work were to be submitted to and approved by the secretary of agriculture. These requirements of matching funds, cooperation of federal and state agencies in planning and carrying out the work, and the provision for contributions by state, county, college, local authority, or individual contributions from within the state, were unique in legislation up to that time. The Cooperative Extension Service was the result. Today it remains a unique educational institution.

Starting Up.   The specific requirements for cooperation in developing and carrying out programs led to a number of administrative problems that had to be solved before the Smith-Lever Act could become fully operative. The executive committee of the Association of

American Agricultural Colleges and Experiment Stations and the department officials who had been assigned responsibility for administering the act met and agreed that there should be a memorandum of
understanding between the department and each responsible college. A
tentative draft was prepared by the director of the Office of Experiment
Stations and submitted for review. The executive committee of the
association and the secretary of agriculture approved a final draft and
it then was sent to each of the responsible colleges. In 1914 the draft
was accepted by all of the states except Arizona and California. The
University of Arizona accepted later, but the University of Illinois
withdrew. These states feared federal domination of Extension work.
However, both California and Illinois maintained cooperative relations
with the department in the same manner as the other states.

FEDERAL-STATE AGREEMENTS.   The 1914 agreements were important in that they provided the structure for the development of the
Cooperative Extension Service. They have been amended and rewrit-
ten, but the basic ideas they contained have remained the same for
seventy-five years. The agreement with each state provided that not
Smith-Lever Extension work exclusively but all Extension work by the
department in the state would be carried on through the state college of
agriculture. Agents appointed for cooperative Extension work who received department funds were to be joint employees of the department
and the colleges, but their appointments were not subject to department approval. The secretary of agriculture agreed to set up an Office
of Extension Work to represent him in supervision of the work. Each
college agreed in turn to set up a separate Extension division with a
leader satisfactory to the secretary of agriculture to administer state
and federal funds and to cooperate with the department in all Extension work in agriculture and home economics it should be authorized
to conduct.

The first draft of the agreement, and the final version as well,
reflected much of the thinking of Alfred Charles True, then director of
the Office of Experiment Stations, in encouraging both sound research
and education. Beginning in 1902 he served as dean of the association's
Graduate School of Agriculture, established to provide for more graduate training. By 1912, five summer sessions of this graduate school
had been held on various university campuses. True assisted and en-

couraged the introduction and expansion of agricultural education in elementary and secondary schools and at the undergraduate and graduate college levels. True also became interested in farmers institutes and asked Congress for funds to appoint a farmers institute specialist. This was done on April 1, 1903, and from then on the Office of Experiment Stations assisted farmers institutes.

The 1914 agreements had called for the Department of Agriculture to establish an Office of Extension Work, with the idea probably coming from True. However, the work was divided into two units, the Office of Extension Work in the South, headed by Bradford Knapp, and the Office of Extension Work in the North and West, headed by Clarence B. Smith. This division reflected the differences in the ways Extension had developed in the South and in the North. A State Relations Committee, headed by True, was appointed to review proposals for Extension work, whether from within the department or from the state colleges. A States Relations Service, headed by True, was established on July 1, 1915, with the Office of Extension Work in the South and the Office of Extension Work in the North and West becoming units in the new service, each retaining a measure of independence.

During the next few years agents in the South, where first loyalty had been to the department, had to learn to work through the colleges. Bradford Knapp observed that the successful farmer his father Seaman A. Knapp had hired as a county agent, while valuable in introducing Extension work, could not stay far enough in advance of the other farmers in the county to remain a competent teacher. Knapp began to replace this type of county agent with those who had both farm experience and college training.

Agents in the North were, for the most part, college-trained people working either for the colleges or for local groups but with help from the colleges. The work varied greatly from county to county. The big difference with these agents was that when any part of their salary came from department funds, they had federal commissions, were subject to the administrative regulations of the federal civil service, and were required to make weekly and yearly reports on their work.

These and other problems were handled over a period of years. It was not until 1921 that the southern and northern offices were consolidated into the Office of Extension Work. Nevertheless, as True said in his presidential address to the Association of American Agricultural Colleges and Experiment Stations in November, 1914: "Carried to its logical conclusion this means that the colleges and department will before long have a definite existence as educating agencies in practically every county of the United States."

Getting to Work.   Reporting on the first year of Extension under the Smith-Lever Act, the secretary of agriculture said that the general lines for the whole country had been well marked out. They included the county agricultural agents, the boys' and girls' clubs, the movable schools, and the supporting work of the college and department specialists. A large portion of the Extension funds available had been spent on the county agent system. More than 1,000, or about one-third of the counties had men as agents, 680 of whom were in the fifteen southern states, where there were also 355 women employed. There were 50 black agents in eleven states. The northern and western states had 350 male agents. Home economics work in the North was done by women who went out from the colleges, but this activity was just beginning.

COUNTY AGENTS.   County agents worked primarily to teach farmers how to increase agricultural production, although they did some educational work on purchasing and marketing. They instructed farmers on building silos, helped inoculate hogs, secured the construction of dipping vats to control cattle ticks, instructed on hillside terracing to control erosion, organized cow-testing and breeding associations, conducted demonstrations on improving crops and livestock, and visited farms.

YOUTH CLUBS.   Boys' and girls' clubs continued under the new law. In the South they were associated with the county agent system, while in other states they were conducted independently, although usually with some relationship to the state agricultural college. The most popular projects were growing winter legumes, raising pigs and poultry, growing corn and potatoes, and gardening and canning. Demonstrations of home canning of fruits and vegetables attracted many women and men. Some 110,000 boys and girls were enrolled in the southern states during 1915, and 150,000 in the northern and western states. However, there was still a large number of rural young people who were not being reached.

As noted previously, the institute movement declined as the county agent system developed, but a number of institutes were conducted in 1915 and for several years thereafter. They were sponsored in some states by the agricultural colleges and in others by the state departments of agriculture. Agricultural short courses and movable schools under the direction of the agricultural colleges continued to reach a number of rural people.

SPECIALISTS.   The number of Extension specialists connected with the agricultural colleges grew steadily in all the states as funds for their work increased through the Smith-Lever Act. The major projects in which subject-matter specialists were employed were dairying, animal husbandry, poultry, agronomy, horticulture, agricultural engineering, farm management, marketing, rural organization, and home economics. There were also specialists in the agencies of the Department of Agriculture working along similar lines. Some of the state specialists participated in institutes, meetings of farm organizations, and movable schools. And, just as they are doing seventy-five years later, specialists were responding to requests from county agents to meet with farmers in particular localities where special problems or opportunities had arisen. They also wrote bulletins and pamphlets to be distributed by county agents.

The trends evident in 1915 continued through 1916 and into 1917. As the system developed, some administrative aspects worked out very well, while problems arose in others. One that worked out well was the project agreement, the plan of work that was to be submitted by the state director of Extension and approved by the secretary of agriculture before funds were released. These agreements usually were comprehensive and relevant, even though they sometimes proposed more work than could be accomplished by the available staff. On the other hand, the requirement for weekly and yearly reports from each county agent was a tribulation for many agents who were more interested in "doing" than in reporting. There is reason to believe that many reports were only approximations of what actually took place.

There were, however, problems of greater importance. In 1916 the

Extension Committee on Organization and Policy (ECOP), which had succeeded the Committee on Extension Organization and Policy of the American Association of Agricultural Colleges and Experiment Stations, asked to meet with the director and Extension chiefs of the States Relations Service to discuss these problems. The conferences, held at Amherst, Massachusetts, in July 1916 produced a number of agreements, most of which increased the autonomy of the state Extension services. These agreements provided: all work within the states should be done through the directors of Extension, and there should be no communication between the States Relations Service and workers within a state except as delegated by the director; the state Extension services would be obliged only to assist the department with its educational work, excluding regulatory functions; the States Relations Service and the committee would inform the secretary of agriculture of duties or assignments outside their "power or jurisdiction"; and the States Relations Service would have no power to appoint subject-matter specialists to operate within the individual states. Agreement was also reached on several procedural questions. These agreements were well received and undoubtedly promoted better relations. Of course, other problems would arise, but a precedent had been set for solving problems through negotiation.

In the view of Alfred C. True and of many others since, the first three years of operation under the Smith-Lever Act settled the principles and methods for the successful and permanent establishment of a national system of Extension work in agriculture and home economics. In that system, federal, state, and county forces were to cooperate closely and many thousands of farm men, women, and children were to participate. True was correct in his assessment, except that the participants were to number in the millions rather than in the thousands. Nevertheless, there remained work to be done and difficulties to be overcome. In fact, some uncertain times arose in the period between 1914 and 1917.

Extension in the States

NORTHERN AND WESTERN STATES.   A number of northern and western states had an Extension structure based in the state land-grant universities existing before 1914. For example, Indiana had held

farmers' institutes from 1882 on. Beginning in 1889 the work was supervised by W. E. Latta, a professor of agriculture at Purdue University, and in 1905 the Indiana General Assembly appropriated funds for
Extension work in the Agricultural Experiment Station. Extension continued with year-to-year support until 1913, when it was established on
a permanent basis at Purdue University. However, county agents were
appointed annually by the county boards of education. They thus became short-term political employees, with all that this implies. It was
not until 1937 that the general assembly passed a law providing for the
appointment of county agents, home demonstration agents, and 4-H
agents by the Board of Trustees of Purdue University. The first corn
club for boys in Indiana was organized in 1905, and in 1912 Z. M.
Smith was appointed state leader for boys' and girls' club work. By
1915 there were twenty-eight local youth club leaders in Indiana. Talks
on home economics and family living were given at farmers institutes
as early as 1899, and in 1914 Lella Gaddis was named the first state
leader of home demonstration work.

Indiana is of interest in the early development of Extension because much of the structure that the state developed and adopted before the Smith-Lever Act was passed was very like that adopted nationwide after 1914. There were, of course, other states that were
developing extension programs in connection with their land-grant institutions, including Pennsylvania, New York, and Massachusetts.
County agent work in cooperation with the land-grant institutions and
with the Office of Farm Management of the U.S. Department of Agriculture began in several states in the period 1910–1912 or earlier. These
states included Colorado, Idaho, Illinois, Kansas, Michigan, Minnesota, Missouri, Ohio, Washington, West Virginia, Wisconsin, and
Wyoming.

Some states, such as Montana, had taken only limited actions
before 1914. Large in area and small in population, Montana did not
have the resources or the population to support a major effort without
federal help. The state land-grant university was established in 1894,
with farmers institutes being held the same year. In 1911, with money
granted by the American Flax Association, the state agricultural experiment station hired Milburn L. Wilson to promote flax growing in the
state. M. L., as he was widely called, later became Administrator of the
Federal Extension Service. A Department of Agricultural Extension
was approved by the state legislature in 1913 and the first two county

agents were hired. Thus Montana had just managed to get the framework in place to start programs under the Smith-Lever Act when it became law.

SOUTHERN STATES.   In contrast to northern and western states, most southern states had been working on Extension directly with the U.S. Department of Agriculture, under the program set up by Seaman A. Knapp. The Smith-Lever Act established a cooperative program that included the land-grant universities. The act thus brought about some adjustments in southern Extension and its management.

The farmers institute movement in Florida began in 1899, under the sponsorship of many groups. However, the superintendent of the institutes was responsible to the director of the agricultural experiment station. In 1909 the director of the station became the superintendent of the institutes. The institutes became active just as the state's farmers were beginning the greatest advances in crop production Florida had ever seen. This may have been a coincidence, but many people credited the institutes with showing the way.

While the funds appropriated by the Florida state legislature in 1909 were used for farmers institutes, the appropriation qualified Florida for federal funds for cooperative demonstration work. The federal government sent a representative to Florida, with headquarters at Live Oak, to develop a demonstration program. The number of Extension agents reporting to the federal representative increased from two men in 1909 to thirty-six men and fourteen women in 1913.

The two programs—the institutes directed from the state agricultural experiment station and the demonstration work directed by an agent of the United States Department of Agriculture—apparently existed side by side with relatively little friction. The potential conflict was resolved in 1915, when Florida accepted the provisions of the Smith-Lever Act. The director of the experiment stations, P. H. Rolfs, who was also director of the farmers institutes, became the state's first Extension director. Many of the county agents who had been employed in the demonstration work transferred to the new state-directed Extension service. Most of their duties remained the same.

It seemed to many early agents in Florida that their primary duty was to vaccinate hogs. County agents in Florida, as elsewhere, encouraged farmers to improve their practices in growing corn, peanuts,

Seaman A. Knapp, called "father of Extension," initiated the demonstration method of providing practical and useful information to the public, particularly to rural people.

President Woodrow Wilson signed the Smith-Lever Act on May 8, 1914, making the Extension Service the educational arm of the U.S. Department of Agriculture. Senator Hoke K. Smith of Georgia was the senatorial sponsor of the bill.

Congressman Asbury F. Lever of South Carolina was the House of Representatives sponsor of the bill.

A.C. True
(1914-1923)

C.W. Pugsley
(1923)

C.W. Warburton
(1923-1940)

M.L. Wilson
(1940-1953)

C.M. Ferguson
(1953-1960)

P.V. Kepner
(1960-1961)

E.T. York, Jr.
(1961-1963)

Lloyd H. Davis
(1963-1970)

Edwin L. Kirby
(1970-1977)

W. Neill Schaller
(1977-1979)

Mary Nell Greenwood
(1979-1986)

Myron D. Johnsrud
(1986-

Twelve directors and administrators, although the first two did not have that title, have guided the development and growth of the Cooperative Extension System of the U.S. Department of Agriculture from 1914 to the present time.

Headquarters of the U.S. Department of Agriculture, Washington, D.C., and the national headquarters of the Extension Service System. Administrators are located in the North Building (*on left*) and the remaining 175 Extension staff members are in the South Building. (USDA photo)

The Walter C. Porter farm, Terrell, Texas, Seaman A. Knapp's first demonstration farm, is still farmed by the Porter family. (*Left to right*) Dawn Duncan, county Extension agent for home economics; Bill Porter, Harry Porter, and Wylie Roberts, county Extension agents for agriculture. (Texas Extension Service photo)

W. C. Stallings (*center*) was appointed county agent of Smith County, Texas, on November 12, 1906, the first county Extension agent in the nation to serve only one county. (Texas Extension Service photo)

In a letter to Seaman A. Knapp, November 9, 1906, Booker T. Washington of Tuskegee Institute agreed to assign Thomas M. Campbell (*left*) to Extension work, operating an agricultural demonstration wagon in several Alabama counties. Campbell was one of the nation's first Extension agents and the first black agent. The "Knapp Agricultural Truck" (*below*) and the "Jessup Wagon," developed by T. M. Campbell and others between 1906 and 1910, took information on such subjects as vaccinating hogs to prevent cholera to black farm families. (Tuskegee Institute photos)

The Massachusetts Agricultural College called their movable school the "Traveling Instructor." Alstair MacDougall began the school in 1913. (Alstair MacDougall photo)

The "Nutrition Van Go" is a 25-foot customized van created in the 1980s by Pennsylvania State University's Nutrition Education Center. Extension home economists help schedule the van, which is equipped with a microcomputer, film strips, slide projectors, a video player, and information materials. (Pennsylvania State University photo)

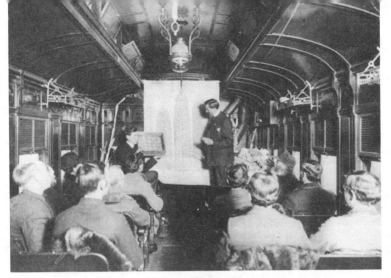

Perry G. Holden, Iowa State College, conceived the idea in 1903 of a "demonstration train" (*above*) with speakers discussing seed corn selection and other subjects at several stops each day. In 1911 sixty-two trains carried seventy-two lecturers 35,000 miles and reached almost a million people. (Iowa State University photo)   A "demonstration train" (*below*) drew crowds such as this one in Yakima County, Washington, in 1927, with forty-three stops and an audience of sixty thousand. (Washington State University Library photo)

Early Extension home agents, with equipment for a meeting, drove their model-T Ford to reach farm families. "Devotion to duty" (*below*) described the early Extension home agents. Here the agent drove a team hitched to a buggy to reach farm families. (Extension Service, USDA photos)

A cooking class being given in 1920 by a New Jersey Extension Service home economist. (Photo by George H. Pound, New Jersey Agricultural Experiment Station Extension Service)

In the 1930s the telephone and the radio speeded up transfer of needed information from the county agent to the farm and ranch family.

THEN: This Montana county agent's office typified the Extension base of operations in 1919. The county agent always has had the telephone at his fingertips to keep in touch with local people and their problems.

NOW: The unit director, Chesterfield County Extension Service, Virginia, has ten computers tied together in a local area network to speed up communications with instant data available to the county Extension staff, local clientele, and state staff.

and other crops, and to consider buying and using improved farm implements. Boys' corn clubs were popular. The home demonstration agents, first called canning club agents in Florida, worked with girls' tomato, garden, and canning clubs. Everyone on the staff worked with the county and state fairs.

As in most other states, agents in Florida had to prove their worth. Farmers at first looked upon the agents with suspicion. They hesitated to take advice from some younger person with little to offer but book learning. In Florida, unlike some other states, this new program received little support from businessmen and the general public. A hog cholera control program, however, won considerable support among farmers. The agents' work during World War I brought them a wide general acceptance.

When Florida accepted the provisions of the Smith-Lever Act in 1915, it created a separate program of Extension work for blacks. Its headquarters were at Florida A. & M. University in Tallahassee, although it was under the direct supervision of the Extension Division of the University of Florida. As early as 1901, Florida A. & M. University, then known as the State Normal and Industrial School for Colored Students, began holding annual farmers educational conferences. In 1902 the Florida state legislature appropriated six hundred dollars to hold institutes for black farmers. The first black county demonstration agent, Frank Robinson, was appointed in 1913 under the federal demonstration program. As work developed under the Smith-Lever Act, boys' and girls' club leaders and home demonstration agents were appointed. In 1920, when blacks made up 34 percent of the rural population, 5 percent of Extension funds was spent for work among them.

Extension began somewhat differently in Kentucky. Farmers institutes were directed by the commissioner of agriculture, although speakers often were secured from the agricultural experiment station. In 1907 the U.S. Department of Agriculture assigned a dairy specialist to the experiment station to work among Kentucky's dairy farmers. This program continued until the Smith-Lever Act became effective. Shortly thereafter, experiment station staff began organizing boys' corn clubs in which boys were instructed on improved methods of producing corn and encouraged to show the results of their work at fairs and farmers conventions. The first county Extension agent, federally funded, was appointed in 1912. In 1913 Helen B. Wolcott was appointed state agent to organize Extension work in home economics.

In 1913 representatives of the U.S. Department of Agriculture, Western Kentucky Normal School, Eastern Kentucky Normal School, the commissioner of agriculture, and the University of Kentucky agreed to locate Extension work in several parts of the state with divided supervision. After passage of the Smith-Lever Act, the secretary of agriculture and the president of the University of Kentucky agreed that all Extension work in agriculture and home economics in the state would be carried on by a superintendent of Extension in the university, with the arrangement superseding the agreement of 1913. In 1919 the dean of the College of Agriculture was designated director of all the work in the Agricultural College, including Extension. While Extension work with black farmers was the responsibility of the University of Kentucky, it was carried out by Kentucky State University, then known as the Kentucky State Normal and Industrial Institute School for Colored Persons, at Frankfort. In 1920, of a total of eighty-three Extension workers in the state, five were black.

Even though the number of black agents was limited throughout the nation, efforts by particular individuals often brought substantial improvements in their counties. For example, Otis S. O'Neal was appointed a county agent for Houston and Peach Counties, Georgia, in 1914, a position he held until his retirement in 1951. He was based at Fort Valley School, now Fort Valley State College. O'Neal saw that farmers must turn from total dependence upon cotton, producing some of their own food as a vital first step if they were to move out of poverty. He began teaching families, usually on a one-to-one basis, just how to go about producing and canning fruits and vegetables, raising poultry and hogs, and curing meat. In 1916 he dramatized his efforts by putting on what became an annual event, a "Ham and Egg Show," that won the support of the farmers and the community. With persistent effort he gave many farm families the knowledge they needed to improve substantially their farming and their lives.

The transition in the South from Extension programs largely financed by the U.S. Department of Agriculture and directed from there, with some financial help from the General Education Board, required compromise, particularly between land-grant universities and the department. The effort was successful and the system has continued to improve farming and rural life in the South for seventy-five years.

Looking Ahead.   In 1914 the goal of establishing a nationally coordinated program of agricultural education became a reality with the passage of the Smith-Lever Act. The accomplishment was an outgrowth of the work of the agricultural colleges and experiment stations on the one hand, and an increasing national awareness of the importance of education on the other. Many educators and farm leaders worked for several years to secure passage of the act.

The provisions of the act soon were adopted by all the states. There were problems to be worked out concerning, first, the relationships of the state agricultural colleges and the United States Department of Agriculture, and second, the relationships between the counties and the states. Still another problem was securing the interest and support of farmers and their families. During the first three years of operation under the act, many of these problems were solved. By 1917 a cooperative Extension organization had been established in every state.

The new service was to be tested very soon in ways never imagined by the people who had worked so hard for the law in the first decade and a half of the century. Yet this testing would resolve some of the problems still remaining and offer an opportunity for growth that would dramatically change Extension.

CHAPTER FOUR

War and Depression:
The First Years under Smith-Lever

Introduction.   In 1914, the same year that the Smith-Lever Act established the Cooperative Extension System, World War I broke out in Europe. Three years later the United States entered the war. Extension, which was well established in some states but just getting under way in others, was to undertake a major role in the war effort. First and foremost, Extension's responsibility was to help farmers increase the production of essential crops, particularly wheat. County agents were assigned responsibility for allocating fertilizer and farm machinery to farmers. With many people entering the armed forces and taking jobs in war industries, farm labor shortages occurred. County agents helped solve this problem by recruiting labor from nontraditional sources.

Extension home economists and boys' and girls' club agents taught both farm and urban homemakers and young people how to use food wisely and preserve excess food. They encouraged home gardens. Their efforts helped people save food essential to the military effort. Many members of the boys' and girls' clubs also produced considerable quantities of farm products.

World War I brought a rapid growth in Extension and helped it win acceptance. However, beginning in the summer of 1920, Extension faced another crisis when agriculture entered into a long-term depression. For about fourteen years, with some ups and downs, farming was subject to difficult economic circumstances. Extension agents emphasized more efficient production, stressed the importance of marketing, and urged diversification. Home economists educated homemakers on the economical management of households and on "making do" with what one had.

The 1920s saw the organization of the American Farm Bureau Federation, the establishment of home economics as a profession, the growth of 4-H, and the development of an educational philosophy and methodology in Extension.

This chapter traces the development of Extension and its programs for the first two decades after the passage of the Smith-Lever Act.

World War I and Extension. When World War I began in Europe in 1914, the United States was a nation of decreasing export surpluses, a stable agricultural population, and a moderately increasing physical output of farm products through the increasing efficiency of farm labor, equipment, and organization. Prices of farm products were advancing at a slightly higher rate than those of other commodities. Generally, the farm economy was in a state of equilibrium with the rest of the economy.

After the United States entered the war, a farmer walking into a county Extension office saw a brightly colored poster. It pictured soldiers charging with fixed bayonets. Bold black lettering said: "Your Country Calls—Save Food with a Silo." Or, in Illinois, a paternalistic Uncle Sam was saying: "Son! Do you know that your seed corn will grow?" with a follow-up message urging the farmer to test his seed corn. The young people were not left out. Posters in Connecticut urged: "School Boys of Connecticut! Help the Farmers with the Harvest!" And the girls and women were also urged to do their part by posters saying, "Can All You Can" and "War Gardens Over the Top."

The wartime posters illustrated how the Cooperative Extension Service, established as an educational agency on a nationwide basis only three years earlier, could become an effective instrument for quickly attaining national goals. The major goal was to increase the nation's production of food, particularly wheat, even as people were leaving the farms to join the armed services or to work in war industries. That goal was achieved.

INCREASING WHEAT PRODUCTION.   The first year of the war in Europe did not greatly affect American agriculture, although the area of wheat sown in the fall of 1914 increased by about 5 million acres and in the spring of 1915 by nearly 2 million acres over the previous year. Increases in planting and a favorable year led to the largest wheat crop ever harvested in the United States. The next year, 1916, saw both a poor harvest and a sharply increased demand by the European allies. By 1917, when the United States entered the war, the government was prepared to do everything possible to increase wheat production, including guarantees of minimum prices for the 1917 and 1918 crops. The Extension Service was an important factor, too, in increasing wheat acreage from an average of 47 million acres for the period 1909 to 1913 to 74 million in 1919, and the crop from 690 million bushels to 952 million during the same period.

Helping farmers increase wheat production was just one of the wartime tasks assigned to Extension. Congress passed two major laws relating to food and agriculture, the Food and Fuel Control Act and the Food Production Act, both signed into law on August 10, 1917, by President Woodrow Wilson. The Food Control Act authorized the president to set up a Food Administration, headed by Herbert Hoover, which would control the handling and distribution of food. The Food Production Act gave the Department of Agriculture responsibility for encouraging the production of commodities, as well as moving them to market and conserving perishable products by canning, drying, and preserving. The county agent was called upon to work for both agencies, although his efforts had no official legal sanction except that the Food Production Act provided an emergency appropriation of $4,348,400 (increased to $6,100,000 in 1918) for "the further development of the Extension Service." The total appropriation for Extension work rose from $3,597,235 in 1915 to $11,302,764 in 1918, and to nearly $17,000,000 in 1921.

GROWTH IN EXTENSION.   The number of counties having agricultural agents increased from 928 in 1914 to 2,435 in 1918. The total Extension staff grew from 2,601 in 1915 to 6,728 in 1918. On June 30, 1917, there were 1,466 county agents, with 66 black agents among them. By October 1917, more than 1,600 emergency agents, including

600 women, had been appointed under authority of the Food Production Act appropriation.

What did these new Extension people do? Judging by their reports, the answer is everything. The war brought a common objective to the agents and transformed their diffuse local programs into a unified national program. Their effective work greatly enhanced their prestige and increased their morale. Instead of being book farmers, they were the patriotic leaders of numerous war campaigns, service agents for many branches of the federal government, and propagandists of a high order.

The major responsibility of the county agent's war work was to campaign for increased production. In the wheat campaign, for example, agents taught farmers better methods of production. In addition, in states making allotments of wheat acreage on a county basis, the agents made farm-to-farm visits to secure pledges from farmers to increase their wheat acreage to meet or exceed the county quota. Other campaigns were carried on to increase the production of corn, oats, barley, and rye. Pork, mutton, poultry, and egg production campaigns also were sponsored by county agents.

Under the Food Control Act of 1917 the president was authorized to buy nitrate of soda and distribute it to farmers to increase production. This responsibility was assigned to the Department of Agriculture and, at the local level, to county agents. Agents usually handled local allocations under the Food Control Act of other fertilizers and farm equipment.

FARM LABOR PROBLEMS.   Crops that were planted had to be harvested. Farmers were in a difficult position in attempting to increase production at the same time men were leaving the farm to join the armed forces or to work in war industries in the cities. About 1.1 million men and women left the farms for the military. County agents were very active in helping solve the problems of farm labor. Nearly all of them served on local draft boards, often being responsible for deciding which farm men should be drafted and which deferred. Everyone in the local Extension offices — county agents, home demonstration agents, and boys' and girls' club agents — worked to meet the labor shortages. They helped organize and place people in the Women's Land

Army and the Boys' Working Reserve. Both of these organizations provided farmers with labor, usually people working in crews during planting and harvesting seasons. They helped organize businessmen into Shock Troops and Twilight Crews to aid farmers by working evenings and weekends during the harvest season. Black agents in Alabama organized rural blacks into the United States Saturday Service League, a movement that spread to several states. Its members did farm work, usually harvesting, on weekends. In 1918, reported the secretary of agriculture, more than 45,000 workers were recruited to help farmers with the wheat harvest. The potato crop in two counties in Texas was saved through the help of businessmen. In Illinois 35,000 people were registered for harvest work. This story was repeated across America.

FOOD USE AND GARDENS.   Second in importance to increased production was the wise use and preservation of food and the raising of additional food for home use in gardens. Farm boys and girls were encouraged to join garden and canning clubs, while city youngsters also were encouraged to plant gardens. In Allegheny County, Pennsylvania, more than 15,000 urban war gardens were planted, and more than 125 canning and drying demonstrations were held for a total of 6,000 women. Home demonstration agents carried on campaigns to save wheat, sugar, and meat by using them carefully. They urged families to serve more milk and cheese as substitutes for meat. Women were urged to save wheat by using more rye, oats, and corn in bread baking.

In general, much of the work centered around practical demonstrations of substitutions for scarce foods and methods of food preservation. Numerous canning centers were established where women could come both to learn and to do their canning. For example, in Florida in 1917 both white and black women were taught canning procedures. The next year, under the supervision of Florida A. & M. University (then Florida A. & M. College), 15 black home demonstrators were hired with federal emergency funds to teach methods of food preservation. The demonstrators enrolled more than 1,600 black women in canning clubs. The Extension Service at the University of Florida did similar work with white women.

There were other wartime activities as well. The influenza epidemic of 1918 spread into every North Carolina community. Each faced a shortage of doctors, nurses, dieticians, and other health workers to care for the sick. Home demonstration agents took the lead in organizing groups to help in every way possible during the emergency. In many instances they served as nurses and dieticians.

SERVICE FUNCTIONS. County agents, home demonstration agents, and club agents were called upon to carry out service functions for many governmental and private agencies. They solicited for Liberty Loans, War Savings Stamps, and Red Cross drives. They helped the War Department locate horses and mules for direct purchase for army use and helped secure hay and straw. They headed metal, paper, and other salvage drives. They conducted surveys and reported on agricultural conditions. They surveyed materials used for fuel and supplied the Fuel Administration with lists of fuel dealers and public buildings using coal. Agents held thousands of mass meetings, not only to encourage food production and preservation, but also to explain the issues of the war and to enlist support for the many war programs and activities.

In summary, World War I brought a rapid growth in the Extension service, with increased funding and personnel. It strengthened the influence of the federal government on county agent work, even though the Extension divisions in the state agricultural colleges benefited similarly from the increased funding. The war provided a common objective for diverse aims and programs and it greatly increased the contacts of the county agent. Finally, because Extension came through in a national crisis, its prestige and its acceptability to the American people grew.

AFTERMATH OF WAR. The armistice ending World War I was signed on November 11, 1918. Many thousands of people who had served in the armed forces or who had been working in factories producing war goods began to come back to farming. However, many others did not return. The farm population totaled 31.6 million in 1920, about 30 percent of the total population. Some people had returned to the farm, but never again was the farm population to reach its 1916 peak of 32.5 million people. In 1920 there were 6.5 million farms averaging 148 acres each. Persons on farms had an annual income from farming of $8,368. Agricultural products made up about 45 percent of the nation's total exports. Farmers on the whole had prospered during the war, but the situation was about to change, even though farm prices remained high during 1919.

Exports declined sharply in the summer of 1920, and farm prices fell even more. In general, prices of major farm products declined by about 50 percent between 1919 and 1921. For a decade, with some ups and downs, prices tended downward, reaching a low point in 1932. This was the situation facing Extension as it moved from a prosperous wartime to a troubled peacetime.

A Time of Transition.   Extension itself faced problems; its character had changed during the war. Instead of emphasizing education, it had become a service agency for individuals and organizations and for the federal government. This had been necessary while the nation devoted its energies to winning the war. When the war was over, the economic situation of many farmers became so difficult that Extension had to work with them on both production and marketing problems. Would Extension work at these problems as a force for education or would it continue as a service agency?

Extension first had to deal with questions of finance and personnel. The large federal emergency appropriation was available until July 1, 1919. However, it was uncertain what funds would be available after that date. So, as all good bureaucrats must, both federal and state Extension directors began to cut back on expenditures. Only part of the emergency fund was used. In addition, as the Food Administration, the Council of National Defense, and other wartime agencies closed down their operations, there was some argument that Extension, too, should come to an end. In most counties, though, farmers had been so impressed with the agents' activities that additional local funds were raised to keep them on the payroll. This was less true of home demonstration agents, most of whom had been first employed during the war. After a great deal of uncertainty Congress appropriated a total of $2 million for Extension for 1920, less than half the $4.6 million spent in 1919. However, additional state, county, and local funding brought total Extension funding for 1920 very close to the 1919 level. The cost of paying and maintaining an agent had increased enough, however, that some cutbacks still were necessary.

Rise of the Farm Bureau.   Local support for county agents, even before the passage of the Smith-Lever Act, had come from diverse groups. Some were made up of farmers and others primarily of businessmen, while some were farm organizations already in operation. The first group calling itself a farm bureau was set up by the Chamber of Commerce of Binghamton, New York, in 1911. The work was taken over in 1914 by the Broome County Farm Improvement Association, made up mainly of farmers. In 1912 a farmers' organization similar to later farm bureaus was organized in Pettis County, Missouri, and began cooperating with the Missouri College of Agriculture and the U.S. Department of Agriculture in both finance and program planning.

County organizations similar to that in Pettis County developed under various names in many counties, mainly in the northern and western states. They provided a nucleus of leaders to assist the county agent in carrying out Extension projects and to supplement his financial support. The Smith-Lever Act specifically allowed contributions from private individuals as part of state matching funds. The organizations themselves usually required a nominal membership fee, but would raise additional money in various ways. In 1916 the name "county farm bureau" was adopted for these groups at a meeting of state county agent leaders from the northern and western states.

Federal, state, and county Extension workers planned and undertook the organization of farm bureaus. Many states required that one be organized before an agent was assigned to a county. By 1919 there were eight hundred county farm bureaus and twenty-two state federations. Early on, the Office of Extension Work North and South defined a county farm bureau as "an institution for the development of a county program of work in agriculture and home economics and for cooperation with state and federal agencies in the development of profitable farm management and efficient and wholesome home and community life."

As county bureaus gained in influence and put more money into the Extension office, some of them began to consider the county agent an employee. At the same time, many were not deeply interested in the development of educational programs but wanted the county agents just to manage the cooperative buying of supplies and selling of products. These developments led to many problems. Some farm bureaus wanted these services limited to their members, even though the county agent was a public servant. Even where this was not true, many county agents still were under pressure to buy and sell for farmers, and local dealers resented such activities by agents. In 1918 State Relations Service Director Alfred C. True ruled that county agents were to confine their activities with cooperative associations to educational matters. They could advise on organizing and operating a cooperative association but were to leave to the association all actual business transactions.

STATE FARM BUREAUS.   The first state federation of farm bureaus was organized in Missouri in March 1915. It was followed in May by one in Massachusetts. These first state organizations essentially were educational federations to promote the efficiency of local bureaus. The Illinois Agricultural Association, organized in 1916, added business activities and legislation to its primary functions. At its first meeting legislative matters were the principal business. The Iowa Farm Bureau Federation was founded in 1918 with James R. Howard its first president. Howard, then a farmer, had been a teacher, a banker, and a wartime emergency county demonstration agent. As an agent, he undertook the organization of farm bureaus as his main assignment. Earlier, he had organized a farm bureau in his home county as a necessary step to securing the appointment of a county Extension agent. In his first address as president of the state farm bureau Howard, although himself an educator, made it clear that in his opinion the state organization should go far beyond the Extension Service's educational programs. It should look after farm business interests, such as dealing with meat-packers and railroads. As an activist organization, it should use its power to influence legislation, but it should remain politically nonpartisan.

The experience of Minnesota with the farm bureau is similar to that of a number of other states. At the end of the war county farm bureaus in Minnesota supplied a strong base of support for Extension, just as many Extension agents had provided aid to farm bureaus in organizing and in securing members. The state legislature passed a law on April 24, 1919, which made organization of a county farm bureau mandatory before county or state funds would be made available for county Extension work. The farm bureau was to approve the appointment of any county agent and to approve the expenditure of county funds for Extension work. These provisions remained in effect for about thirty-five years. As state and national farm bureaus were organized and as they entered into noneducational activities, the mandatory involvement of the farm bureau in Extension created some problems. The state Extension director stated that the county agent should not solicit membership in farm bureaus or operate business associations established by the bureaus, but this was difficult in Minnesota in light of the 1919 act. However, the farm bureau did provide an often effective base of support for Extension.

THE AMERICAN FARM BUREAU FEDERATION.   Early in 1919 a group of men from twelve states met at Cornell University to consider the formation of a national farm bureau federation. Howard attended, as did Extension leaders of the Department of Agriculture. The group agreed to call a broader meeting in Chicago in November 1919 to formally organize the national federation. The 1919 convention agreed on an organization to become permanent when its constitution was ratified by at least ten states, and to establish headquarters in Chicago, with a representative in Washington. Howard was elected the first president. The new federation, which became permanent in 1920, almost at once became a driving force in working with the farm bloc, a group of senators and congressmen pledged to the welfare of the American farmer over partisan political considerations.

Working with the farm bloc, the American Farm Bureau Federation persuaded Congress to fund the Extension service at a level that permitted gradual expansion. At the same time the farm bureau counted on Extension to organize farmers into strong, effective farm bureaus. The Department of Agriculture attempted to confine the county agent's relations with the county farm bureau to impartial educational activities. In 1921 the State Relations Service of the USDA and the American Farm Bureau Federation signed a formal memorandum defining the relationships between the county agent and the county farm bureau, emphasizing their educational nature. The memorandum was followed in 1922 by a statement of Secretary of Agriculture Henry C. Wallace. Wallace emphasized county agents were public teachers and that it was not part of their official duties to carry out for individuals or organizations actual operations of production or marketing operations, nor was it proper for them to act as organizers or managers of farmers associations. While it may seem a simple matter to handle such questions by an agreement or a memorandum, the county agent was in reality responsible to local and state governments rather than to the federal agencies. The question of farm bureau and Extension relationships would continue to be a problem in some states for several years.

Reorganization of the Federal Extension Office.   The relationship with the farm bureau was not the only problem facing federal Extension leaders. The division of responsibility between the Office of Extension Work in the South and the Office of Extension Work in the North and West, with their leaders' different approaches to problems and to relations with the state college Extension offices, had created difficulties. Alfred C. True, as director of their coordinating agency, the States Relations Service, had attempted with little success to bring about agreement, at least in principle, in carrying out the responsibilities of the Smith-Lever Act. In 1920 the Association of Land Grant Colleges recommended that the two offices be combined. The retirement of Bradford C. Knapp, chief of the southern Extension office, opened the way. On October 1, 1921, the two were combined as the Office of Extension Work, with Clarence B. Smith as chief. The new office remained a part of the States Relations Service until 1923, when True retired. At that time Clyde W. Warburton was appointed director of Extension work and the Extension Service became an agency reporting to the secretary of agriculture. Warburton held the post until 1940.

LINES OF WORK.   As cooperative Extension work had developed, three main lines of work were reflected in federal, state, and county Extension offices: county agricultural agent work, home demonstration work, and the boys' and girls' club work. Federal and state leaders in these different lines began conferring directly with each other to the extent that state Extension directors were being bypassed. This situation came to a head when Charles W. Pugsley, formerly director of Extension in Nebraska, became assistant secretary of agriculture. At his direction and with the concurrence of the Association of Land-Grant Colleges, the divisions in the federal office relating to county agents, home demonstration agents, and boys' and girls' club work were abolished. New subject-matter divisions were established. After the 1923 reorganizations, the federal office had four divisions: (1) division of projects, inspection, and methods; (2) division of subject-matter specialists; (3) division of reports and studies of the efficiency of extension work; and (4) division of visual instruction and editorial work. The reorganizations of 1921 and 1923 were accompanied by a clear, definite understanding that all the department's business with the state Extension services would be coordinated through the Extension directors at the agricultural colleges.

Fighting the Depression. As Extension at several levels reorganized and began working with farm bureaus, and with C. W. Warburton heading the federal office, it faced the problem of helping farmers overcome the effects of a continuing farm depression. Farm prices were going down even as the rest of the economy was prospering and the prices farmers paid were going up. Warburton had experience working with distressed farmers. In 1921 he had been called from his job as an agronomist in the Bureau of Plant Industry to take charge of field work for a seed-grain loan program for farmers hit by drought in western states.

FARMERS COOPERATIVES. During the 1920s many farmers, the American Farm Bureau Federation, and the Department of Agriculture saw farmers cooperatives as a major force for overcoming the farm depression. The farm bloc in Congress, with strong encouragement from the federation and the secretary of agriculture, passed the Capper-Volstead Act, exempting agricultural cooperatives from some aspects of the antitrust laws. The federation became involved in some very large cooperative projects that failed but had more success with smaller cooperatives. The Extension Service was also active in the cooperative movement. Secretary of Agriculture Henry C. Wallace wrote in 1924 that the "need for strong cooperative marketing associations cannot be overemphasized." He advised, though, that the relationship of the government to cooperatives should be one of service. Government should help farmers market their crops by supplying information they could not get for themselves.

County agents took part in the organization and promotion of many successful marketing associations. These included wool pools, creameries, truck marketing associations, poultry and egg marketing associations, livestock shipping associations, seed associations, and fertilizer associations. County agents were active in establishing the Dairymen's League of New York and large cotton associations in the southern states. In 1923 agents worked with 926,000 farm families and 6,000 cooperative associations on marketing problems. In spite of the advice of state and federal leaders, county agents sometimes acted as managers for local cooperatives, particularly those that were too small to afford a manager.

Cooperatives were encouraged throughout the 1920s. In 1926 Congress created a Division of Cooperative Marketing in the Bureau of Agricultural Economics. The division took on some of the advisory functions previously carried out by Extension. In 1929 Congress created the Federal Farm Board to encourage producers to organize effective marketing cooperatives and to aid in preventing and controlling surpluses in any agricultural commodity through orderly production and distribution. Although the farm board was an independent agency, Extension was involved in its duties. County agents were responsible for explaining the functions of the board and for helping cooperatives meet the organizational requirements it set up. They also worked with farmers in the Federal Farm Board's program to reduce wheat and cotton production to the proper level to meet effective demand. Federal and state leaders, subject-matter specialists, county agents, and local leaders met to draw up long-term plans for farmers to adjust their production and marketing activities to national needs and to survive the continuing agricultural depression. The Federal Farm Board got under way just as the farm depression broadened into a great national depression. Its stabilization programs failed, but a number of the cooperatives it organized with the help of Extension survived.

EFFICIENT PRODUCTION AND NEW TECHNOLOGY.   Extension always has encouraged farmers to produce as efficiently and at as low a cost as possible. County agents stressed the need for farm records and accounts as a base for adopting more effective practices. For example, the Dairy Herd Improvement Associations, often organized with leadership from the county agent, showed farmers that by keeping careful records of dairy production and carrying out relevant breeding programs, they could upgrade the productivity and profitability of their herds. In 1923 the Department of Agriculture began issuing outlook materials on trends in production and the demand for major agricultural commodities. The materials were revised by the agricultural colleges to fit each particular state and they then were distributed to farmers by county agents.

New technologies were developing in agriculture. While some farmers, because of depressed conditions, felt they could not afford to make changes, others, often with the advice of the county agent, adopted the new technologies. Among the new technologies none was more revolutionary or more expensive to adopt than was the tractor powered by an internal combustion engine. There were 246,000 of these tractors on American farms in 1920 and 920,000 in 1930. The farmer who purchased a tractor was changing his way of farming. He had to buy other machinery to be used with the tractor and he had to buy fuel. Horses were of little use henceforth, and the land used formerly to pasture horses and raise feed for them was now available for other crops.

Many farmers learned about tractors and other machines as well as about improved crops and livestock at their county and state fairs. Extension workers traditionally have been key people in both county and state fairs and often have had the primary responsibility for their management. In Indiana, for example, the state Extension director is a member of the board of directors of the state fair. In Wisconsin, H. G. Seyforth, Pierce County's first Extension agent, served as president, secretary, director, and advisor of the county fair for fifty-five years. He was a livestock and poultry judge at many county fairs and was president and director of the Wisconsin Association of Fairs. Although there is disagreement about the value of fairs as educational tools, they certainly have promoted information exchange and brought rural people together.

Midwestern corn producers faced another decision — whether or not to adopt hybrid seed corn. The new corn seed greatly increased yields, but the farmer had to buy seed every year since the hybrid did not reproduce satisfactorily. County agents were called upon for advice. In 1930 less than .001 percent of the corn crop was grown from hybrid seed; in 1940 hybrid seed accounted for 30 percent of the crop, and in 1960, 96 percent.

THE FARM MANAGEMENT APPROACH.   A farmer adopting these and other new technologies found himself facing many problems. He needed better farm management, not just a change in a particular operation. County agents took the forefront in helping individual farmers draw up farm management plans. Material for this training was available because both the state colleges and the USDA were emphasizing farm management as one way out of the farm depression for the individual farmer.

Some studies showed that even in the depression, capable farmers were making a living. About 1919 Henry C. Taylor, professor of agricultural economics at the University of Wisconsin, sought to apply the principles he was teaching to an actual operation. He purchased a farm in the midst of many unsuccessful farms near Madison. He set to work to handle the crops, machinery, and farming methods in accordance with the best principles of farm management. Taylor succeeded in establishing a successful dairy farm. The tenant soon had a contract to purchase the farm and eventually became the owner. Taylor then proposed to a foundation that it finance a corporation to continuously develop single-family farms that a tenant, by adopting good management practices, would become able to purchase.

On a trip to Montana in 1923, after he had become chief of the newly established Bureau of Agricultural Economics in the Department of Agriculture, Taylor found that M. L. Wilson, then Extension economist at Montana State College, had studied a number of northern Montana ranches that had prospered in spite of the depression. In 1924, after discussions between Taylor and Wilson, the Fairway Farms Corporation was established in Montana. The corporation planned to buy farms, establish tenant farm families on them, and by teaching the tenants to apply proven methods of efficient farm management, enable the tenants to buy the farm. At the same time the farms would be a demonstration of successful farm management. County agents and the state Extension office were both involved in locating suitable farms and farm families, and then in working with the families to make the farms profitable. As Taylor and Wilson put it, the goal was "to facilitate the climbing of the agricultural ladder." A series of severe droughts hit before most of the tenant-purchase contracts were completed, but, one way or another, a number of farm families did purchase their farms. After seeing the impact of both the depression and the droughts, M. L. Wilson became convinced that so long as major regions of the nation were subject to catastrophic forces, their problems were of national concern.

In the 1920s Arizona suffered a continuing farm depression that was deepened by periods of drought. Most of the state's dryland farmers were forced out of operation. Extension agents taught farmers something about marketing and helped farm groups organize both buying and selling cooperatives. Nevertheless, the situation was very difficult for most farmers although those raising long-staple cotton on irrigated acreage in the Salt River Valley did reasonably well. Arizona home economists taught women to cope with some of the problems resulting from the depression. Good nutrition, canning surplus foods, house gardening, home poultry production, home nursing, furniture refinishing, and sewing with gunny and flour sacks helped some farm families survive the years of economic depression and drought.

Farm Women in the Depression.   The better farm management programs took account of the farm women and indeed of the farm family in determining what could and should be done on a particular farm. Farm women traditionally maintained the household and cared for the children, but a survey made in 1920 by the Office for Extension Work in the North and West showed that farm women also made contributions to the economic well-being of the farm. Some 85 percent cared for chickens, 25 percent for livestock, and 56 percent for gardens; 36 percent milked cows; 33 percent made butter to sell; and 24 percent engaged in field work for an average period of about seven weeks. About a third of the women kept farm accounts. About 79 percent of the women used kerosene lamps, 61 percent carried water from an outside well, and most cooked on kitchen ranges and heated the house with stoves burning wood or coal. The average home was six miles from a high school, three miles from a church, five miles from a market, and five and a half miles from a doctor.

HOME DEMONSTRATION WORK.   The significance of home demonstration and related work with farm women was obvious. The improvement of home equipment, particularly providing running water, power, and modern heating; safeguarding family health, including better food selection and sanitation; and developing more income from such home industries as butter and eggs offered great opportunities for bettering farm women's lives. The number of home demonstration agents had declined at the end of the war but was again increasing by 1922. There was some question whether or not there should be separate farm bureaus or other local organizations for women, and in some states this arrangement existed. However, over a period of a few years the idea of separate organizations for women was dropped. The work itself was carried on in the counties by resident women agents, by district agents serving more than one county, or by agricultural agents with the assistance of home economics specialists from the agricultural colleges. The number of voluntary local leaders increased rapidly. They added much to the program, just as they were doing in boys' and girls' club work.

Home Economics Becomes a Profession.   The first home demonstration agents often were school teachers who were hired for the summer or who moved into Extension full time from teaching. The Smith-Hughes Act of 1917 provided federal funds to pay part of the salaries of home economics teachers in the secondary schools and funds for training teachers of home economics and other vocational subjects. This led to the establishment of home economics departments in a number of colleges and universities and provided a source of trained home demonstration agents. While teachers usually made higher salaries than home demonstration agents, prospects for moving up the ladder were better in Extension. However, the attrition rate was high in both occupations since many organizations had policies against hiring married women. When a woman got married, she was expected to quit her job.

Many state agricultural colleges were limited to male students and some were segregated by race. Segregation by either race or sex or by both created problems for women as well as for blacks in obtaining an education qualifying them for Extension work. It was even more difficult for a woman or a black to hold an Extension job in a college limited to white male students.

The establishment of the American Home Economics Association in 1914 and the development of home economics as a profession is credited largely to Martha van Rensselaer and Flora Rose of Cornell University. The establishment of the Bureau of Home Economics in 1923 in the U.S. Department of Agriculture under the leadership of Louise Stanley further strengthened home economics as a profession.

NUTRITION RESEARCH.   The field of nutrition developed separately from both home economics and Extension. It grew out of chemistry, with scientists at Wesleyan University and the Sheffield Scientific School of Yale University all active in the work. Wilbur O. Atwater of Wesleyan University was the leader. Some of his concepts and research findings still have validity. He was the first head of the Department of Agriculture's Office of Experiment Stations at a time when farmers institutes were getting under way. However, his interest was in nutritional research rather than in administration or education. He returned to Wesleyan University, still as an employee of the department, and continued his studies of nutrition.

Thus in the 1920s home economics and nutrition came to be recognized as professional fields and both contributed to Extension. The women who came into Extension work early and made it a lifetime career had rural backgrounds, a good basic education, good communication skills, and a sense of mission. They acquired technical information as needed and accumulated knowledge with experience. By the late 1920s many had moved into administrative positions. The new home demonstration agents they were hiring had been educated in home economics and, often, in nutrition. Home economics and nutrition research had helped make home demonstration agents true professionals.

The Rise of 4-H.   In 1917 Gertrude Warren, a home economics teacher at Teacher's College of Columbia University, joined the Office of Extension Work in the North and West to expand canning and food conservation programs to meet wartime needs. Under her direction and with the efforts of many state and local leaders, the movement expanded greatly, particularly among young people, even reaching into many cities through canning and gardening clubs. The clubs worked with Extension but had many names and many different structures.

In the early 1900s O. H. Benson and Jessie Field of Iowa had begun using a three-leaf clover emblem for awards in boys' and girls' clubs. Each clover leaf bore an H, the H's standing for head, heart, and hands. In 1910 Benson went to Washington to work with Knapp's Office of Farmers' Cooperative Demonstration Work. At about that time he began using the four-leaf clover, with the fourth H designated as health. In 1918 Warren began using the name 4-H with the clover symbol as a coordinating force, even though the name was not recognized universally until 1924.

A STRUCTURE FOR THE CLUBS.   With the end of the war and of emergency funding, enrollment in the clubs dropped sharply. Northern and Western 4-H leaders meeting in Kansas City in 1919 felt that an institutional framework was needed to focus membership loyalties beyond the individual's pigs, corn, or canning project. They agreed upon a general structure for clubs. A local club finally was defined as a group of at least five members working on a similar project with a local leader. Each club had to have officers and a program of demonstration activities. A club meeting these requirements would then receive a charter signed by the secretary of agriculture, the state Extension director, and the state club leader.

As the organizational framework was put into place, two problems became evident. The first was the relationship of the clubs to the farm bureaus. In some states, farm bureaus rather than Extension services hired club leaders. However, this problem became less important as the relationships between the farm bureaus and Extension were clarified.

The major potential conflict lay in the relationships between the clubs and vocational education programs in the schools. However, as A. C. True saw it, there was plenty of opportunity for both club leaders and vocational teachers. The school program was more formal and was directed by national and state officials. Club work was flexible, determined by local needs and desires, and capable of reaching many more young people. As they have developed over the years, both club work related to Extension and vocational work in the schools have been important in the development of American youth.

By the time of the 1919 meeting, Warren was promoting other projects besides canning and gardening. She suggested clothing, garment making, cooking, and baking for girls. She also suggested that simple outlines be developed by club leaders for projects. Each project would last two or three years, but would achieve some practical result each year. The project idea, developed over the years, did much to make 4-H a vital, growing organization.

FINANCING 4-H.   While the 1919 meeting provided a general structure for the clubs, financing was another problem. Private support seemed to be at least part of the answer. Impetus for a nationwide support program came through the efforts of Guy L. Noble, an employee of the Armour Packing Company of Chicago. For several years businesses in some states and communities had been giving sporadic support to the youth clubs, often by awarding prizes to winners of contests for growing corn, raising hogs, or canning, for example. Noble persuaded the Armour Packing Company to offer prizes of trips to the Chicago International Livestock Exposition to winners of state pig club contests. He discovered that others were giving similar awards. In 1921 Noble and E. N. Hopkins of the Meredith Publishing Company organized the National Committee on Boys' and Girls' Club Work, including representatives of packing companies, publishers, and the American Farm Bureau Federation. The committee agreed that Noble would become executive secretary with an office furnished by the Farm Bureau. The committee was incorporated in 1924. It had four objectives: to promote club demonstrations before state associations, to publicize club work, to encourage bank loans to young people in club work, and to coordinate donations and other efforts by private sponsors. Funding was slow but the annual club tours to Chicago became increasingly successful. In 1923 the tours were renamed the National 4-H Club Congress.

Even as private support was being increased, public support through the Extension Service held steady despite the rapidly increasing cost of maintaining the program. Nevertheless, club work continued and became more institutionalized despite the loss of membership and the inability of Extension to hire additional agents. Although the continuing agricultural depression discouraged some club members, just as it was discouraging their parents, two other developments strengthened club work. First, following successful experiences in Arkansas, local clubs were being encouraged to design their own programs, including the financing. Second, at the suggestion of Milton Danziger who had been in the Cooperative Extension Service, Horace A. Moses, president of the Strathmore Paper Company, established the International 4-H Leadership Training School at the Eastern States Exposition at Springfield, Massachusetts. The first session was held in 1923. This, together with state adult and junior leadership programs, created a pool of experienced and motivated club leaders for the future.

4-H CAMPING.   A few years later interest in 4-H camping led to another means of rewarding and encouraging junior leaders. As early as 1907 a camp for boys was held in Missouri. Campers were instructed in new farm methods. Several states began holding camps, with West Virginia leading the way in formalizing camping as a part of the 4-H movement. By 1921 that state had established a permanent campsite. Camping offered a certain informality and companionship in club work that influenced the level of enthusiasm for more formal programs and offered an opportunity for many young people to develop their leadership abilities. This camping movement culminated in 1927 with a national 4-H camp in Washington, D.C., sponsored by the Department of Agriculture to reward and develop junior leaders in club work, to introduce club members to their national government, and to provide an annual meeting for state leaders.

The same year that the national 4-H camp was first held, Noble and the business leadership of the National Committee on Boys' and Girls' Club Work assisted in securing increased appropriations for Extension work. Noble and a number of representatives of farm organizations, bankers groups, and breeder associations testified in favor of a bill increasing federal funding of Extension by $6 million. Three young 4-H people from Maryland also testified, explaining their projects to the committee. In 1928 a compromise bill, the Capper-Ketchum Act, providing an increase of $1.38 million a year for Extension, became law. For the first time, boys' and girls' club work was specifically mentioned.

Developing an Educational Methodology.   In 1930 two leaders of the Office of Cooperative Extension Work, Clarence B. Smith and Meredith C. Wilson, published *The Agricultural Extension System of the United States.* It is clear from their volume that an educational philosophy and methodology had been developed in Extension for Extension during the first decade and a half after passage of the Smith-Lever Act.

The aim of Extension teaching, according to Smith and Wilson, was to influence farm men and women to make desirable changes. Extension, though, was a completely voluntary program. Thus Extension programs had to meet the real needs of rural people. At the same time, continued confidence in the Extension Service depended upon the change brought about by the teaching program.

The methods of Extension teaching could be grouped as objective, oral, and written. In addition, Extension teaching was spread by indirect means. Objective teaching by method and results demonstrations, exhibits, lantern slides, and motion pictures relied upon the old adage that "seeing is believing." The demonstration, as a fundamental method of teaching farm and home practices, was written into the Smith-Lever Act. In fact, Extension was first known as farm demonstration or home demonstration work in some sections of the country.

DEMONSTRATION.   Two types of demonstration, the result and the method, were recognized by 1930. A method demonstration was a demonstration given by an Extension worker or other trained leader to a group to show them how to carry out a practice. It might be some such activity as pruning, canning, or poultry culling. A result demonstration was a demonstration carried on by a farmer, farm woman, boy or girl, under the direction of the Extension Service, involving a substantial period of time and records of results and comparisons. Growing an acre of cotton or corn, rearranging a kitchen, or raising a pig or a calf are examples of possible result demonstrations. Generally, while result demonstrations could be very effective for the people the agent was working with, they placed a heavy demand on an Extension agent's time. The method demonstration had a distinct advantage in that many more people could be reached with the same expenditure of Extension time and effort. However, after World War II, as farming became more complex, result demonstrations, or what was sometimes called applied research, grew once again in importance.

EXHIBITS.   Extension agents gave much time and effort to exhibits, yet surveys made in the late 1920s indicated that exhibits had little influence in inducing farmers and their families to change any of their practices. Their greatest value was in stimulating interest and fostering goodwill for Extension. The state and federal offices had large collections of photographs and lantern slides. These helped agents make orderly presentations that held the attention of audiences. Posters and charts added another dimension to objective methods of teaching. Film strips and motion pictures were just coming into use and appeared to offer great possibilities. However, their usefulness was severely limited by the lack of electricity for lighting in the country districts where most Extension meetings were held.

FARM AND HOME VISITS.   Farm and home visits were the most effective of the oral methods of Extension teaching. In most counties there were too many farmers and too few agents to make this the sole method. Nevertheless, it was imperative, according to Smith and Wilson, that each agent make some farm and home visits, both to have some specific examples of achievement to describe and to have some field contact upon which to base discussions. When a farmer or a farm woman made an office visit to an agent, it showed confidence in the agent and the likelihood that the agent's recommendations would be followed. However, to conduct successful office calls, the agent had to be familiar with conditions in the field.

MEETINGS.   Meetings were second only to method demonstrations in bringing about the adoption of improved farm practices in the late 1920s. Through talks at field meetings, farmers institutes, and other community meetings, the county agent could bring information regarding improvements in farming and farm life to large numbers of people. The personal acquaintance between the county agent and the farmers developed at these meetings strengthened the agent's influence. Meetings, of course, took many forms. There were field or barn meetings where the material discussed was at hand. Farmers institutes and agricultural trains continued to be effective as vehicles for oral methods of Extension teaching. The farm and home weeks sponsored by most agricultural colleges, during which farm people spent a week at the college attending lectures and demonstrations, were popular. Two devices rather new in rural areas—the telephone and the radio—were being used in many states and counties to keep rural people informed on Extension activities. The United States Department of Agriculture was doing innovative work with the radio as an educational tool.

PRINTED MATERIAL.   When people need definite and detailed information, they want written or printed material. In 1927 the agricultural colleges published some 1,600 bulletins and circulars and distributed 17 million copies of them. The Department of Agriculture distributed another 22 million publications, most of which were Extension in nature. A 1927 study of farms in Minnesota, Wisconsin, and Ohio showed that 62 percent of the farmers had received bulletins; 82 percent receiving them reported reading them and 48 percent had made some practical application of the information contained in them. While bulletins were not among the most important methods of influencing farmers, they did reach and help a large number.

NEWSPAPERS AND MAGAZINES.   In the 1920s, just as in the 1980s, many farm people reported that they got their information on farm and home practices from newspapers and farm journals. Then as now, very few realized that the information they were getting had been given to the papers and journals by the Extension Service. This was a quick and inexpensive way to get information to people, which is one reason it has continued. County agents also put out circular letters when that seemed appropriate and answered a considerable number of letters from individuals.

Finally, as Smith and Wilson pointed out, the passing on of Extension information from neighbor to neighbor was one of the most powerful forces at work in bringing about wider acceptance of improved practices. This could hardly be called a method of Extension teaching, but it was certainly effective.

Extension in Place.   By the early 1930s, even as the nation and its farmers were sliding deeper into depression, the Extension Service had become firmly established as a cooperative educational force, working on county, state, and federal levels. Extension had proven its worth during World War I. After the war the farm bureau movement had stimulated Extension, and in turn, had been stimulated by it. Home demonstration and youth work had become established as a part of rural life. By 1930 an Extension philosophy and methodology had been developed and recognized. In 1930 about three-fourths of rural counties in the United States had county agents, one-third had home demonstration agents, and one-eighth had agents devoting full time to youth work or 4-H. However, the Great Depression made it difficult to continue expansion as tax revenues declined at every level of government. But change was on the way. The New Deal of the 1930s would both challenge and strengthen Extension at the county, state and federal levels.

CHAPTER FIVE

The New Deal and
World War II, 1933–1945

Introduction.   As the nation and its farmers sank deeper into depression, it was evident that farmers needed more than cooperatives and efficient management, useful though these were. Although there were many proposals for government intervention in the 1920s, the Federal Farm Board was the only such proposal adopted. This changed with the New Deal in 1933. With the change came a challenge to and an opportunity for Extension. The challenge to Extension was to preserve its integrity as an educational institution while helping to carry out such programs as price support, production control, and rural electrification. On the other hand, Extension had the opportunity to serve as the educational force for the new programs. In so doing, it could augment a staff seriously depleted during the Great Depression, using funds allocated by the new agencies. For the most part, Extension met the challenge and took advantage of the opportunities.

Hardly had the rigors of the Great Depression been overcome when Extension and the nation were faced with World War II. Once again, Extension turned in large part from education to action, using emergency funds to enlarge its staff. Extension worked with farmers, farm families, and 4-H club members to secure the production increases essential to the war effort. It carried out a large-scale farm labor recruitment program and allocated fertilizer and farm machinery.

Among their wide-ranging activities, Extension home economists taught housewives how to make the best use of available food to insure adequate nutrition, how to maintain household machines and equipment, and how to deal with the rationing of food and other materials. The home economists were responsible for a large-scale urban gardening program, often with help from 4-H. They also carried on such activities as selling war bonds and assisting the Red Cross.

Congress and the public recognized the value of Extension's wartime efforts. The Bankhead-Flannagan Act of 1945 and the Research and Marketing Act of 1946 provided for substantial increases in appropriations for Extension and research.

This chapter traces the activities of Extension during the New Deal and follows with a discussion of Extension's contributions to the nation during World War II.

The Coming of the New Deal.   On January 25, 1933, even before Franklin Delano Roosevelt was inaugurated as president, the president of the American Farm Bureau Federation had given an ominous warning: "Unless something is done for the American farmer we will have revolution in the countryside within less than 12 months." The Farm Holiday Association, a radical grass roots farm organization in the Midwest, seemed to threaten violence. It proposed that Midwest farmers stop the movement of food products to market and force a halt in farm foreclosures.

With President Roosevelt and Secretary of Agriculture Henry A. Wallace urging action, Congress passed the Agricultural Adjustment Act, signed into law on May 12, 1933. Basically, the act offered farmers guaranteed prices for their major crops if they would cut back on acreage farmed or on the amount of a commodity produced. This remained the key idea behind price support legislation through the 1980s. The 1933 act was declared unconstitutional in 1936 but was replaced by the Soil Conservation and Domestic Allotment Act and then by the Agricultural Adjustment Act of 1938. These laws, much amended and modified, have remained in effect through the 1980s. They, like the 1933 act, have sought to restore farm prices by adjusting production to demand.

The Agricultural Adjustment Act was followed by legislation authorizing the Farm Credit Administration, the Resettlement Administration, the Rural Electrification Administration, and the Soil Conservation Service. The Tennessee Valley Authority, although not a part of USDA, was another New Deal agency having a major impact on Extension. All these agencies have continued into the 1980s, although the Resettlement Administration's emphasis shifted and it has become the Farmers Home Administration. The name Agricultural Adjustment Administration (AAA) was changed several times. The agency eventually became the Agricultural Stabilization and Conservation Service.

EXTENSION AND THE AGRICULTURAL ADJUSTMENT ADMINISTRATION.   The AAA made the county agent an important part of its innovative and controversial program. It added to, and in some areas virtually replaced programs designed to increase productivity. It related traditional farm-management work to the achievement of the national goal of a planned agriculture. The county agent, in much of his work, became a promoter rather than an educator. He became an administrator rather than a teacher as he was assigned responsibility for programs that offered farmers large rewards for cooperation and imposed penalties for noncompliance as well.

The Soil Conservation and Domestic Allotment Act replaced the Agricultural Adjustment Act of 1933 and was incorporated into the Agricultural Adjustment Act of 1938. After this move, the county agent in many cases was called upon first to determine and then to evaluate compliance with "good farm management practices" related to soil conservation. This meant that the county agent could see to it that farmers were rewarded for carrying out some of his earlier teachings. It also meant that the agent was responsible for withholding benefits in some cases.

When the AAA was established, it immediately faced a number of pressing deadlines dictated by the financial emergency and the natural cycle of agricultural production. It quickly turned to Extension for help. It was imperative the program reach every farmer, and the Cooperative Extension Service was the only agricultural agency with representatives in virtually every farm county.

Some Extension leaders, both national and state, opposed making the county agent a program manager and a promoter rather than an educator. On the other hand, some opposition arose to the use of Extension agents on the charge that they would be unsympathetic to the programs and would not carry them out effectively. For example, a group of newly elected Democratic congressmen from Iowa requested that the Secretary of Agriculture not use state Extension leaders and county agents in carrying out the program. The congressmen considered those personnel to be Republicans who would be opposed to federal production adjustment goals. In some states where the farm bureau was strong, the endorsement of the Agricultural Adjustment Act by the American Farm Bureau Federation eased the strain. Some state Extension directors also believed that cooperation was necessary to keep the AAA from establishing a competing organization in every farm county in the nation.

The problem also eased with the contribution of funds by the AAA to hire county and assistant county agents, beginning in 1933. Extension, like everything else, had been badly hurt by the Depression. Many states and counties had been forced to cut staffs and discontinue offices. The New Deal offered an opportunity to turn the situation around. The first county agents and assistant agents appointed from emergency funds were appointed through the federal Civil Service Commission but were responsible to state and county officials who had no voice in their appointments. The civil service method of making appointments was discontinued after six months.

With the discontinuance of these federal appointments, the AAA transferred funds to the federal Extension Service. It in turn allocated them to the states for the employment of additional county agents and assistants, for travel and other expenses, and for clerical assistance. In the southern states, where the county agents had assumed most of the responsibility for operating the programs, additional funds were allotted. While it is difficult to determine how much money was transferred and spent, during 1934–1935 about $20 million dollars were transferred and about the same amount was available through regular funding with AAA funds. The number of regularly appointed Extension personnel was increased by 1,171 from June 30, 1933, to January 30, 1935.

The amount and type of work done by Extension for the AAA varied greatly from state to state and even to some extent among counties in the same state. Every agent was responsible for the educational phases of the program, but this responsibility was interpreted in different ways. At the very least, an agent held meetings to explain the law and the regulations surrounding it. Many agents, with the aid of state and federal material, pointed out the need for the program and showed how the farmer could benefit from it. Some agents were enthusiastic; others were not.

After farmers were informed of the program, the county agent set up the local organization for getting it into operation. County and township committees were selected or elected to administer the program. The county agent served as an advisor or as secretary to the committee. In some programs and in some states, the agent ran the program for its first year, but Extension's direct involvement ended after a few years.

The county agent often was involved in acreage allotments and in resolving questions about the division of payments between landowners and tenants on farms operated by tenants. This latter issue arose with recurring frequency in the South, and its resolution was particularly difficult. In many instances, according to farm tenants associations and social workers, white landowners received their black tenants' share of payments as well as their own payments. The problem was serious in the early years of the program, but it was corrected by Congress in later legislation and when the AAA began making payments directly to tenants. Furthermore, it was charged that county agents collected farm bureau dues before releasing checks to small farmers or tenants, even though the individual farmer might never have joined the farm bureau. But, as Gladys L. Baker, an authority on the county agent during this period, has written: "Any criticism of the agent in such cases, however, must take cognizance of the tremendous size of his administrative job, the continuous pressure exerted on him for speed, and his dependence upon the dominant political and economic class."

When the commodity programs were first replaced and then supplemented by the agricultural conservation program, the county agent still was called upon to give leadership to the effort. Many agents, though, felt more at home with the conservation program since it paid farmers to do what the agents had been urging for many years.

In 1934 the Department of Agriculture began sponsoring discussion groups among farmers through the AAA and then through the Bureau of Agricultural Economics. Most of the work was done by Extension. These groups began as a rural education movement to give farmers the factual background needed to discuss and reach decisions regarding agricultural policy. Some Extension services already had similar programs, based upon local and state concerns. However, the department put a great deal of effort into expanding those programs.

The discussion project was initiated in 1934–1935 when nine state Extension services began carrying on a cooperative experimental project with the AAA to promote forum and discussion groups among rural people. Broadcasts covering particular topics were made over the NBC radio network. These were backed up by written material distributed to farmers through state and county Extension offices. This particular project never aroused great enthusiasm among Extension leaders or county agents. County agents, in particular, felt they had enough specific work without this additional, ill-defined task. Eventually, Congress cut off all money for the discussion project. However, some states and communities continued to carry on public affairs discussions, although their programs were no longer directed from Washington.

EXTENSION AND THE SOIL CONSERVATION SERVICE.   The agricultural conservation program of the Agricultural Adjustment Administration sought to relate production control to good soil management practices, including reducing acreage devoted to "soil-depleting" crops. The programs of the Soil Conservation Service (SCS), the 1935 successor to the Soil Erosion Service established in 1933, were more permanent in nature. They attempted not only to stop further soil erosion but also to restore eroded lands, sometimes by moving substantial amounts of earth with heavy equipment.

Extension and the state agricultural experiment stations had established educational and research bases upon which a national soil conservation program could be built. Liberty Hyde Bailey, one of the founders of modern Extension, wrote eloquently during World War I of the wickedness of wounding the land and of the dire consequences that were bound to follow. Between 1914 and 1932, largely through the efforts of the state Extension services, millions of acres of land were terraced as an erosion control measure.

During the 1920s Extension in many states also had encouraged farmers to plant and cultivate trees as a soil conservation measure and as a commercial crop. The effort had met with only marginal success. In Maine, for example, farmers used their woodlots to meet their own needs or sold off all the timber. They seldom were interested in trees as a crop. Extension aroused more interest in this area when it acted to meet an emergency. In September 1938 a hurricane downed more than a hundred million board feet of timber, mostly pine, in southwestern Maine. Without assistance the owners would have lost much of the timber. Extension helped set up the Northeastern Salvage Administration to purchase and hold the logs in pond storage until they could be manufactured and marketed in an orderly manner. Extension continued to advise and assist farmers in the devastated area and effectively helped salvage downed timber in more than a thousand woodlots.

In the years immediately following World War II, the demand for timber led to substantial increases in its value. A number of farmers in Maine turned to commercial tree production. This industry has continued to the present day.

In Kansas, where conditions for timber production are about as different from those in Maine as they can be, there has always been concern about trees as windbreaks as well as for timber. The state agricultural experiment station at Fort Hays began experimental tree plantings shortly after it was established. A state forester was appointed in 1910. He worked closely with Kansas State Agricultural College and traveled over the state encouraging farmers to plant trees. A part-time Extension forester was appointed in 1935, with the position becoming full-time in 1941. During this period, particular attention was given to planting trees as windbreaks and as a soil conservation measure. After World War II the state forester and Extension forester assignments were combined. As had occurred in Maine, the demand for and high price of timber led many farmers to turn to commercial farm woodlots. By 1975 Kansas had nineteen Extension foresters.

When soil conservation was established as a national program, one central issue was whether assistance would be provided directly to farmers by a national agency or carried out through state and county Extension services. The Association of Land-Grant Colleges and Universities in 1934 urged Secretary of Agriculture Henry A. Wallace to have the program administered by the agricultural colleges. In 1935 an interbureau committee of the USDA recommended that the SCS be put in the traditional Extension-USDA pattern. The committee proposed that soil conservation specialists be added to the staffs of county agricultural agents and work under the joint direction of the SCS regional officer and the state Extension directors. The secretary, however, decided to have the soil conservation program administered locally through soil conservation districts, which were organized by Extension. Extension provided the districts with educational help and SCS provided technical assistance. While this decision has remained in place, it was the subject of controversy for many years. Many state Extension directors, backed by the American Farm Bureau Federation, recommended that Congress give full responsibility for soil conservation work to Extension. In spite of the controversy, however, Extension and SCS work together on many projects.

EXTENSION AND FARM CREDIT.   In the 1930s, just as in the 1980s, most farmers faced credit problems and many of them were driven out of business. Extension became active and effective in this area. County agents educated farmers about the different types of credit available, particularly when new Farm Credit Administration and Farm Security Administration (the predecessor to the Farmers Home Administration) programs were established. Emergency feed-and-seed loans were administered by local committees. The county agent usually recommended individuals for committee membership and sometimes supervised its office work.

Even more important, the county agent as a trusted member of the community recommended members for and sometimes directed the work of debt-adjustment committees. These committees were established by the Farm Credit Administration, first on a voluntary basis and later as required by law. They attempted, very often successfully, to persuade farm debtors and their creditors to readjust their relationships. In some cases creditors were willing to scale down the debts contracted in a time of high prices and land values to conform with the changes in farm purchasing power and land values. In other cases interest rates were lowered and the time for repayment extended. These committees were credited with helping many farmers readjust their debts and thus continue farming.

The Farm Credit Administration and the Extension services in several states cooperated to offer training schools for county leaders to learn sound uses of credit in farming. In several states they also offered training in keeping farm records.

County agents sometimes worked with the Rural Rehabilitation Division of the Farm Security Administration. In this capacity they helped select tenants and other less well-off farmers who, with the proper guidance, might be able to succeed in farming. The selection was sometimes made by a Farm Security representative and sometimes by a committee, with the county agent acting as an advisor. This effort brought county agents into contact with a segment of the farm population with which they previously had few dealings. The program varied a great deal from state to state. In some southern states black agents working through the 1890 colleges gave assistance when blacks were involved in programs.

EXTENSION AND THE RURAL ELECTRIFICATION ADMINISTRATION. The Rural Electrification Administration (REA) began in 1935 as an emergency relief project. Within a year it had become a lending program, working primarily with local rural electric cooperatives. REA experienced difficulty in reaching people in rural communities who wanted to obtain electricity but did not know how to do so. However, Extension agents had been working with farmers on electrifying their farms since the 1920s. The agricultural agents had seen electricity as a source of power for such operations as pumping water, mixing feed, and operating milking machines. Home economists knew the advantages of electric lighting and running water in the home and the availability of electricity to operate appliances. Thus Extension was ready to give full cooperation to the program.

Extension staff members distributed information, headed tours of electrified farms, and taught farmers something about wiring and installation. Most important of all, though, they helped rural people organize electric cooperatives to work with REA. For example, on June 28, 1935, county agent Ralph Wayne of Meeker County, Minnesota, and former county agent Frank Marshall, with the help of the Meeker County Farm Bureau Federation, organized the first rural electric cooperative in Minnesota. The cooperative submitted a loan application to REA, and the first lines were energized in November 1936. The first REA cooperative lines in Wisconsin were built in Richland County in 1936–1937, with the Richland county agent serving as president of the cooperative. Similar activities took place across the nation.

After the electric cooperatives were organized, county agents held educational meetings on problems of safety, problems in wiring farm buildings, effective lighting, and how electricity could be used. Similarly, home economists met with homemakers clubs and other groups, providing educational programs on electric lighting, home water systems, safety, the purchase and care of appliances, home freezing of meats and vegetables and other matters that today people take pretty much for granted.

Over the years rural electrification became one of the most highly regarded of the New Deal farm programs. Its success was due in part to the educational efforts of Extension. When REA began, 10 percent of the nation's farms had electricity. By 1940, more than 30 percent were electrified, and today about 99 percent are electrified. Only very isolated farms are without central station electric service. Rural electrification has been a major factor in improving the quality of life in rural America.

EXTENSION AND THE TENNESSEE VALLEY AUTHORITY.   Congress approved the Tennessee Valley Authority Act in 1933 to promote navigation, soil conservation, and flood control and to produce cheap electricity. Rather than create a new staff to work with rural people in the Tennessee River Valley, the Tennessee Valley Authority (TVA) chose to contract with the Extension Services in the seven valley states to administer a program in soil conservation, working with individual landowners. These added employees were Extension Service personnel and were responsible to the state Extension directors rather than to TVA. Some of the first contractual employees helped families relocate to make way for the construction of Norris Dam.

Shortly after TVA was established, the land-grant universities in the region advised the agency to: (1) Improve farmers' skills in producing crops and managing farms; (2) supply farmers with plant nutrients (especially phosphate); and (3) improve farmers' access to resources needed to operate a farm. With the home economics and 4-H programs already in place, this became the basic method adopted by Extension to teach farmers, farm families, and young people that beneficial economic and social changes were possible.

County cooperatives, organized with the guidance and counsel of county agents, became the chief vehicle for change. They were responsible for such activities as promoting the use of fertilizer, increasing electrical consumption, administering emergency relief funds in the early 1930s, selecting test demonstration farmers, purchasing farm supplies, operating terracing and pond-building machinery, conducting seed-cleaning operations, and producing and distributing ground limestone. The cooperatives, with these varied responsibilities and with the help of the county agents, served as training schools for local farm leadership. Although black Extension staffs were too small to have a major impact on programs, the Tennessee Valley Authority transferred funds to some of the 1890 colleges to provide leadership for gardening programs in both rural and urban areas.

The ordinary farmer in the Tennessee Valley benefited substantially from TVA's and Extension's program of agricultural development, even though he did not completely catch up with the rest of the country economically. The area was well on the way to achieving erosion control by 1941. New fertilizers had been developed and put into use. In relation to the national average, farm income had improved. By the end of World War II most farm homes in the area were electrified and families enjoyed a better standard of living.

EXTENSION AND OTHER NEW DEAL PROGRAMS.   Many New Deal programs, in addition to those previously discussed, became at least in part the responsibility of the county agent. In drought-stricken areas, the county agent usually served as the county drought director. Here duties ranged all the way from making surveys of needs to helping obtain supplies of feed for livestock.

Other relief programs included encouraging the cultivation of subsistence gardens, in both rural and urban areas, and teaching the necessary gardening skills. In working with families on relief, home demonstration agents emphasized the conservation and preservation of food. For example, in South Carolina they and state nutrition specialists trained assistants financed through Works Progress Administration (WPA) relief funds to carry on special nutrition work with needy families—a program similar to the Extension Expanded Food and Nutrition Educational Program (EFNEP) of the 1970s and 1980s.

COORDINATION IN FEDERAL-STATE RELATIONSHIPS.   Problems of coordination were eased by an overriding sense of the need to act to overcome the Depression, by the appropriation of emergency funds to strengthen Extension and to assist it in carrying out the New Deal programs, and by the staffing of many New Deal agencies with former state and county Extension personnel who were able to work closely with their former colleagues. But as time went by and the Depression began to fade, questions of responsibility came to the fore.

At the 1937 convention of the land-grant colleges, the Extension Committee on Organization and Policy of the Land-Grant College Association expressed concern over the relationship of the state and county Extension services to New Deal agencies, particularly the Agricultural Adjustment Administration and the Soil Conservation Service. The committee wanted assurance that "the Land-Grant College be designated as the sole agency for leadership in research and extension education in all so-called action or other programs dealing with individual farmers. . . . "

Committees of the Land-Grant College Association and of the USDA studied the problem. Finally, in July 1938 representatives of the colleges and of the USDA, meeting at Mount Weather, Virginia, reached an agreement. The USDA was to continue administering action programs from Washington but was to work with the colleges in jointly setting up state and county land-use planning committees in all states and agricultural counties. At the state level, the director of Extension was to serve as chairman of a land-use planning committee. State committees were to be composed of representatives of USDA agencies carrying out programs in the state and counties, along with a number of farm people. Similar committees were to be set up in counties and communities. The term "land-use planning" meant democratic participation of farm men and women in planning action programs; adaptation of national policies and programs to varying local conditions; coordination of the many bureau and division activities into one broad comprehensive program; and coordination of federal, state, county, and local action on agricultural problems. Although the perhaps overly elaborate concept of the land-use planning committee never achieved all of its goals, it did at least for a time assure Extension that it had a vital longtime role in agricultural programs. But whatever chance of success the planning concept had came to an end with the eruption of World War II.

THE IMPACT OF THE NEW DEAL ON EXTENSION.   The Depression and subsequent New Deal programs were a challenge to Extension. In some states the Depression brought severe cutbacks. New Deal emergency money helped keep Extension alive and growing. Nevertheless, some New Deal programs threatened Extension's position by going directly to farmers with combinations of action and education. Extension, for the most part, adapted to the needs of the times, often working with the new programs. Without giving up its integrity as an educational institution, it did what it had to do to help the nation overcome the worst depression in its history.

Extension and World War II. When the Japanese attacked Pearl Harbor on December 7, 1941, the Cooperative Extension Service was in a position to give immediate wartime service to the nation and to its farmers. It had been strengthened by the transfer of funds from New Deal agencies, it was an active participant in building up American agriculture to meet the Allies' demands for food, and it held a position of leadership in land-use planning and related committees.

REORGANIZATION AT THE FEDERAL LEVEL. Changes had taken place in the federal Extension Service. It had been reorganized in 1939 into three new divisions — Subject Matter, Field Coordination, and Extension Information. In 1940 Milburn L. Wilson succeeded Clyde W. Warburton as director. Warburton had held the office for seventeen years. During his administration, many differences between the federal and state agencies had been ironed out. Warburton was dedicated to keeping Extension an educational agency, but he had been able to adapt to the pressures of the Great Depression. Wilson began his career in Extension as a county agent in Montana. He had held many posts, both at Montana State University and in USDA. He moved from the position of under secretary of agriculture to director of Extension. M. L., as he was known to virtually everyone, young and old, was a man of broad ideas, with an interest in developing a philosophical base for action. He was to remain director for thirteen years.

Farm exports had declined sharply in 1939 and 1940. USDA and state university administrators and economists were saying that the United States should learn to live at home and produce for the domestic market, a message that Extension carried to American farmers. But by mid-1940, the possibility of a German victory shocked the American people into emphasizing national defense and aid to the Allies. By the end of 1940 the USDA, for the first time since 1933, was actively encouraging increased production. By March 5, 1941, the department had received requests from the British for $500 million worth of American farm products. The passage of the Lend-Lease Act of March 11, 1941, which in reality made it possible to give supplies to the British, made it clear that more food would be needed to meet these demands.

In July 1941 the USDA established an Interbureau Production Goals Committee. In September the committee issued a report calling for the increased production of a number of essential commodities. The goals were revised upward in January 1942, as the United States became involved in the war. The full educational and informational facilities of the department were marshalled to sell the new production goals to American farmers. In addition to an intensive press and radio campaign, a county-by-county and farm-by-farm campaign to get farmers to sign up for goals was conducted by the Extension Service, the Agricultural Adjustment Administration, and the Farm Security Administration. Farmers were assured that they would not be faced with unreasonably low prices or unmarketable surpluses during the war or immediately following the end of hostilities. The sign-ups were successful.

Secretary of Agriculture Claude R. Wickard established state and county defense (later war) boards. These were headed by AAA personnel, Wickard explained, because "the AAA is the only action agency that has personnel available in every state and every county," and "AAA employees are administratively responsible to the Secretary of Agriculture." State and county land-use planning committees were first bypassed and then abolished.

WARTIME ASSIGNMENT TO EXTENSION. The state and county war boards provided coordination between department agencies in the field, but Secretary Wickard reaffirmed the responsibilities of the Extension Service as the educational arm of USDA by issuing on February 11, 1942, what has become known as "The Extension Service Charter." The charter stated: "The Extension Service is responsible for all group or general educational work essential to a fundamental understanding of all action programs" and that the educational program "must, without exception, include all that is necessary to an understanding by rural people of each program individually and of all programs as a unified whole." Early in 1943 the War Food Administration was established within the USDA but with its administrator directly responsible to the president. The Extension Service became part of the new agency, a recognition of its importance to the war effort.

PRODUCTION FOR WAR.   Throughout the war, Extension encouraged farmers to meet production goals. Extension personnel advised farmers of the goals, explaining what signing up meant so far as price supports and allocations of such production needs as fertilizer were concerned. They then provided farmers the best available knowledge on production. Sometimes they found a need to educate farmers on how to produce the commodities most needed in the war effort rather than to continue to produce what they had in the past. For example, in order to encourage the production of more soybeans, flaxseed, cottonseed, and peanuts, particularly by farmers who had not been producing these crops, county agents stressed information on yields, varieties, and cultural practices. The agents were helped by more than 620,000 volunteer neighborhood leaders.

Farmers needed machinery, fertilizer, and labor to meet their production goals. Extension took the lead in reporting their requirements and then in allocating what scarce supplies were available. County agents helped allocate such fertilizer as was available and encouraged farmers to make the best use of it. Extension schools and meetings advised farmers and farm women how to maintain and repair their farm machinery and electrical and household equipment. Farmers were encouraged to share scarce machinery and to put their machines to work for other farmers whenever possible. Extension also took the lead in scrap metal drives to collect and turn in unused and worn out machinery. On the whole, more work was done by machine during the war than had been the case previously, thanks to the careful allocation and maintenance of available supplies.

While machines were instrumental in meeting farm labor shortages, it still was necessary for the War Food Administration to carry out a major farm labor program. The Office of Labor was established to bring in and manage foreign workers and to be responsible for interstate workers. Extension was assigned responsibility for domestic farm labor. That responsibility had many aspects. For example, the county agent usually was either a member of his local draft board or relied upon by the board to furnish information so the board could determine whether a particular farm worker should be drafted for military service or be deferred.

FARM LABOR PROGRAMS.   The federal and state Extension services were accountable for all intrastate agricultural labor, including the Women's Land Army and the Victory Farm Volunteers, programs similar to those conducted in World War I. Although by definition the Women's Land Army included all women working on farms, the action program recruited women from villages, towns, and even cities for year-round, seasonal or emergency short-term assignments on farms. The program varied from state to state, depending partly on the type of agriculture, partly on the acuteness of the need for labor, and partly on local attitudes toward nonfarm women doing farm work. These women were particularly useful in harvesting fruit and vegetable crops. Work with the Women's Land Army was carried out primarily by Extension home economists.

The Victory Farm Volunteers program was aimed at the nation's youth; it employed high school and college students during summer vacations. Much of this work was channeled through 4-H clubs, with many 4-H members joining the Victory Farm Volunteers. In some areas school vacation periods were adjusted to coincide with periods of greatest need for seasonal labor. The labor programs were decentralized, with the federal Extension office serving in an advisory and coordinating capacity.

The Extension Service also carried on training programs for inexperienced farm labor, for work leaders of labor crews, and for farmers to improve employer-employee relations and to increase efficiency in labor use. The Extension Service operated a farm labor placement service and was responsible for determining the number of laborers required and the date and approximate duration of their service.

Late in 1941 the USDA and the Office of Defense Health and Welfare Services launched a victory garden program. Many agencies participated, and Extension was given particular responsibility for gardens in rural areas. Home economists and 4-H leaders often took the lead. The 1890 Extension agents were deeply involved as well. Extension instructed city families on how to tend their gardens, and information programs were carried by the press and radio on a continuing basis. Special programs were undertaken to provide seed, fertilizer, and simple gardening tools for victory gardens. Business, industry, and local governments cooperated to provide space for community garden projects in urban areas. An estimated 15 million families planted victory gardens in 1942, and in 1943 some 20 million victory gardens produced more than 40 percent of the vegetables grown for fresh consumption that year. Production from this source continued at high levels in 1944 and 1945. The victory garden program was one of the most popular programs developed in the war period.

Increasing production was vital to the nation and to the world, but it had a particular importance to Hawaii. The islands had not been self-sufficient in food before the attack on Pearl Harbor, and the war sharply reduced available shipping, making it harder to import food. Early in 1942 several units of farm machinery were sent to Hawaii to be lent to farmers. Extension agents taught farmers to use the new machinery effectively to produce food and feed crops. Among other activities, the agents issued permits to buy tires and insecticides, inspected weekly consignments of fresh vegetables for the army, helped determine which farmers would receive occupational deferments from military service, and enforced rules meant to conserve gasoline and tires. They interpreted rules of the military governor's office for non-English-speaking aliens and conducted an Americanization program.

Home economists taught the principles of nutrition and home management to be followed during the emergency, just as home economists were doing on the mainland. But in addition, they taught homemakers how to ventilate blacked-out rooms, how to find substitutes for unobtainable foods, how to make soap, how to make emergency use of the coconut, and how to comply with possible evacuation orders.

Nearly every type of material was in short supply, so Extension's word was to repair it, patch it, or make it at home. 4-H club members learned to make their own clothes and to make household furnishings and other items from scrap material. Hawaii's 4-H club members increased the islands' food supply during the final year of the war by raising more than 5,000 rabbits and 16,000 Muscovy ducks and by growing 41 acres of vegetables in their home and community gardens.

The Department of Agriculture and the War Food Administration were justifiably proud of the food production achievements of World War II, achievements in which Extension had a major role. Each year for five years, total food production increased. In 1944, according to the food administration, food production was 38 percent above the 1935–1939 average. Increased production occurred mainly in foods most needed by the United States and its Allies. Acreage of oil-bearing seeds increased 42.6 percent and vegetables for processing 91 percent. Meat production increased annually during the war years, reaching a peak of 24.6 billion pounds in 1944—more than 50 percent above the 1935–1939 average of 16.2 billion pounds—but it fell off 2 billion pounds in 1945 because reserve supplies of feed grains had been used up. Milk production increased from an annual prewar average of 107.9 billion pounds to 123 billion pounds in 1945. The supply actually available for human consumption was increased far more than this by the shift in marketing from farm-separated cream to whole milk, and the consequent cutback in feeding skim milk to hogs and poultry. In 1945 wholesale deliveries of whole milk by farmers were more than 55 percent above prewar levels. Production of poultry and eggs increased greatly in 1942, 1943, and 1944, but fell in 1945 due to feed shortages.

In addition to increasing food production, an effort was made to increase timber production, although this was a longer-term project. In Mississippi, for example, 7 million tree seedlings were planted in 1943, mainly by 4-H club boys.

MEETING FAMILY NEEDS.   Even though food production increased during the war, so did needs. During much of the time from 1943 through 1945, many food products were rationed. Rationing created greater demands than ever before on Extension to teach families how to conserve and preserve food. With emergency funds Extension employed war food assistants to demonstrate ways of preserving food efficiently and safely, as well as to provide information on nutrition.

Extension home economists and assistants trained rural and city people in up-to-date methods of canning, freezing, dehydrating, brining and storing vegetables, fruits, and meats. A nationwide program was organized by Extension to test pressure cookers for safety. Major efforts were concentrated on home canning, although home economists directed a number of community canning centers. The time when freezing would displace much home canning was still in the future, yet increased help on freezing was given in the northeastern and southern states where new locker plants had been established.

There were, of course, unusual circumstances in various parts of the nation. For example, Fabiolo Cabeza de Baca, home economist in Santa Fe County, New Mexico, organized Indian and Hispanic women and families who previously had not been involved in Extension. She worked with other families as well, and when World War II began was reaching 80 percent of the families in the county, an unusual achievement in crossing ethnic barriers. De Baca encouraged women to plant gardens and to can or sell surpluses, to learn nutrition, to exchange field labor with neighbors, to raise poultry, to make clothing, and to undertake home repairs.

Shortages of many kinds resulted from the war. Home economists and 4-H staff members and volunteer leaders taught women and young people how to make and repair clothing, how to care for and repair household appliances, and even how to make simple pieces of furniture. One popular program was making cotton mattresses. During the 1930s surplus cotton and cotton cloth had been made available, usually through Extension, for use by needy people to make cotton mattresses. In the 1930s Tuskegee Institute provided instruction in mattress making to 1890 colleges' home economists, many of whom in turn taught the skill to their counterparts from the 1862 institutions. Whatever way they learned the skill, home economists throughout the country taught families mattress making. When World War II began, large quantities of cotton and cotton ticking were stored in warehouses. Extension home economists revived the project in many parts of the nation. In just the state of Michigan, for example, Extension reported that nearly 50,000 mattresses and 28,000 comforters were made in one year during the war.

4-H AND WORLD WAR II.   When the war began, 4-H established seven national war goals. Three of the goals dealt directly with the production of more food and other products for the prosecution of the war. The other goals were aimed at helping young people define their responsibilities in the community. These four goals committed 4-H'ers to interpreting the "nation's war aims to the community," to practicing democratic procedures, to acquiring deeper appreciation for democratic society, and to becoming informed about the economic and social forces "now at work and steps to take in developing the Good Neighbor spirit at home and abroad." Enrollments increased during the war. At the end of 1942, 4-H had enrolled over 650,000 new members for a total of 1.5 million. These members, through victory gardens and production-oriented projects, contributed significantly to the increased harvest of food and fiber. Throughout the country 4-H clubs adopted the slogan "Food for Freedom." With the military and defense industries draining older youth from the farm, younger 4-H members took on added responsibility. In nearly every project category, 4-H'ers recorded impressive increases in levels of agricultural production over the previous year. In 1942 4-H'ers were directly responsible for over 77,000 head of dairy cattle, 246,000 swine, and 210,000 head of other livestock. Field crop production also increased. 4-H contributed over 40,000 tons of forage crops and 109,000 bushels of root crops. In Texas alone, it was estimated that 4-H members produced enough food and fiber to supply 17,000 fighting men.

4-H also joined numerous campaigns to collect scrap iron and aluminum and to conserve the use of scarce items essential to the war effort. 4-H clubs in some states organized specific projects. In Texas and other states, 4-H engaged in a massive program to decrease livestock losses from disease and improper care. Massachusetts club members canned more than a quarter million jars of food in 1944. Many 4-H club members joined the Victory Farm Volunteers as noted previously; they not only worked but also taught city youngsters how to do farm work. In 1943 nearly 85,000 Michigan students worked as farm volunteers.

With the end of the war, 4-H could look with pride upon its achievements. Its members, like Extension and American farmers, had responded to the emergency.

OTHER WARTIME ACTIVITIES.   County agents, home demonstration agents, and 4-H agents, as well as many volunteers, were called upon to perform a myriad of war-related duties. They sold war bonds, assisted with fire-control programs, helped to control diseases and insects, encouraged housewives to save kitchen fat for soap, organized transportation pools to get products to market, advised with purchasing and marketing cooperatives, and carried on scores of other activities. Once again, Extension proved that it would come through for the nation in an emergency situation.

PLANNING FOR POSTWAR ADJUSTMENT.   In 1945 Extension programs increasingly addressed postwar problems. Congress, in part because it valued Extension's wartime work and in part because it recognized education would have to play a large part in postwar adjustments, passed the Bankhead-Flannagan Act. The measure authorized a $12.5 million increase in federal funds over a three-year period. These were to be matched by state funds. Most of the funds were to be used in the counties, particularly to strengthen home demonstration, 4-H club, and black Extension work.

Postwar planning dealt with many topics. Returning veterans should have the opportunity to return to farming. Readjustment of production to meet peacetime needs was essential. Rural health and sanitation required improvement. Well informed Extension workers led discussions of these and other needs.

In 1945 the Department of State asked the USDA to distribute information and hold discussions with farmers on the proposed United Nations and Food and Agriculture Organization. In rural areas responsibility for the program was assigned to Extension, which distributed a discussion guide nationwide. This was followed by discussion meetings in which rural people themselves came to conclusions about how peace could be maintained.

Also in 1945 the USDA sponsored a postwar planning conference involving state and district supervisors of Extension work with blacks. In planning for the advancement of agriculture among blacks, the conference considered the role of Extension in a proposed cotton program, in food production and conservation for home use, in a program for farm youth, and in assistance for veterans and displaced war workers. Thus Extension was beginning to move away from some of its wartime action programs and back to its more traditional educational responsibilities.

The Emergencies End.   Extension helped the nation survive two major emergencies, the Great Depression of the 1930s and World War II in the 1940s. Extension had come through in these emergencies. Now it would be called upon to assist veterans to return to or enter farming, to teach rural families how to reestablish themselves after the disruptions of war, to encourage young people in 4-H and in other groups to turn from wartime to peacetime projects and activities, and to provide knowledge helpful to farmers and rural families in adjusting to the tremendous changes that research would bring to their lives.

CHAPTER SIX

Extension and the Farmer: Insuring Our Food Supply

Introduction. The Smith-Lever Act of 1914 charged the Cooperative Extension Service with improving agricultural production. At that time a single farm worker was supplying food and fiber for seven persons. Today, each American farm worker supplies farm products for ninety-three people—a figure six times higher than it was in 1950. Americans have a safe, sure supply of food at less cost in take-home pay than do the people of any other industrialized nation in the world. This increase in production and productivity resulted from the efforts of Extension and government research people working together with the American farmer, with substantial contributions from the private sector.

The chapter begins with a review of the importance of farming to the American economy and a comparison of agricultural production in 1950 and in 1986. It continues with a description of the agricultural revolution stimulated by Extension and the state agricultural experiment stations and what that revolution has meant to the American farmer. The benefits American and world consumers derive from this increase in productivity are discussed. The major theme of the chapter is the work of Extension in educating farmers and farm families in using the new production technologies developed by the state agricultural experiment stations and by other research institutions to solve their farming problems.

Agriculture and the American Economy.   The continuing concern of the American people with agricultural production reflects an awareness of both the need for an adequate food supply and the place of agriculture in the general economy. Although World War II put strains on farm production, Americans generally did not go hungry. However, for about fifteen years after the war ended, a number of writers argued that many parts of the world, even eventually the United States, faced famine because of rapidly growing populations.

ENOUGH FOOD.   A series of droughts did bring famine to the Indian subcontinent in the 1960s. Food shipments from the United States and other nations saved millions of people from starvation. Droughts also caused famines in Ethiopia and the Sahel region of Africa in the mid-1980s. However, the doomsayers of the 1960s have been proven wrong. The world as a whole is not faced with any threat of famine, largely because of advances in agricultural production and productivity.

The second reason for continuing concern with agricultural production lies in its importance to the nation's economy. Even though farmers make up only a small part of the work force today, agriculture is the nation's largest industry. Farm assets have totaled about $1 trillion in recent years. The nation's food and fiber system has accounted for about 18 to 20 percent of the total gross national product, that is, the total value of all production in the United States.

AGRICULTURE IN THE ECONOMY.   Agriculture is the nation's largest employer. Around 21 million people work in some phase of agriculture, from growing food and fiber to selling it at the supermarket. Nearly one out of every five jobs in private enterprise is in some aspect of agriculture. Farming itself requires some 2.1 million workers. About 18.9 million people are employed in storing, transporting, processing, and merchandising America's farm products.

The American farmer is a consumer and taxpayer as well as a producer. When farmers experience economic difficulty, as many did in the mid-1980s, businesses in rural communities suffer, as do workers in such industries as farm machinery and fertilizer. The rural communities themselves are hurt by eroding tax bases and collections, with a consequent decline in public services.

American Farm Production in 1950 and in 1986.   In 1950 25 million Americans out of a total population of 151 million lived on farms, compared with 5.2 million of a 241 million population in 1986. The number of farms declined from 5.4 million in 1950 to 2.2 million in 1986, and the average size increased from 216 acres to 455 acres. The total acreage in farms remained about the same, 1.2 billion acres in 1950 and 1.0 billion acres in 1986.

Fewer farmers cultivating about the same amount of land produced larger quantities of products than almost anyone had believed possible. Wheat production rose from 1.0 billion bushels in 1950 to 2.4 billion bushels in 1986. Corn production increased from 3.1 billion bushels to 8.9 billion bushels and rice from 39 million hundredweight to 135 million hundredweight. Milk production rose from 117 billion pounds in 1950 to 144 billion pounds in 1986. Some 9 billion pounds of beef were produced in 1950 compared to 24 billion in 1986. Soybean production increased from 299 million bushels in 1950 to 2 billion bushels in 1986.

INCREASED PRODUCTIVITY.   This production increase resulted from rising productivity rather than from increased acreage, except in the case of soybeans, where there has been a large increase in acreage. For example, the average yield of wheat was 16 bushels an acre in 1950 and 37 in 1986. The average corn yield rose from 37 bushels an acre to 118, while soybeans went from 21 to 34.

A Revolution in Agricultural Production.   One of the nation's outstanding production economists, Sherman E. Johnson, foresaw the coming change. He wrote in 1949 that the adoption of combinations of improved farm practices could bring about major changes in farm productivity. As agricultural scientists and Extension workers found in the early 1950s, the improvement of every part of the farm operation resulted in a vastly greater increase in productivity than might be expected if the increases resulting from each individual improvement were added up. For example, in producing a particular crop the best seed might increase production 10 percent, the use of fertilizer 10 percent, the use of suitable mechanical power 5 percent, the chemical control of pests and diseases 10 percent, and the application of soil conserving technologies 5 percent, for a total of 40 percent. However, when all the best practices were used together, productivity increased 80 to 100 percent or even more. About one-half of the increase resulted from new technology and the other one-half from better farm management in putting these technologies together.

THE PACKAGE OF PRACTICES.   The concept of looking at every part of the farm operation and doing what was possible to improve each part became known as the package of practices. Experimental work in producing hybrid corn in North Carolina was the first widely publicized indicator of the value of the concept. These experiments, combining the application of the most productive levels of nitrogen fertilizer, the use of hybrid seed, adherence to suitable conservation practices, use of appropriate mechanical power, and the effective control of pests and diseases, resulted in yields of more than 80 bushels per acre compared with usual yields of 15 to 20 bushels. The North Carolina Extension staff got word of these results to the state's farmers, and the idea was soon being adopted in other states. The package of practices concept, or the application of systems analysis to farming, was to be the most important force in increasing farm productivity for the next two decades. It would bring about a true revolution in American agriculture.

IMPACT ON FARMING.   This change in American agriculture, brought about by the close cooperation of Extension and research in working with farmers, peaked in the 1960s and then gave way to evolutionary rather than revolutionary change. The rate of productivity growth in the 1970s was substantially below that of the 1950s and the 1960s. Extension had persuaded farmers to apply the accumulated scientific knowledge and to apply new knowledge as it became available. As a consequence, productivity was increasing steadily but without spectacular jumps.

At the same time farmers were tied more closely to costs and returns. As new technologies were added to production agriculture, farmers purchased such means of production as machinery, fuels, chemicals, and improved seed and livestock. The day had long since passed when the farmer raised horses as his source of power, fed them with farm-produced hay and grain, fertilized his fields with manure, and saved seed and breeding stock he had produced on the farm.

As new practices were being widely adopted in the 1950s and 1960s, Extension found that the management skills and techniques used by many farmers were not adequate to handle the economic decisions they faced through adopting these technologies. By the 1980s the greatest tasks faced by Extension in the area of agricultural production were to educate farm families in management skills and in ways to deal with the farm depression. These educational efforts involved virtually everyone in a farm family since the entire family usually was involved in production.

PRODUCTION AND THE EXTENSION STAFF.   Just as most of the farm family was involved in production, so was most of the Extension staff. For example, the agricultural agent might conduct educational programs on new machinery or pesticides, the home economist might teach computer use as well as nutrition, and the 4-H agent often was the primary force in introducing new or more effective tools of change. Although there was some variation from state to state, Extension generally planned to devote about 44 percent of its staff time and other resources to agricultural production from 1988 to 1991.

Computers in Agricultural Production.   Computers, which were just coming into wide use in business and industrial production in the 1960s, seemed to be an appropriate tool for improving farm management. The farm family, with help from the Extension staff, could use the computer, for example, to determine what amounts of fertilizer and other chemicals applied to crops would realize the greatest returns; to plan which dairy, hog, or poultry rations the farmer should use considering the relative prices of possible components; to decide when to market livestock, considering market prices and the costs of holding; to decide what crops to plant in the light of the future price outlook and the impact of government programs; and to store the farm records needed for effective management. With access to a computer and to relevant programs, farm records could be made more useful and decisions on a wide range of management operations could be made more effectively than ever before.

EXTENSION AND COMPUTER EDUCATION.   Extension in every state has offered education in computer use to its clientele. It has also developed practical programs farm families can use to help solve specific problems in agricultural production.

The Clemson University Extension Service is one example. In 1979 it received a grant to develop computer programs. More than thirty were completed in such subjects as farm budgets, cash-flow statements, and farm records. In 1981 the Kellogg Foundation made a grant that permitted Clemson to put personal computers in twelve of South Carolina's forty-six counties. Within two years every county had a computer, and in 1985 a second portable computer was added to each county office. The system developed into the Clemson University Forestry and Agricultural Computer Network (CUFAN), serving the main Clemson campus, forty-six county Extension offices, five research and education centers, South Carolina State College and a number of state agencies, television stations, and newspapers. In August 1987 users called upon CUFAN for information more than sixteen thousand times. It had become an educational resource for rural and urban citizens as well as for farmers.

A unique computer-oriented educational project was developed by Texas Extension with the assistance of the Kellogg Foundation. The farm, which was called the "Year 2000 Farm," was established on 3,000 acres that had been given to Texas A.&M. University. It was designed to develop and test the application of computer technology to as many management functions as possible on a reasonably large-scale commercial farm. The results of the experiments have been made available to Texas farmers and ranchers and to Extension services throughout the nation.

By the late 1980s the computer was firmly established throughout Extension as an educational tool. Farmers who did not have their own computers had access to them at their county Extension offices. Hundreds of software packages had been developed for guiding farm decisions. Many state Extension services had established computer networks. They provided current research-based economic and technological information to every county office as soon as it was available and gave the county offices immediate access to a wide variety of educational packages.

Extension and Commercial Agriculture. In 1986 95,000 farms, or 4.3 percent of the nation's total of 2.2 million, sold farm products valued at $250,000 or more. These are generally classed as large farms. About 210,000 farms, or 9.5 percent of the total, had sales of $100,000 to $249,000. Some 294,000 farms, or 13.3 percent of the total, operated with sales of $40,000 to $99,999. Those two groups are viewed as midsize farms. About 1.6 million farms or 73 percent of all farms, had sales of less than $40,000. They are classed as small or noncommercial farms, even though some are commercial operations.

The midsize and large farms, making up 27 percent of the total, are commercial farms, devoted primarily to agricultural production and relying upon that production for basic income. The smaller commercial farms are concentrated in the Midwest: the Corn Belt, Lake States, and Northern Plains. About one-third of the farms specialize in cash grains, with most of the rest in beef, hogs, sheep, and dairy. The larger midsize farms also are concentrated in the Midwest, particularly in the Corn Belt, with about the same commodity distribution as the smaller ones. These farms make up over 10 percent of the farms in the Northeast and Mountain regions. Midsize farms accounted for 23 percent of all farms, 46 percent of the land in farms, 37 percent of agricultural sales, and 39 percent of net cash income from farming in 1986. The smaller farms in this group have been declining in number, while those with sales of over $100,000 have remained stable during the 1980s.

Midsize farms are usually operated by a family, which makes the management decisions and supplies most of the labor. Most of the operators consider farming to be their major occupation, with the families depending upon farming for 85 percent of their income. These are the farms usually referred to as family farms. The families operating them are a major segment of the clientele of Extension.

FARM AND HOME DEVELOPMENT.   In 1954, as a result of an ECOP-USDA Extension report and a special appropriation by Congress, Extension undertook a Farm and Home Development program, primarily to assist midsize farms. The county Extension staff and the farm family, working together, considered the farm and home as a complete unit and charted its overall development on a long-term basis. Specialists from federal agencies, banks, and feed, seed, chemical, and machinery companies were consulted. Attention was given to the type and extent of production, the preferred type of living, building plans, plans for the children's education, and relationships with the community. Consideration also was given to taxes, credit, education, communication, price structure, marketing, and international influences. As N. E. Beers, then director of Extension in Montana, said: "It is a personalized approach which has been tailored to suit the needs and desires of each of the many families with whom Extension has worked."

Minnesota Extension found that farm and home development work reached different kinds of farm families. Of the 1,799 families in the program in 1961, 198 were new farmers, 397 were regarded as low-income families, 205 were part-time farmers, and 999 were midlevel and large family farmers.

Michigan added forty agricultural and twenty home economics agents to its staff during the decade to carry out intensive efforts in farm and home development. Their actions reached about 5 percent of the state's farm families. A major difficulty was that the program required a large commitment of staff time to each family. Nevertheless, the program, sometimes called "Better Farming — Better Living," benefited a number of farm families.

EXTENSION AND THE FARM CRISIS.   By the mid 1980s many of America's commercial farmers were facing an agricultural crisis, and they turned to Extension for assistance. County agents taught farmers how to adjust their farming operations by cutting costs, shifting to different crops, finding new markets, or taking other steps that would improve income. Agents also were active in establishing debt adjustment committees. These committees, often chaired by the county agent, worked with financial institutions and the farmers to get agreements on adjusting debts so the farmer could stay in farming. Many county Extension offices employed a staff member trained in farm finance who worked directly with a farmer in developing financial plans for surviving the crisis. Extension, as discussed in a later chapter, worked with families to handle problems arising from the economic situation.

Iowa was one of the states affected most directly by the crisis. Iowa's farmers are primarily commercial family farmers, operating midsize farms, but there are also a number of large farms in the state. The sharp drop in farm prices in the 1980s and the continuing farm depression forced many Iowa farmers to give up farming, while many others needed help to survive. Iowa Extension gave top priority to a program called ASSIST, designed to educate rural families to deal with the financial situation. All units in Extension—production agents, home economists, 4-H agents, and community development specialists—contributed. One ASSIST goal was to create awareness of the farm financial situation through documentary tape presentations and discussions. Farm Aid, ASSIST'S financial management component, provided nearly 3,500 families in 1985–1986 with free confidential computer analyses of their farm financial situations. This service helped farmers learn to use all available data in making production and financial decisions. Farm families also were encouraged to give more attention to marketing strategies and to producing for the market. More than 10,000 producers attended Extension meetings and workshops on marketing in 1985–1986. More than half the participants reported later that they had modified their marketing practices.

Extension in every state gave particular attention to improving production and marketing during the crisis of the 1980s. For example, many midsize Maryland farmers, like those in other states, faced such problems as overinvestment in machinery, inadequate planning, and a lack of accounting and decision-making techniques. To meet their requirements, the Extension staff held a statewide series of seminars covering cash flow, farm budgets, business analysis, and other subjects. The continuing agricultural depression deepened in 1986 when the worst drought in many years hit the state. Extension responded with detailed financial counseling for individual farmers and with a sophisticated computer software package for farm financial planning. Extension was also called upon to carry out an emergency educational program to help poultry farmers, in conjunction with poultry specialists and veterinarians, bring an avian influenza epidemic under control.

LARGE FARMS.   Most large farms, which make up 4.3 percent
of all farms, are in the Corn Belt. The Pacific and the Mountain regions have more large farms as a percentage of their total farms than
any other region, with those in the Pacific region being concentrated in
California. The Southeastern and Delta states have a number of large
farms. Some 24 percent of all large farms specialize in beef, hogs, and
sheep; 22 percent in cash grains; and 15 percent in dairy. Large farms
accounted for nearly a quarter of gross cash farm income and more
than half of net cash income in 1984. They operated 24 percent of the
acres in farms.

The Farm and Home Development and the financial crisis programs were available to farmers in every state, including those having
large farms. Large-farm operators participated in many Extension programs and Extension often looked to them for community leadership.
In some instances the operators of large farms would go directly to the
regional or state Extension or experiment station specialists to obtain
the help they needed. At the same time some larger farms, particularly
corporation farms with hired managers, either had their own commodity specialists or looked to private consulting or management firms for
advice and assistance. However, these private specialists and consultants usually received their training from the land-grant institutions and
Extension. In several states Extension has offered training for field men
employed by the consulting firms. In general, Extension provided education to enable the farmer to solve his problems, while consulting and
management firms transferred technology to the farmer.

EXTENSION AND FARM MECHANIZATION.   Extension, drawing
upon research in the agricultural experiment stations and elsewhere,
has sought to educate farmers on methods of increasing production
and productivity. Computer analysis is one such method. Another is
mechanization of tasks formerly carried out by hand labor. While
mechanization has reduced physical drudgery, at least to some extent
on all farms, it has been particularly adaptable to large crop-producing
farms employing substantial numbers of workers. Since the machines
replaced field workers, they cut labor costs and made the farms less
dependent upon the workers.

California has been a leader in the mechanization of agriculture.

There, mechanization has ended much of the drudgery of farm life. At the same time, as in all states, it has reduced employment opportunities in mechanized crops such as cotton, sugar beets, carrots and canning tomatoes. However, with the development of new crops and agriculturally related industries, total agricultural employment in California has increased in recent years.

Mechanization has always been criticized, at least since the days of the Luddites. These were British workmen who between 1811 and 1816 rioted and destroyed textile machinery in the belief that the machinery would diminish employment.

In 1972 Jim Hightower in his widely circulated book, *Hard Tomatoes, Hard Times,* charged that the land-grant system had by its emphasis on production technology favored the development of large commercial units while ignoring the needs of small farmers and rural communities. In 1979 the California Rural Legal Assistance organization filed a suit against the University of California for failure to consider the impact on farm workers of labor-displacing technologies, alleged misuse of Hatch Act funds, and inappropriate research activities by Extension personnel.

In this controversy, Extension's deliberate program changes over time seemed, to some critics, not enough. Production technology did indeed continue to be the strong central focus of California's Extension work, yet by the end of the 1970s four elements of change were in place: Greatly enhanced environmental awareness, shifting of some program costs to agricultural industry groups, diversification of gender and ethnicity in Extension staffing, and increased outreach to underrepresented minorities and the nonagricultural population.

MID-SIZE FARMS.   Many of Extension's agricultural programs, while useful on farms of any size, are particularly helpful to operators of midsize or family farms. For example, experiment stations have been developing new varieties of crops to fit particular circumstances such as location and markets. Extension has been advising farmers on their availability.

Extension also has been working with midsize farm operators on postharvest technology and farm storage. Each year large amounts of farm commodities decline in value or are lost because of poor postharvest handling and inadequate farm storage. Extension has emphasized that taking care of a crop after it has been harvested can add substantially to the income from that crop.

Dairying, carried on in virtually every agricultural county on many midsize as well as large farms, is a major concern of Extension. Research and Extension have emphasized dairy herd improvement, the use of productive sires, improved sanitation, artificial breeding associations, and efficient feeding practices. In 1950 the average dairy cow produced 5,314 pounds of milk, in 1984, 12,495 pounds. The increase resulted from adoption of improved practices. Artificial breeding associations have been of particular help to the midsize dairy farmer by providing his herd access to proven production sires. The first such association in the United States was organized in New Jersey in 1938 under the leadership of the New Jersey Cooperative Extension Service.

Feeding the cows is an aspect of dairying that can mean success or failure for the farmer. Keeping balance in an equation that must consider nutritional needs of the cow, expected production from a particular ration, costs of different components of the ration, and returns from the sale of milk is a complex matter. However, research has provided formulas for selecting the most favorable composition of the ration under any given set of circumstances. Computers are useful in making the calculations. Extension agents teach dairy farmers how to use the formulas to arrive at the optimum ration at a particular period in time.

Most agricultural research is "size neutral" in that it can be applied to large, midsize, or small farms. Extension agents adapt the principles to particular farm situations. The appropriate delivery of unbiased research information, as in these situations, is a key function of Extension work.

Extension and Small and Part-time Farming.   Most small farms are also part-time farms in that the farm family depends upon off-farm income for a living. In 1986 more than one-half of small farm operators had a major occupation other than farming.

Small farms make up 73 percent of total farms, operate 30 percent of the land, and account for less than 10 percent of the sales. They account for 16 percent of the cash expenses and 3 percent of the total net cash income from farming. Small farms earned an average of $950 in 1986 in net cash income from farming; small-farm operators averaged $22,500 from off-farm sources. More than 50 percent of small farms specialize in beef, hogs, and sheep and another 16 percent in cash grains. A number of small farms produce alternative or specialty crops.

SMALL FARM PROGRAMS. Over the years state Extension Services have offered their programs to all farm operators, making no particular distinction between small and other farms. In recent years, however, there has been a shift. A Cooperative Extension Service survey made in 1985 showed that thirty-eight of the fifty-six states and territories had programs specifically designed for small-farm families. Seven other states indicated that some staff effort was devoted to this group of farmers. Fifteen of the thirty-eight states and territories with small-farm programs had programs specifically designed for minority small farm families. Only eleven states and territories indicated no small-farm family programs were being conducted in 1985. Some 90 percent of the general small-farm family programs and 85 percent of the minority farm-family programs have originated since 1970.

In a majority of the states, small-farm family programs focus on agricultural production and marketing and, to a lesser degree, on home food production. This is also true of the minority small-farm family Extension programs. In both programs there is some emphasis on home-based industry and off-farm employment, subjects usually not mentioned in programs for commercial farmers. However, the greatest needs are in the traditional areas of improved production, marketing, and management skills. These are followed by the increased demand for markets, financial and business planning and management, improved product quality, and alternative enterprises.

SMALL FARM PROGRAMS FOR MINORITIES. Of the fifteen small-farm programs in 1986 specifically designed for minorities, five were primarily for nonblack clientele—two for Hispanics, one for Native Americans, one in Puerto Rico, and one in the trust territory of Micronesia. Ten were targeted primarily to black families. In addition, plans of work for two states implied that black families operating small farms were their major audience. In eight states—Alabama, Florida,

Georgia, Kentucky, Louisiana, Maryland, Oklahoma, and South Carolina—the 1890 land-grant institutions and Tuskegee University provide
leadership for these programs. In four states—Arkansas, Mississippi,
Missouri, and Tennessee—leadership for minority small-farm family
Extension programs is provided by the 1862 land-grant university, with
participation by the 1890 universities. All of the states in Extension's
southern region conduct small-farm family education programs, although some are not designated as minority programs. For example, in
1985 North Carolina Extension had twenty-two professional staff years
assigned to small-farm projects. Although this was not designated as
minority programming, much of the work was with black farm families.

The primary emphasis of minority small-farm family Extension
programs is in traditional agricultural fields, including both agricultural production and marketing and home food production. Total
family resource management is also emphasized in several of these
programs. Other concerns include generating home-based industry, local community development, and off-farm employment.

MEETING THE NEEDS OF SMALL FARMERS.   It is often said that
small-farm families are harder to reach with Extension programs than
are the more traditional farm-family audiences. The 1985 survey indicated that Extension was using both traditional and nontraditional
methods to reach small-farm families. Among nontraditional methods,
some twenty-five states reported one-on-one visits or consultations.
On-farm result demonstrations were carried out in Arkansas, Florida,
Kentucky, Missouri, Mississippi, North Carolina, and Tennessee. Special funding for demonstration projects was provided by the Tennessee
Valley Authority, Heifer Project International, and a state 4-H Foundation.

The continuing Michigan family farm project includes three long-
term research and Extension demonstration farms of 5, 10, and 40
acres, with funding provided by the W. K. Kellogg Foundation. Direct
marketing projects for small farm products were carried out in Arkansas, Colorado, Louisiana, Maryland, South Carolina, and other states,
and wholesale vegetable marketing was conducted in Louisiana. Montana conducted programs for Native Americans in home meetings with

four or five farmers at a time, and at tribal celebrations. Other nontraditional methods as well as traditional ones also were used.

Lincoln University reported in 1986 that 87 percent of Missouri's farms were small-acreage operations. The objective of Extension's small-family farm program there was to help raise the living standards of this segment of Missouri's rural population by reducing their expenses and increasing their income through new management practices. The program involved 1,078 participants, including 85 minority families. Each family used about 6 acres of cropland. The average farm-derived income per family was $3,000. The success of the program as a whole indicated that an intensive effort by Extension could improve the productivity of small farms.

SOME LESSONS LEARNED.   Experience in other states, according to the 1985 survey, also leads to the conclusion that targeted small-farm family programs are effective. One-on-one program contact is costly, but the social benefits appear to outweigh the program costs. In several states, work with paraprofessionals shows that when given adequate training and supervision they are effective in group and one-on-one education. The survey also demonstrated that because small farmers are engaged in a variety of enterprises, Extension's educational program must include a variety of efforts and options. Finally, given adequate program resources, small-farm families willingly participate in educational programs targeted to their needs.

While these targeted programs were successful, they reached only a limited number of the small farms in any state. There have been neither adequate program resources nor sufficient public interest to make the programs widely effective.

Extension and Alternative Production Programs.   In recent years, partly in reaction to the agricultural depression of the 1980s, Extension has been encouraging research to develop new farm products or to revitalize the production of existing ones. California Extension, for example, has been educating small farmers on the production of Oriental vegetables and other little-known crops, while

North Carolina Extension has worked with ginseng production. Several states have undertaken educational programs on aquaculture, or the production of fish. Others have emphasized forestry products, as discussed in a subsequent chapter. Extension Services have given attention to direct marketing and "pick your own" enterprises, even though the number of these that can be successful is limited.

AQUACULTURE.   The commercial production of fish has been carried out on a small scale for a number of years. Trout production for the restaurant trade is an example. However, in recent years Extension in several states has worked with farmers to build up both production and demand for farm-raised fish. This effort has been particularly successful in Mississippi and Arkansas, where pond-raised catfish now are produced for a national market. Mississippi has some 90,000 water acres and Arkansas 20,000 in catfish production. This is a prime example of diversification and pursuing alternative agricultural opportunities. Research in the land-grant universities in these and other states may lead to other successful fisheries enterprises.

Several land-grant universities participate in the Sea Grant program inaugurated by the Department of Commerce in the late 1960s. Under the program, financed by the Department of Commerce, the university and the department agree to develop ocean resources through a partnership of government, industry, and education. The university is responsible for research and education, with the educational responsibility usually assigned to the Extension Service. Oregon State University, for example, received its first Sea Grant funding in 1968, although its Extension Service had been carrying on a public marine science education program since the early 1960s. By the 1980s, eighteen full- and part-time Extension staff were conducting educational programs at the coastal ports, the ports on the Columbia and Snake rivers, and the salmon streams east of the Cascade Mountains.

DIRECT MARKETING AND PICK YOUR OWN.   Along rural roads leading out from towns and cities, stands at which farm families — usually youngsters — offer fresh fruits and vegetables are an American tradition. Many Extension Services have built upon this tradition and offer instruction on how best to carry on such enterprises. Some producers join together and operate farmers markets in towns and cities, often with the county agent helping to establish them. Extension also works with farmers on establishing direct-mail marketing of such products as Wisconsin cheese, Vermont maple syrup, Georgia pecans, Florida grapefruit, and California almonds. Some such businesses are operated by farmer cooperatives.

The "pick your own" idea has spread rapidly, and many farms near urban areas now offer customers the opportunity to harvest fruits and vegetables or to cut Christmas trees. Several Extension Services offer educational materials and consultation on establishing and managing such enterprises. Tuskegee University has been particularly active in this area. Booker Whatley, now retired from Tuskegee, developed a model pick-your-own farm plan. His farm, rather small in size, would concentrate on high-value and high-quality farm commodities maturing over as long a period as possible. While relatively few such farms have been established, several Extension Services use modified versions of the plan.

Meeting Today's Needs.

ALTERNATIVE METHODS OF PRODUCTION. For many years the agricultural experiment stations have been testing different methods of agricultural production. Extension has been carrying the results of such research to farmers. Some alternative methods have received particular attention in the 1980s, in part because they reduce production costs and in part because they protect the environment. Many county agents are working with innovative farmers who, for example, want to cut costs by cutting back on the amount of purchased production materials such as fertilizer, pesticides, and fuel to such an extent that losses in production are offset by savings in outlays for materials. More research and education are needed in this area, and some is being carried out. For example, the Pennsylvania Extension Service and the agricultural experiment station are cooperating with a private foundation on alternative methods of farm production.

SUSTAINABLE AGRICULTURE.   The concept of "sustainable agriculture" is possibly a program of the future. Concern has grown among research workers and Extension leaders that many of modern agriculture's practices cannot be maintained over time. Several state Extension Service staff members are studying the question. For example, in 1987 California Extension appointed a sustainable agriculture specialist. He was to work with other specialists and farm advisors on strategies to minimize conventional use of chemical pesticides and fertilizers and of such nonrenewable resources as fossil fuels.

Biotechnology as a tool for agricultural production is receiving attention in the late 1980s. Many of the agricultural experiment stations are applying the new technique as a research tool for increasing agricultural productivity, guarding against any threats it may pose to the environment and to plant and animal life. Extension is being called upon to keep farm families advised of developments.

INTEGRATED PEST MANAGEMENT.   A new effective pesticide, DDT, came into use after World War II and soon was followed by others which, like DDT, persisted in the environment. They were widely adopted. Then in 1962 Rachel Carson, a well-known biologist and author, published her book, *Silent Spring,* an indictment of the widespread use of chemicals to control insects, animal, and plant diseases and weeds.

Carson stated, with some exaggeration, that the use of modern pesticides was polluting our air and water, poisoning our soils and many of the food crops grown on them, killing fish and wildlife, and endangering man through the gradual build-up of toxic substances. There was immediate public reaction and legislation was passed at various levels to control the use of the chemicals. The state experiment stations undertook studies to determine the long-term effects of pesticides, to find replacements for those thought to be dangerous to man, and to find more effective natural controls. Farmers called upon Extension for advice.

The state Extension specialists sent material urging moderation in the use of chemicals out to county agents. Extension created a pesticide education, safety, and applicator training program, designed to help commercial pesticide applicators and farmers understand and comply with pesticide use laws. Then Extension, with an earmarked appropriation from Congress, took the lead in developing an integrated pest-management program. The program was to reduce the use and level of pesticides in the environment, reduce reliance on pesticides, and improve farm profits by increasing production through more efficient pesticide use. This integrated approach was developed by researchers from many disciplines. Extension's educational efforts led to its widespread adoption.

Arizona Extension, for example, developed a program in four counties which reached 143 farmers operating 60,000 acres of cropland, several applicators, and several field representatives of pesticide suppliers. Through the program, effective pest control was achieved with fewer pesticides and applications. Farmers saved $45 an acre or a total of $2.7 million for the program participants, and progress was made in protecting the environment.

Extension is continuing to educate farmers on the most efficient and safest use of pesticides and other chemicals.

EXTENSION AND FARM SAFETY.   Farming and ranching are dangerous occupations. For that reason, Extension has emphasized farm safety for many years. In the early 1970s nine states had a full-time safety specialist on their staffs. In 1975 Congress appropriated funds earmarked for farm safety, and every state then undertook a program. The work with earmarked funds continued in the 1980s. Extension undertook programs aimed at educating every farmer and farm family about the dangers in farming and the need to be careful. While there is no way to determine the effectiveness of the program, farming and ranch fatalities declined from 2,300 in 1971 to 1,600 in 1984. Injuries were reduced from 200,000 a year to 170,000 a year. Deaths per 100,000 workers declined from 52 per year to 46, compared with 60 per 100,000 workers in mining and 39 in construction.

Improving farm safety carries economic benefits as well as relief from suffering and death. For example, Idaho Extension, through the media and public meetings, undertook an educational program to increase public awareness of the need for safety. While again it is impossible to determine the impact of the Extension program, Idaho experienced a 34 percent reduction in agricultural accident fatalities between 1975 and 1984. The overall reduction in farm accidents saved farmers and ranchers an estimated $5 million in medical expenses.

URBAN GARDENING.   Gardening is not a major project in Extension as a whole, yet its importance traditionally has been recognized. During times of war and economic depression, gardens have made substantial contributions to our food supply. Although gardening programs usually have been directed by horticultural or agricultural agents, home gardens have been recommended strongly by home economists as a source of vegetables and fruit for a nutritious diet and many Extension Homemakers clubs have had garden projects. Gardens were among the first projects stressed in 4-H, and gardening still is part of the program of many 4-H clubs. Garden clubs with their Master Gardeners, as accomplished gardeners who meet specific goals are called, are a source of capable volunteers to work in Extension garden projects.

In 1977 Congress directed Extension to earmark $1.5 million from existing appropriations to be used for gardening programs in major cities. The funds were allocated to the six largest cities in proportion to their populations. The program was so successful that mayors of many cities asked for its continuation and expansion. Congress responded by appropriating relatively small sums, even though in the 1980s the Office of Management and Budget recommended abolishing the program as an economy measure.

In 1985 the urban gardening program was active in twenty-one cities. In addition to a federal appropriation of $3.5 million, local governments and private agencies contributed another $1 million. A staff of 171 conducted the program, with help from 2,300 volunteers. Some 186,000 participants worked an area equivalent to more than 670 acres, from which about $20 million in produce was harvested.

Philadelphia, as an example, was one of the first cities to begin an active urban gardening program. In 1985 it received twice as much support elsewhere as it got from the USDA. The staff used innovative techniques like raised beds and introduced fruit growing and fish farming. Bridgeport, Connecticut, was added to the program in 1985, with $75,000 in USDA funds. For every dollar of that amount, participants raised $3 worth of produce. More than 90 percent of the participants were low-income minorities and urban dwellers.

In 1978 the Cooperative Extension Service of the University of the District of Columbia began an urban gardening program. Some 225,400 persons were participating by 1986. In 1988 Extension inaugurated a "Tip-A-Phone" service. Interested persons could dial a number and have a choice of recorded messages dealing with such subjects as vegetable production, horticulture, plant pests and diseases, and conserving natural resources.

Extension and Natural Resources.   Farming is dependent upon good water, fertile soil, and clean air. Extension seeks to educate the people of the nation about the benefits from preserving the quality of the water, conserving the soil, and protecting the quality of the air. These goals are essential, both for farming and for the future well-being of the nation.

WATER.   More than 95 percent of the nation's rural residents drink groundwater, as does more than one-half of the total population. There are reasons, according to reports of Extension's national initiatives task force, for Extension to conduct public education programs on the importance of high-quality water to life, well-being, and agricultural production; on the benefits of using water resources wisely; on the impacts of agricultural and other chemicals on water quality; on methods of conserving water supplies; and on the development of appropriate policies to assure adequate supplies of quality water. These programs should be delivered to the audiences most affected, notably rural residents and local government officials.

In the 1980s Extension received limited funding through the Rural Clean Water Act. These funds were used to carry out educational programs to reduce sediment in lakes and streams and to manage nutrients and pesticides to reduce runoff into water supplies. Extension seeks to teach agricultural producers to monitor their fertilizer needs through the use of soil tests, to use pesticides judiciously, and to reduce erosion through such management practices as contour farming, conservation tillage, and the use of soil-conserving crops.

SOIL CONSERVATION.   From its very beginnings Extension has urged all Americans, especially farmers, to conserve their soil. This is a theme that runs through and is discussed in connection with most Extension programs. In the 1980s Extension is teaching farmers and other public and private land users and managers to develop and apply cost-effective soil conservation technologies and systems, thus reducing off-site effects and ensuring the long-term productivity of soil resources.

Extension has carried out educational programs on conservation tillage to enable farmers to make informed decisions on controlling soil erosion and on adopting particular conservation tillage practices. Some practices are more suited to particular soil types and cropping patterns than to others. Many farmers have adopted soil-conserving tillage practices as a consequence of Extension programs.

RENEWABLE NATURAL RESOURCES.   During the 1980s Congress provided funding through the Renewable Resources Extension Act for educational programs on renewable natural resources. In 1988 all states were participating. More than half of the program funding went to forest management. An additional one-third was divided between forest harvesting, processing, and marketing; fish and wildlife management; and range management. The balance of the program focused on environmental management, public policy, and outdoor recreation. Several of these programs are related to rural development activities and are discussed in a subsequent chapter.

Extension is working through its educational programs to protect and sustain the abundance and diversity of renewable natural resources. It is teaching producers, local governments, and industries to identify renewable resource market opportunities and develop profitable and competitive marketing strategies for natural resource goods and services. Its programs aim to increase the short- and long-term productivity of privately held renewable natural resources. To meet these goals, Extension is aiding elected officials and decision makers formulate and implement informed and dynamic natural resource policies.

Lessons for Tomorrow.   In the years since World War II, Extension's programs have helped American farmers achieve the greatest increases in agricultural productivity the world has ever seen. Extension's educational work in farm management has been particularly effective in increasing production and productivity. The American consumer has been the major beneficiary, enjoying a diversified supply of safe, healthful food at a lower cost in disposable income than do consumers in any other nation in the world. Extension has the responsibility to continue to work with the nation's farmers to insure the food supply.

However, there are costs. The number of farms has declined sharply and the size of commercial farms has increased. The farmer, dependent upon a wide range of purchased products to carry on his work, seems to be caught up in "boom and bust" cycles, and with every "bust" there are still fewer farmers. As the number of farmers declines, rural communities also decline and cannot provide services.

The turning point in the structure of farming came at the end of World War II, when Extension workers encouraged farmers to adopt the new technology developed by the public and private agricultural research establishments. The improvement of every aspect of the farm operation through application of this technology and effective farm management were the basic sources of the increases in productivity that have changed farming and rural life. As Extension's next seventy-five years began, it was researching whether or not this type of agriculture can be sustained.

Extension's success in production agriculture has been most striking with the larger commercial farmers. Extension leaders agree that this relationship must be maintained but greater effort should be made to reach small and part-time farmers, a much larger if less influential constituency. Beginning in the 1970s a majority of the state Extension Services undertook special programs to reach this group. In the past, most small farmers never took the first step to work with Extension, or they were discouraged by the county agent's recommendations for improvements that were for them financially impossible. Extension has learned that it often must take the first step to reach the small farmer and that its recommendations often must be tailored to the needs of the small farm. More attention is being paid to alternative types of agriculture in meeting those needs.

Over the next several years Extension must, according to an ECOP-USDA task force, improve the economic efficiency and integration of the total agricultural system from producer to consumer. It must integrate marketing strategies into the production management system and, realizing that American agriculture competes in a global economy, it must provide farmers with accurate information and education to adjust profitably to global changes in supply and demand. At the same time it must balance human wellness, nutrition, and environmental concerns with competitiveness and profitability goals.

Extension has the tools to meet these challenges. And if the past foretells the future, it has the people and the support to continue to do its part to assure Americans of an abundant supply of the food and fiber they need.

State and local demonstration agents sponsored youth clubs for several years before the Extension Service was created. These included corn clubs, canning clubs, corn-growing contests, exhibits at county fairs, gardens, and soil testing. (USDA photo)

Demonstrating how to vaccinate calves to prevent blackleg was part of the job for Extension county agents in Richland County, Montana, in 1919. (Extension Service, USDA photo)

The county agent tour to see demonstration plots of improved crops and livestock breeding and feeding practices on farms in Indiana was a popular and effective way in the 1920s to transfer knowledge from the research laboratory to the farm.

"Quick, flexible and economical transportation is vital to the successful county agent" said this national advertisement recommending the Chevrolet Utility Coupe as "ideal for county agents" for country roads and stormy weather. (Photo courtesy Bob Davis)

M. L. Wilson (*left to right*), director of Extension Work, Chester Bowles, administrator of the Office of Price Administration, and H. H. Williamson, agricultural advisor for OPA, discuss Extension's World War II responsibility for disseminating information about price control. (USDA photo)

Five secretaries of agriculture discussed Extension policy and other matters at the USDA Teleconference Center on June 19, 1985. They are (*left to right*) John Block, 1981–1986; Bob Bergland, 1977–1981; Earl Butz, 1971–1976; Clifford Hardin, 1969–1971; and Orville Freeman, 1961–1969. (USDA photo)

Opposite: Extension paraprofessionals knocking on doors in neighborhoods needing improved knowledge of food and nutrition is one of the strong features of the Expanded Food and Nutrition Education Program (EFNEP). (Extension Service, USDA photo)

Above: An EFNEP paraprofessional instructs Maryland consumers on efficient buying practices. (Photo Maryland Cooperative Extension Service)

Right: The Expanded Food and Nutrition Education Program (EFNEP) focuses on low-income families needing information on nutrition, diet, food preparation, and food buying. (Extension Service, USDA photo)

Above: EFNEP also features nutrition education for youth, hoping to improve their lifetime diets. (Extension Service, USDA photo)

Left: Children learn about wool from a specialist at the North Carolina A&T State University Farm. (Photo North Carolina A&T University Agricultural Extension Program)

"Rural Route" was the name of the hot line conducted by the Illinois Cooperative Extension Service during the farm crisis of the mid-1980s. During the first two years of the program, over 2,700 farm families in Illinois received help in dealing with their financial situations. Other states had similar programs. (Illinois Cooperative Extension Service photo)

Integrated Pest Management (IPM) scout uses a sweep net to determine insect population count. IPM, an environmentally and economically sound method of protecting crops, has been widely adopted.

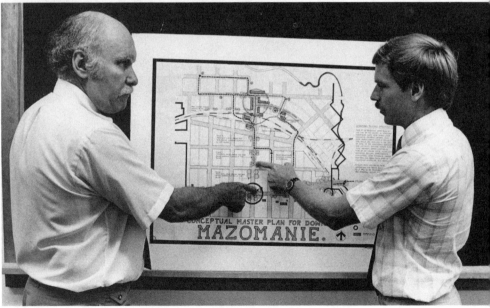

An Extension landscape architect and an architecture professor, University of Wisconsin, lead a planning and design team that works with local business people and Extension agents on revitalization projects. (University of Wisconsin photo)

J. C. Penney (*center*) visited with 4-H members on the Mall during the National 4-H Conference in Washington, D.C., in 1969. (National 4-H Council photo)

Sometimes company stops to visit before 4-H campers are ready for visitors! (Virginia Cooperative Extension Service photo)

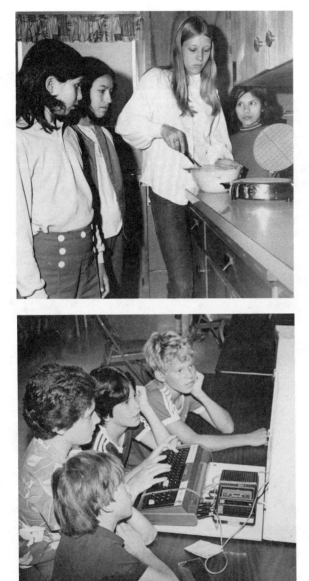

A junior 4-H leader, Dayton, Washington, invited children of Mexican migrant workers to a class on food preparation. (Washington State University Extension Service photo)

Computers at 4-H camps and meetings in Kentucky and other states are a part of today's Extension 4-H program to teach technology transfer to youth as well as to adults. (Kentucky Extension Service photo)

Young Alaskans from rural villages are participating in the Alaska Summer Computer Camp offered by the Alaska Native Human Resource Development Program and the Extension Service. (Alaska Cooperative Extension Service, Jim Smith photo)

CHAPTER SEVEN

Building a Stronger Society: Home, Health, and Nutrition

Introduction. The Smith-Lever Act of 1914 directed Extension to "aid in diffusing . . . useful and practical information on subjects relating to agriculture and home economics." Other subjects have been added to Extension's responsibilities since, but agriculture and home economics have remained at the heart of the law.

Home economics, like farming and rural life, has changed as communities, the nation, and the world have changed. The Smith-Lever Act stated that Extension should give "instruction and practical demonstrations in agriculture and home economics." In recent years, the focus of education has shifted. Nevertheless, the basic concerns of home economics — the physical, psychological and economic well-being of the family — do not change. The way each of these concerns has been addressed in current research has evolved with changes in society and in the research base. The means of transmitting knowledge to Americans who need it also has changed.

This chapter briefly reviews the work of home economists through World War II, discusses farm and rural life in 1950 and the changes that have taken place in families since then, lists recommendations by the Extension Committee on Organization and Policy (ECOP) and other groups, discusses home economists' recent activities in meeting needs, and takes a brief look at recommendations made by home economists and ECOP for the future.

Background.   When Secretary of Agriculture David F. Houston reported on the first year's operation of the Smith-Lever Act, he stated that "women county agents" had worked on topics related to the physical well-being of families — home conveniences, eradication of flies and mosquitoes, proper preparation of food, care of poultry, and marketing of eggs. Approximately fifty thousand homes had been visited, and those families had been given helpful suggestions. Six thousand farm women had presented special demonstrations in home improvement to fellow homemakers. In the 1980s home economists worked on issues associated with the economic, physical, and psychological well-being of families. Life for farm women, and for rural women as well, had become much more complex. Business management of the farm, nutrition as the important consideration in food preparation, community improvement, family stress, and off-farm employment became topics of concern in the 1980s.

Between the passage of the Smith-Lever Act and the end of World War II, Extension home economists built a positive reputation. They won nationwide recognition for their community work in World War I, helped rural families cope with the Depression of the 1920s and early 1930s, took an active part in New Deal programs, and contributed to overcoming the national emergency of World War II. As a means of expanding their contacts and educational programs, they developed volunteer leaders and homemakers clubs for educational programs. At the same time they broadened their programs to help rural Americans deal with change and became the leaders in educating families on the relationships between nutrition and health.

Between World War I and World War II, in many small offices agents divided time between home economics and 4-H. Larger offices employed home economists, youth, and agricultural agents. In the largest offices there often was a staff of Extension home economists, each specializing in a single topic such as nutrition, housing, clothing, or family relations.

Family Needs in the Postwar World.   In 1950, according to Director M. L. Wilson, Extension's 3,500 county home economists and assistants, aided by other Extension employees and 450,000 volunteer local leaders, encouraged more than 3,000,000 families to make improvements in their homemaking and family living. New homemakers, young mothers, and older women with new problems maintained a constant demand for basic information on such home economics subjects as foods and nutrition, health, clothing, child development, family relationships, home furnishings and equipment, home management, family financial planning, and housing.

Demands upon Extension home economists led to increased use of mass communications and a declining emphasis upon individual contacts. Homemakers clubs and volunteers continued their substantial contributions.

After the war years home economists became active in family housing education, focusing on such basics as electricity, water and sewage systems, and the selection, construction, and care of furnishings. Home demonstration agents at South Carolina State College, for example, opened a farm demonstration home that provided first-hand experience in better rural living for farm families. Some families actually had an opportunity to spend a brief vacation period living there. Through this experience, they developed ideas for improving their own homes.

The Farm and Home Development program, discussed in a previous chapter, was conducted by home economics and agriculture staff members. They worked together to plan programs involving all farm and family resources. These programs included every member of the farm family and dealt with farm and home goals concurrently.

A Changing Family in a Changing World.   As Extension celebrated the seventy-fifth anniversary of its efforts to provide educational service to the family, the family was experiencing rapid and in some instances traumatic change. Between 1960 and 1986 the number of families in the United States increased from 45 to 64 million. The number headed by a man with no wife present increased from 1.3 million to 2.4 million, and those headed by a woman with no husband present increased from 4.6 million to 10.2 million. In 1986 some 14 million children were living in single-parent homes. The percentage of elderly people in the population was increasing; and for women there were more opportunities for employment outside the home. The economic structure had changed to such an extent that women were virtually forced to seek employment outside the home to maintain the economic stability of the family.

Stress in families manifested itself in child abuse and family violence, juvenile delinquency, divorce, teenage pregnancy, drug and alcohol abuse, and bankruptcies.

Changing family structures and life-styles are creating changes in nutrition, diet, and health. Demand has increased for food that one can prepare quickly after getting home from the job. People eat more often in restaurants and food service facilities outside the home, and they are taking advantage of the wider variety of foods available throughout the year. People are more conscious of the relationship between diet and health.

As these changes occur in families, home economists are involved in identifying the role of Extension in helping Americans deal with them. There are three basic concerns. What programs should Extension undertake? Who should Extension reach? How can Extension best use the organization, the staff, and the knowledge it possesses?

Expanding Horizons.   The Home Economics Subcommittee of the Extension Committee on Organization and Policy (ECOP) published its first focus study, *Extension Home Economics Focus on the Family,* in 1967. The study was an attempt to increase awareness and understanding of the forces influencing family stability. Values were changing. Society witnessed a greater materialism, a shift away from ethical values, liberalized sexual mores, increased mobility of families, changing roles of family members, and a rising rate of gainful employment among wives and mothers. Poverty was greatest among rural families and families headed by women. Authors of the focus report concluded that family members were no longer dependent upon one another for most needs, from food and shelter to recreation and protection. These needs were now mostly provided for by the business community.

According to the report, Extension home economics should concentrate on educational programs to help families (1) understand and provide for maximum mental, emotional, and physical development of children; (2) guide young people from birth through adulthood; (3) acquire skills critical to the quality of family life, including management of financial resources; (4) maintain satisfying personal relationships inside and outside the home; (5) adjust to the retirement years; and (6) accept and adjust to the expanding and changing roles of family members.

In 1968 the U.S. Department of Agriculture (USDA) and National Association of State Universities and Land-Grant Colleges (NASULGC) Study Committee on Cooperative Extension issued a report entitled *A People and A Spirit*. The report recognized that Extension's quality of living programs, specifically home economics and 4-H, had assumed a broadened perspective. The committee recommended that Extension increase attention to "disadvantaged youth and adults in rural slums and urban ghettos, potential school dropouts, young families and unemployed out-of-school young adults."

A number of other studies followed these reports, virtually all of them holding it important that home economists stress nutrition and family relationships. These studies emphasized that home economics priorities could and should change to meet problems resulting from the rapidly changing social and economic environment.

VIEWS OF THE USERS.   In 1981 a National Extension Homemakers Study was conducted by the National Extension Homemakers Council (NEHC) to explore future directions for that organization and for Extension. The NEHC is a nonprofit educational organization made up of thirty thousand organized clubs in forty-four states and two territories, with a membership of some one-half million persons. Shortly after the Cooperative Extension Act was established, home economists from the state universities began to take educational material to women in counties that had no home economist. The home economists organized classes, which soon became clubs meeting semimonthly or monthly in members' homes. Very quickly these home demonstration or homemakers clubs began to depend upon volunteer leaders who were trained by a county home economist on a particular subject and who then in turn trained members of their own individual clubs.

As more clubs were organized, county and state affiliations were formed. In 1934 Grace Frysinger, home economist with the federal Extension Service, organized a Rural Homemakers Conference with representatives of several state home economics Extension groups. This resulted, after some additional meetings, in the organization in 1936 of the National Home Demonstration Council. In 1963, the name was changed to the present National Extension Homemakers Council.

The Council's objectives in 1981 included improving the quality of family living in cooperation with Extension and the USDA, improving home and community life, promoting the preservation of the American home, and bringing about better international understanding. Members acted on what they believed, each contributing an average of fifty-six hours annually in volunteer services. One-third of the club members had developed skills they used to earn supplementary family income. Through their club activities about two-thirds had acquired skills useful in voluntary projects.

The 1981 study indicated that members of homemakers clubs were interested in the basic subjects associated with the selection, use, and care of goods, and in family-life concerns. They also had expanded their horizons to citizenship community activities and national and international interests associated with quality of life for themselves and their families.

RECOMMENDATIONS FOR THE 1980s.   In 1983 a Joint USDA-NA-SULGC Committee on the Future of Cooperative Extension recommended that home economics/family living be strengthened as a major continuing area. Home economics/family-living programs, said the committee, should provide educational programs that help individuals and families identify their needs, conserve their resources, achieve a desired level of living, and become informed participants in the evaluation and formulation of public policy. The programs should continue to stress leadership development and training of voluntary leaders as a means of expanding their effectiveness. At that time the educational work of home economics professionals was being multiplied by the efforts of more than 600,000 volunteers in both rural and urban areas throughout the nation. Most of those volunteers were recruited and trained through homemakers clubs. The recommendations strengthened the position of those who believed that at least some of Extension's activities should be expanded to urban areas.

Improving Nutrition, Diet, and Health.   Food in its many aspects has long been a touchstone of home economics. Food is essential to human life, but it is more. Food has been the subject of poetry, novels, and learned tomes. The need for an assured supply of food has led to exploration, invention, and war. Food is the foundation upon which education and research in nutrition and diet are based. Ultimately, it is the key to solving or preventing many health problems.

Knowledge about the relationships between diet and many health problems facing Americans, much of it learned from Extension home economists, has had two consequences: The demand for particular agricultural products has changed, and the demand for reliable and understandable advice about dietary practices has increased. All segments of the food system, from producer to consumer, make decisions that affect the nature of the food supply. These decisions reflect changing consumer needs; changes in technology in food production, processing, and distribution; and research findings related to food, nutrition, and health. In recent decades the economic success of the food industry has become more closely related to the nutritional quality and safety of the products offered to consumers.

Extension home economists have always encouraged consumers to make the best possible use of the food supply. In the early days of Extension, this included conducting cooking classes, instructing on auxiliary programs associated with remodeling kitchens, taking needed sanitary measures, and teaching canning as a way of preserving food for future use. Home economists gave educational programs on such subjects as the relationships between pellagra and diet or between hookworm and sanitation. The Depression years of the 1930s saw food distribution programs, with Extension helping families take advantage of them. World War II was characterized by food shortages and rationing, with Extension home economists working with rationing boards and educating Americans about how best to use the supplies available. By the 1960s it seemed that most people enjoyed a good diet at a reasonable cost. Nevertheless, millions of Americans were living at or below the poverty level.

The Expanded Food and Nutrition Education Program.
As knowledge of the problem of hunger in an affluent America became widespread, private organizations and the federal government — mainly the Department of Agriculture with its donated food and food stamp programs — began supplying food to the needy. However, there still were problems. Many families lacked knowledge of nutrition and its relation to health. Such families often were isolated from sources of information, either because of their geographic location or because they were isolated from community resources. Existing educational institutions were not reaching out to these families. Food and nutrition education programs directed to the poor were needed to help them acquire the knowledge and skills to improve their diets.

In the early 1960s Extension financed a number of pilot studies that suggested some of these needs could be met through educational programs for low-income families using paraprofessional nutrition aides. Employees who lived in the communities in which they worked would work with families in a one-to-one setting or in small groups. Pilot projects, carried out in Alabama, Massachusetts, Missouri, Rhode Island, and Texas, dealt with different ethnic and racial groups living in urban slums or in isolated rural settings. The results were encouraging. Families of three-quarters of the participating homemakers showed improved eating habits. Two-thirds of the homemakers improved their food preparation skills; one-half increased the amount of milk consumed by their families, served more balanced meals, and used better food buying practices; and one-third improved methods of storing, canning, and freezing foods. The pilot studies led to two major conclusions. An educational program tailored to the interests, needs, competencies, and economic and educational levels of homemakers could be effective in changing families' eating habits. Paraprofessionals, under the supervision of professional home economists, could be trained to teach low-income homemakers effectively and could gain the confidence of needy people because they lived in the same community.

In November 1968 the Department of Agriculture, with the approval of Congress, provided Extension with a $10 million grant from Section 32 funds. The money, allocated from customs receipts for the removal of surplus agricultural products, was to initiate the Expanded Food and Nutrition Education Program (EFNEP).

The initial funding for EFNEP permitted every state to have

several program sites for testing the one-on-one concept and others developed in the pilot programs. Paraprofessionals employed to teach homemakers at 513 sites were trained and supervised by Extension home economists. Two fundamental principles guided the work: Information must be based on the latest available research and educational methodology, and teaching must be focused to produce measurable behavior change in the target population. Subsequently, allocations of funds were based upon the percentage of people in each state who were living below the poverty level.

While food and nutrition had always been a part of Extension home economics, a program targeted to the poor and a program with considerable emphasis on people living in inner-city slums was a new experience for many Extension staff members.

Pilot studies had shown that the most effective aides were individuals from the same ethnic and cultural backgrounds as the people with whom they were working. Extension maintained this practice. In 1986 some 224,600 homemakers at 813 sites participated in EFNEP. About 2 percent lived on farms, 31 percent in towns of under 10,000 population or in rural areas, 21 percent in towns and cities between 10,000 and 50,000 population, 4 percent in suburbs of large cities, and 42 percent in central cities with populations of over 50,000. Of these homemakers, 39 percent were white, 38 percent were black, 19 percent were Hispanic, 1 percent were American Indian or Alaskan Native, and 3 percent were Asian. The staff included 4,185 paraprofessionals, nearly all of whom were part-time workers, and 50,924 volunteers.

EFNEP won friends for Extension in cities like New York and Philadelphia. Congressional representatives from such cities supported its funding. Many representatives from rural areas also supported it. During the 1980s the federal Office of Management and Budget rather regularly proposed cuts in funding or the outright elimination of EFNEP, but Congress did not agree.

Congressional apprehension that EFNEP would detract attention from agricultural production was also a concern of state Extension directors, who were dedicated to meeting farm needs as their basic responsibility. Extension administrators frequently were called upon to reassure both Congress and Extension's traditional clientele that the EFNEP program was not detracting from work in agricultural production.

Critical Issues and Opportunities in Food and Nutrition. As the new century approached, a bulletin, *Food and Nutrition: The Link between Health and Agriculture*, produced cooperatively by ECOP, Extension Service, USDA, and Cornell Cooperative Extension, reviewed Extension food and nutrition programs and proposed action for the future. The bulletin recognized the critical goal of improving the nutritional and health status of the population. That goal was to be achieved by educating consumers to recognize that most individuals can promote their health by making informed choices from the commonly available food supply. The same is true in the case of infant mortality and low birth weight, problems that could be eased by designing appropriate educational materials targeted to specific audiences.

Obesity is another such problem. Obese individuals are at greater risk of developing a number of health problems, including hypertension and diabetes. Intensive, long-term educational programs addressing behavior modification often are necessary to help people achieve and maintain desirable weight. In 1975 Wisconsin Extension inaugurated an interdisciplinary weight control program called "New Dimensions in Weight." For two years specialists presented the program in informal open meetings throughout the state. As a follow-up, county home economists were provided kits of resource materials to continue with weight control programming. Newsletters on different aspects of weight control were developed and participants received them for a small fee. Many states had similar programs, most of which were very popular. For example, more than 1,600 people participated in an eleven-week Georgia Extension series on weight control.

Controlling obesity contributes to better health. Extension also developed educational messages and programs to bring about changes in dietary habits and life-styles to reduce the risk of such chronic diseases as hypertension, osteoporosis, coronary heart disease, and cancer. Many states have conducted programs that proved dietary habits can be changed with the proper motivation. In 1982, for example, Alabama Extension home economists encouraged individuals to exert more control over their own health through lessons on nutrition, stress, exercise, and weight loss. In 1983 they conducted educational programs on diets and food. In addition to producing news articles, radio and television programs, and newsletters, agents held 255 meetings, reaching about 9,000 people. A survey showed that one-half to three-quarters of the audience felt that the program had helped them learn to eat a greater variety of foods, select foods lower in fat, eat less salt and sugar, and plan meals and snacks to better meet nutritional needs. More than 90 percent stated that Extension programs had helped them save money on groceries, a bonus for nutrition education.

Extension home economists in Rhode Island and other states warned against fads and fraud. The inability to distinguish fads, frauds, and fallacies from reliable information leaves consumers vulnerable to nutritional quackery, a $500 million industry.

Home economists are increasing consumers' knowledge of what is in their food supply so they can make informed decisions regarding risks and benefits. Judging the safety and quality of food has become an increasingly complex task. Technological advances in food production, processing, packaging, and distribution may reduce or add to that complexity. Extension must rely upon research and the work of the regulatory agencies charged with food safety in developing its educational materials.

Cornell Extension has played a major role in bringing the results of this research to the public. Their aim has been to help consumers minimize health risk by providing them information to make intelligent decisions about their dietary practices. One program, "Moving toward Health and Fitness," complemented printed materials with an interactive computer program for analyzing one's diet and level of physical activity. Data indicate that participants increased their knowledge and made positive changes in their diets and levels of physical activity.

Extension home economists provide consumers with the knowledge and skills to make appropriate food selection, handling, and storage decisions to prevent food-borne illnesses. Between 400 and 500 food-borne disease outbreaks, affecting 10,000 to 20,000 people, are reported annually in the United States with many incidents probably not reported. One Extension goal is to increase knowledge of sanitary practices and proper storage of food by consumers, food service workers, processors, and others who handle food to minimize potential health hazards.

HEALTH PROGRAMS.   Extension home economists, particularly in rural and suburban areas, cooperate with others working on health problems. Participation in health fairs is an example. Extension has the resources in organization, knowledge, and skills to implement health education programs. In a number of cases city groups have called upon Extension home economists to help organize urban health education programs, especially in nutritional education. Extension is helping the American consumer achieve better nutrition in the same way that it has helped the American farmer achieve better productivity.

Meeting the Needs: Family and Economic Well-being.   The American family, whether farm, rural, or city, underwent radical changes over two decades, culminating in the 1980s. These changes led to stress and a negative impact upon health and well-being. Extension identified several critical issues relating to change and stress, many of which were not new but had been intensified by economic and social pressures.

FAMILY DISRUPTION AND DISLOCATION.   Loss of a farm or a job, divorce, and death all cause family disruptions. Earlier, two world wars, the Korean War, and the Vietnam War brought family disruptions with which Extension had to deal, while the Great Depression of the late 1920s and early 1930s had many of the same effects as the farm and rural depression of the 1980s.

The decade of the 1950s had been one of transition from war to peace, and it ended on rather a hopeful note. However, changes in farming practices brought about family disruption and dislocation as the number of jobs in farming declined along with the number of farms. Technological change and the decline in farm incomes during the 1960s, according to Director of Extension E. T. York, Jr., led many rural women to take jobs outside the home to supplement low incomes. While this improved their economic position, it also brought on many family and home management problems. The most effective way to deal with these problems, according to Lloyd H. Davis who succeeded York as director in 1963, was to tailor the work in home economics to the particular needs of special groups. This was not always easy to do. Opposing pressures regularly were placed upon home economists and Extension in general. On the one hand, Extension was urged to expand its role, increasing the diversity of its clientele, and expanding its programs to meet the challenges of change. On the other hand, if this expansion departed in any significant way from longtime programs, abrasive criticism arose almost immediately. This conflict often created problems in securing adequate financial support from all of the major sources of funds—county, state, and federal.

The problems of family disruption and dislocation that came to the fore in the 1960s eased somewhat in the 1970s as farming experienced a golden decade of prosperity. While both the number of farms and the farm population continued to decline, the decline occurred at a much reduced rate. Families had more choice about their futures. Home economists and other Extension staff had greater opportunities to expand their programs in the area of family stability. For example, the Cuyahoga County, Ohio, Cooperative Extension Service spearheaded the development of "Woman's World," a television series of twenty-seven programs aimed at the young urban homemaker in the Cleveland metropolitan area and its neighboring counties. The series was accompanied by organized, leader-led discussions at public housing projects and similar sites. The series covered four subjects: Foods and nutrition, child development and care, home furnishings related to children's needs, and family economics and management. Teaching through mass media reached a new audience in an urban area with programs that would improve family stability among the participants.

A Kentucky area Extension agent in foods and nutrition coordinated the efforts of an organization of volunteer leaders. The Neighborhood Organization of Women helped the area agent reach the 1,320 families living in public housing in Fayette County. Each month every new family moving into public housing was visited by the area agent or by a volunteer who gave guidance on home management, meal planning, and stretching the food dollar. This educational program helped provide a sense of family stability for its participants.

Even though farmers generally were prosperous during the 1970s, many farm, rural, and urban families were threatened by inflation. Extension home economists in many states and counties conducted educational programs on improved management of the resources available to the family. Innovative programs included efforts by the University of Arkansas, Pine Bluff, which involved hiring and training nine home management paraprofessionals to work in six counties. Homemakers learned better financial management in a time of inflation while improving their homes and environments.

Early in the 1980s Extension faced a serious problem: How best to meet the needs of farm families and rural communities as farm prices and income declined sharply. Part of a general, nationwide depression that moved toward recovery in a few years, the economic situation of farmers continued to worsen until near the end of the decade. Rural communities and rural people suffered as the farm depression deepened. Acute stress experienced by large numbers of farm families took its toll, with an increase in suicides, family breakups and divorces, school dropouts, alcoholism, and other damaging reactions. While not every farm family was adversely affected, about a third were in desperate circumstances and another third were in serious difficulty. The remaining one-third of farm families were reasonably well off.

Home economists took an active part in developing and carrying out programs to assist those in the worst situations. In some cases, they helped the family find alternative sources of income, either from the farm operation or off the farm. Once again, farm families had to make do with what they had. Here home economists were particularly helpful. Homemakers clubs, with the aid of county home economists, developed programs for remaking clothing and repairing and refurbishing home furnishings. They offered mutual support in dealing with crisis situations, continuing a tradition that is very important in rural areas. Specialists offered training on managing crisis situations in the home, often coordinating such education with the agricultural, rural development, and youth programs that were also providing guidance. The key contribution of home economists was teaching stress management and coping skills.

HOUSING.   Housing has been a concern of Extension home economists from the earliest days. During the 1960s Extension's home economics educational programs on housing gave increased attention to hard-to-reach families — the elderly, disadvantaged, public housing residents, young marrieds, and those who spoke little or no English.

By the end of the 1960s thousands of Missouri families were living in homes that more nearly met their requirements because of educational assistance from the University of Missouri Extension Division. The number included low-income families who were living in homes built with the university's low-cost house plans. About 88 percent of

Missouri's counties included housing in their educational programs in the 1960s.

In Washington state Extension conducted a pilot educational program with commercial small-home builders in Cowlitz County. The county home economist and the state Extension housing specialist, who enlisted help from the university's Department of Architecture and Research, conducted a four-lesson school for small-home builders. These sessions helped home builders come closer to meeting the needs of buyers and made homes more convenient and livable at little or no added cost.

In 1971 a Maryland Extension home economist cooperated with a housing corporation by decorating and furnishing an apartment to serve as a model for incoming residents of a 300-unit complex for families with low to moderate incomes. The success of this project led the corporation involved to work with Extension home economists in other parts of the country to meet the housing needs of lower income families.

In the early 1970s Ponca City, Oklahoma, contracted with Extension to employ, train, and supervise seven part-time housing aides who helped two hundred native American families moving into new homes. After the aides became involved, delinquency in payments dropped by 80 percent, and repair and maintenance costs were also reduced by 80 percent. In Claiborne County, Mississippi, Alcorn University assigned a home management paraprofessional to work with fifty families on a one-to-one basis. All the families attended workshops on refinishing furniture and on food preservation. They also worked with the paraprofessional on better management of their housing facilities.

In the mid-1970s, with energy costs escalating, Extension gave priority to energy conservation in the home, on the farm, and in the community. Home economists pointed out the value of home insulation and proper maintenance in cutting energy costs. Proper care of heating equipment was taught through meetings and printed material. Demonstrations of the results in livability and reduced energy consumption that might be accomplished by home improvements were effective in a number of states. Texas, for example, reported that 290,500 families viewed a thirteen-part television series, "You Can Do It." Some 32,000 homemakers participated in follow-up workshops, institutes, and direct-mail instruction of home care and maintenance skills. Substantial savings resulted. While energy costs fell in the 1980s, farm incomes dropped as well. Extension home economists in nearly every state used publications, the radio, television, and group meetings to help families handle the upkeep of their housing at minimal costs. Educational programs on refinancing home mortgages, handling mortgage payments, and otherwise meeting pressing financial problems were even more important to many families. In Alaska, for example, villagers who were being moved to permanent housing for the first time learned to adjust to mortgage payments and other obligations through Extension programs.

Extension home economists at Tuskegee University pointed out that housing costs had risen by 90 percent between 1970 and 1980, and that more than half a million rural Alabama residents were living in substandard housing as the decade began. Extension worked with the Farmers Home Administration and other agencies to explore innovative housing approaches for the rural disadvantaged. Home economists also taught families how to make the best use of what they had.

ALCOHOL AND DRUG ABUSE.   Although there always has been abuse of alcohol and drugs in American society, this problem recently has become one of the most pervasive issues facing American families and society. Not until the 1970s did Extension home economists consider the problem of major importance. However, that attitude had changed by the early 1970s, because the use of illegal drugs and the abuse of legal drugs were causing national concern.

Many state Extension home economics staffs cooperated with colleagues within the land-grant institutions, with the American Medical Association, with schools, and with others in conducting "drug-problem solving workshops." For example, North Dakota Extension sponsored eight one-day area workshops. Positive community approaches to meet the threat of drug abuse were planned at each workshop. Similarly, Extension in twenty-one Colorado counties cooperated with schools and local and county police to conduct educational programs related to drug abuse. The programs were widely attended. A Youth Enrichment Program conducted annually by home economists at Delaware State College includes classes on drug abuse.

While the control of drug and alcohol abuse is not primarily a responsibility of Extension, home economists and 4-H agents—with their emphasis on health and family well-being—have made important contributions in educating people about the dangers of such abuse as well as how it might be controlled. During the 1980s Extension raised public awareness of drug abuse as a national problem. The Cooperative Extension System has the nationwide staff and the educational technology to increase its contributions. Future programs will depend, at least in part, on local and state needs and on requests for cooperation by regulatory authorities.

A number of state leaders of the National Extension Homemakers Council reported in 1986 that homemakers clubs were carrying on active educational programs in their communities on drug and alcohol abuse. These states included Alabama, Massachusetts, Montana, Tennessee, and Virginia.

FAMILY FINANCIAL STABILITY.   Helping farm and rural families establish economic stability is a long-term goal of Extension. It is related to nearly every Extension program, from more efficient production and marketing to food preservation and household efficiency. Improving resource management skills was stressed during the 1970s and 1980s, with home economics cooperating with many other Extension programs.

Educating rural families to better manage their available resources has taken many forms over the years. The effort changed as needs changed and as Extension developed new techniques for meeting needs. Such was the case in 1973 when the Mississippi Cooperative Extension Service established the first Money Management Center in Jackson, Mississippi, with a grant from the Office of Housing and Rural Development. Work began with families in low-income housing to teach them to manage their money so they could make their rent payments in a timely manner. When the grant funds expired, Mississippi Extension provided funds for the center and expanded it to include work with banks, businesses, churches, and community organizations. Individual consultations were carried out with families as staff time permitted. In 1977 the U.S. Office of Education granted funds to expand the center. A year later a second center was opened in Biloxi. Its program at Keesler Air Force Base contributed to the adoption of a memorandum of understanding in 1985 between the U.S. Department of Agriculture and the Department of Defense for such cooperation. Meanwhile, in

1981 the Farmers Home Administration made a grant to Mississippi Extension to work with borrowers and homeowners delinquent in their payments. This grant ended in 1984, but Mississippi Extension continues to provide funds for a money management center in Tupelo.

A study conducted in 1986 revealed that 87 percent of the participants sampled felt better able to handle finances at the conclusion of counseling and 67 percent felt that their financial situation was better as a result of the program.

By 1977 family resource management programs were found in every state. They accounted for about one-tenth of the total home economics effort. From 1973 through 1976, for example, 237,000 families in Colorado, Indiana, Kentucky, and North Carolina made adjustments in family resource management following participation in estate planning programs. Some 20,740 families in Puerto Rico participated in money-management classes and reported that they were making better use of their funds. About 3,400 homemakers were budgeting, 2,290 low-income families were using credit more wisely, and 3,725 had become better informed about consumer rights.

Looking Ahead.   Effective efforts by Extension home economists to continue to support improved nutrition, diet, health, and family and economic well-being require both planning and action. Recent studies have identified several possible lines of action. One would be to designate Centers of Excellence within Extension. Such centers, representing priority areas in food, nutrition, and health, would need the staff and support to provide leadership for other Extension personnel in bringing programs addressing key issues to the American people. Another step would be to increase cooperation with researchers to assure that Extension's educational programs reflect the best possible advice on how consumers can make informed food choices most relevant to their health and well-being.

Many food, nutrition, and health issues are controversial. Exchanges among professionals in all Extension program areas will be required before educational messages or strategies can be developed. Such dialogue should not, however, be confined to Extension home economists. There is a pressing need to bring to life and expand a nutrition education network. Some interchange is taking place, but much more is needed. Several agencies of the USDA are concerned with issues relating to food, nutrition, and health. They should work closely with Extension home economists to get their messages to the public. Health and nutrition professionals from other government agencies and from the private sector would benefit from such an interchange. Even more to the point, so would the American public.

A family community leadership project in which Extension educates families for local leadership, especially in local government, offers promise for the future. It strengthens both families and communities.

Home economics has been a key part of the Cooperative Extension System from its beginning. As it meets the demands for education in food and nutrition and in family well-being, it will continue to play a vital role. Certainly, never before in the history of our nation have there been more critical issues surrounding the family — single parent households, two-wage earner families, drug and alcohol abuse, youth at risk, and others. Research-based university knowledge, taught to families by Extension, is critical to long-term solutions to such issues.

CHAPTER EIGHT

Building a Stronger Society: Youth and Leadership

Introduction.   Membership in 4-H has a highly positive image among former members and among the American people in general. Former 4-H members are more likely than others in their age groups to participate in and become leaders of community and Extension-related activities. According to studies completed in the late 1980s, 4-H is educating young Americans for effective participation in a practical way in the complex, technology-driven world of today. It has the potential to educate many more young people than it is reaching today.

This chapter begins with a brief review of the background of 4-H and then turns to a discussion of the current goals, organization, and programs of 4-H. The chapter concludes with a brief look at future prospects for 4-H.

Background

BOYS' AND GIRLS' CLUBS.   Boys' and Girls' Clubs, devoted to such agricultural subjects as corn, hogs, gardens, and canning, were the direct predecessors of today's 4-H clubs and were building blocks for Extension. Early leaders included A. B. Graham of Ohio, O. J. Kern and W. B. Otwell of Illinois, O. H. Benson and Jessie Field of Iowa, W. W. Smith of Mississippi, Marie Cromer of South Carolina,

Ella Agnew of Virginia, and Otis O'Neal of Georgia. They saw the need for practical programs for young people. Moreover, they saw that if young people were involved in adopting new and more efficient practices, their parents also would become involved. Their ideas received strong backing when the Country Life Commission of 1908, under the leadership of Liberty Hyde Bailey of Cornell University and Kenyon L. Butterfield of the University of Massachusetts, urged practical agricultural education for young people and the development of new, young rural leadership.

FIELD AGENTS ENCOURAGE GROWTH.   In 1908 and 1910 respectively, Oscar B. Martin of South Carolina and O. H. Benson of Iowa were appointed field agents in the U.S. Department of Agriculture to work with Boys' and Girls' Clubs. Benson, with Jessie Field, had been using three- and four-leaf clover emblems in Iowa, and he brought the idea to Washington. By the end of 1911 the four-leaf clover, with an "H" on each leaf representing "Head, Heart, Hands and Health" respectively, had become a permanent symbol, although the term "4-H club" was not used in a federal document until 1918. In 1912 club and youth demonstration work enrolled 73,000 boys and 23,000 girls.

4-H AND WORLD WAR I.   When the Smith-Lever Act was passed in 1914, Boys' and Girls' Clubs were already firmly established as a part of the new Cooperative Extension Service. They were further strengthened during World War I when Congress appropriated substantial sums to be used by Extension to secure increased food production from America's farmers. With labor shortages on the farms, Extension leaders in virtually every state recognized that a sure way to increase production was to expand club work among rural youth. Club membership stood at 169,000 in 1916. By 1918, a year after the United States had entered the war, it was more than 500,000. Some emergency funding was allocated to the South's 1890 colleges, resulting in a substantial increase in the number of Boys' and Girls' Clubs for black youth. At the war's conclusion, although the special appropriations ended, Boys' and Girls' Clubs were even more firmly established, although membership then declined for a few years before resuming the upward trend.

In 1921 the National Committee on Boys' and Girls' Club Work was established with E. T. Meredith as chairman and Guy Noble as secretary. Based in Chicago, the committee, which changed its name to the National 4-H Service Committee in 1960, served as a vehicle through which private businesses and individuals could contribute to the support of 4-H. It sponsored competitive events and awards programs at various levels, published a national newsletter, and took the lead in arranging annual state and national 4-H congresses for outstanding club members. Questions arose over the respective responsibilities of the committee and of state and federal Extension offices. In 1939 the Extension Committee on Organization and Policy (ECOP) authorized establishment of a subcommittee devoted entirely to 4-H, thus providing a reasonable way to resolve those differences. The subcommittee, representing state and national 4-H offices, became the principal policy-recommending body for future 4-H development. This gave both government and private parties a formal means of communicating recommendations for 4-H programs to a group having the authority to make formal recommendations to ECOP.

For the next thirty years 4-H continued to grow, becoming the best-known of all Extension programs and one of the nation's best-known youth programs. Its contributions to meeting family, community, and national needs during the Great Depression, the New Deal, and World War II won it widespread public support.

Planning for Today and Tomorrow

CHANGING PATTERNS AND NEEDS.   Today, about one-half of members enrolled in 4-H live in large cities and towns and their suburbs and one-half live on farms, in rural areas, and in towns with populations of 10,000 or fewer. Although this shift toward urban enrollments has taken place largely since World War II, there has always been some city and suburban participation. For example, Kent County, Rhode Island, had an urban club in 1906; Texas, Oregon, and New York also had urban clubs in the very early years. These, however, were exceptions.

The needs that 4-H is particularly qualified to meet concern virtually all young people, regardless of place of residence, occupation of parents, or color of skin. Unfortunately, as President Grant A. Shrum, of the National 4-H Council has pointed out, today's young people are at greater risk than ever before in our history. In the late 1980s of all four- and five-year old children—the potential students and workers of the year 2000—one in four is born into poverty, while one in six lives in a family in which neither parent has a job. One in five is at risk of becoming a teen parent; one in six has no health insurance; one in two has a mother working outside the home, with only a small minority having quality child care; and one in seven is at risk of dropping out of school. One out of eight seventeen-year-olds in the United States is functionally illiterate. In addition to the children burdened with these disabilities, many others from all segments of society are in danger of falling victim to alcohol and drug abuse, child abuse, teen suicide, and crime. How to meet and solve these problems has been the subject of studies by committees and others representing 4-H, ECOP, and the U.S. Department of Agriculture (USDA). In general these studies conclude that 4-H has the programs and the leadership to contribute effectively to the solution of the problems identified. To do so, 4-H should work to secure additional support from the community, from state and federal governments, and from private institutions and foundations.

4-H OBJECTIVES.   The objectives of 4-H, according to the 4-H in Century III task force of the ECOP Subcommittee on 4-H, include encouraging young people to develop inquiring minds, an eagerness to learn, and the ability to apply science and technology; to learn practical skills and acquire knowledge; to maintain optimum physical and mental health; and to increase leadership capabilities.

The key to the success of 4-H, said the task force, is volunteer leaders. In turn, the availability of the extensive talents and resources of land-grant college and university subject-matter specialists is one of the keys to the success of volunteer leaders. Providing up-to-date information and teaching methods in agriculture, home economics, community resource development, communications, and other areas, these specialists, working through the Extension field staff, help volunteer leaders become better prepared to work with 4-H youth.

4-H NATIONAL NEEDS ASSESSMENT.   A committee representing the Extension Service, USDA; National 4-H Council; and North Carolina State University with the assistance of state 4-H leaders reported in 1983 that "more than ever, youth need effective educational programs to help them acquire the life skills and knowledge necessary to grow and succeed in a rapidly changing and complex society." The committee concluded that 4-H should assist youth to acquire skills and knowledge in agriculture, home economics, science, and technology. Youth needed the direction 4-H could provide to develop a positive self-image, to learn to respect and get along with people, to develop and practice responsible environmental skills, and to learn and use accepted practices for mental, physical, emotional, and social health. The 4-H program should assist youth to explore and evaluate career and job opportunities, use leisure time productively, and participate in community affairs. Not the least important goal was developing volunteers as individuals and leaders for 4-H and their communities.

To work successfully with youth in meeting these goals, the national needs assessment study identified five major areas of concern: Provide for more effective staff development and training; involve youth, volunteers, and other community leaders more directly in program planning; insure that the curriculum is up-to-date and meets real needs; relate financial and resource needs to national roles and responsibilities; and develop programs to keep professional staff in 4-H while making better use of volunteers and paraprofessionals.

BUILDING BLOCKS FOR THE FUTURE.   In 1986 a panel of leading national and state 4-H leaders, in *4-H Future Focus: 1986–1996,* called for "new vision" to guide the work of the nation's largest informal out-of-school educational program for young people. The panel identified these building blocks for refining and redirecting 4-H: Keeping the focus on youth development education; giving 4-H leadership maximum opportunities to grow in educational leadership skills and management responsibilities; strengthening and expanding relationships in the land-grant university system; and strengthening the bilateral public and private partnership.

The panel recommended that the Cooperative Extension System "pursue vigorously" the mission of the 4-H program, which is "to help youth and volunteers in their development through educational programs using the knowledge and educational base of the land-grant universities and the United States Department of Agriculture." The system must assure that 4-H is accessible to targeted youth — both rural and urban—and must increase the duration of involvement at all age levels.

The multiple interests and changing environment of today's youth, according to the panel, necessitate a wider range of subjects for instruction. A stronger research and knowledge base in less traditional disciplines outside agriculture and home economics also is essential. The 4-H program should draw on any department of the university where knowledge and research can contribute to current and future program needs of youth.

4-H PROFESSIONAL RESEARCH AND KNOWLEDGE PROJECTS.   In 1986 the Extension Service, USDA, awarded a grant to the 4-H unit of the Mississippi State University Extension Service to identify the base of existing research supporting 4-H professionals in their day-to-day efforts. Another grant to the 4-H unit of the Ohio State University Extension Service was earmarked to identify the knowledge base of 4-H youth development. The key knowledge and research areas from which 4-H professionals draw to carry out youth development education were determined to be communication, educational design, youth development, youth program management, and volunteerism. These areas were emphasized in studies of available resources published in 1987. For the first time there is a taxonomy of categories and an assembled body of knowledge providing a base for future youth development programs. The National Agricultural Library is working with the Cooperative Extension System to enter this data in a new electronic data base, which makes this and future material readily available to 4-H workers throughout the nation.

Organizing 4-H for Today's Tasks

CHANGE IN THE FEDERAL OFFICE.   The federal Extension Service established a Division of 4-H and Young Men's and Women's Programs on December 1, 1952; it was renamed the Division of 4-H and Youth Development in 1963. The new division, first headed by Edward W. Aiton, provided some of the recognition for 4-H that the National Association of Extension 4-H Agents, organized in 1946, had been seeking. It emphasized the training of 4-H agents and volunteers as well in new skills associated with human development and in advanced educational techniques. Greater emphasis on the social sciences to enable 4-H workers to keep abreast of the changing interests of club members and to reach out to young people who traditionally had not been a part of 4-H was encouraged.

NATIONAL 4-H COUNCIL.   The need for a mechanism to provide new kinds of training was an important factor in the creation of the National 4-H Club Foundation in 1948 and the subsequent establishment of the National 4-H Center in Chevy Chase, Maryland, as a training facility. After the National 4-H Club Foundation was established, the National Committee on Boys' and Girls' Club Work and the foundation agreed that the foundation would have four major areas of responsibility. It would acquire and develop a National 4-H Center facility; it would support leadership training and development in the United States and abroad; it would support professional improvement for Extension personnel; and it would conduct programs in international education. The National 4-H Center in Chevy Chase, Maryland, opened in 1959, provided a permanent home for National 4-H Conference that had begun in 1927 as the National 4-H Club Camp. The committee continued to be responsible for the annual National 4-H Congress in Chicago. Both organizations, each with its responsibilities, continued to operate for nearly thirty years. However, there appeared to be some duplication of effort and, even more important, both were competing for funding from many of the same private organizations. In 1976 the two combined as National 4-H Council. Norman C. Mindrum, who had directed the committee, was named chief executive officer; Grant A. Shrum, who had headed the foundation, became chief operating officer. In 1979, upon Mindrum's retirement, Shrum was elected chief executive officer. He also became president of National 4-H Council.

State 4-H foundations have been established in a number of states and are currently growing in number and influence. The foundations raise funds and allocate them to various programs and activities and help keep 4-H before the public.

INTEGRATION IN 4-H.   The passage of the Civil Rights Act of 1964 brought an end to legal segregation in 4-H and in Extension as a whole. In 1965 the federal 4-H office issued a memorandum stating: "any 4-H club . . . which is organized and served by Extension in which there now exists racial exclusion, will desegregate its membership no later than December 21, 1965, as a condition for continued assistance. . . . " Carrying out the directive was particularly difficult in states where 4-H meetings were part of the regular school schedule, since some schools continued to be segregated for another ten years. While federal and state Extension staffs did what they could to ease tensions, the real burden fell on county Extension people.

Integration of the Extension staffs from the university to the county level was difficult. However, the problem was eased to some extent in 1972 when Congress began appropriating specific amounts for Extension work in the 1890 colleges and Tuskegee University. This funding remained on a year-to-year basis until 1977. Then Congress in the Food and Agriculture Act provided that not less than 4 percent of the total amount appropriated annually under authority of the Smith-Lever Act should be allocated to the 1890 colleges and Tuskegee University. Effective in 1983, the allocation was increased to 6 percent. These funds have supported an administrator of Extension and usually a small program staff at each of the 1890 colleges and at Tuskegee University.

VOLUNTEERS IN 4-H.   Volunteer workers are at the heart of 4-H. In the traditional county Extension office, one professional staff person or one-half the time of a professional staff worker is devoted to 4-H. That person must have assistance to carry out an effective program, which has traditionally come from volunteers. Today, more women — the traditional volunteer work force — than ever before are employed in full-time jobs and family structures are changing. There simply are not as many people from traditional sources who have the available time to serve as volunteers as there were in earlier years.

New sources of volunteers for 4-H, according to a report sponsored by the ECOP Subcommittee on 4-H, must be developed from among teenagers and young adults, senior citizens, retired persons, members of minority groups, and leaders of community and civic organizations. Such leaders will likely come with new expectations, new skills, and greater demands for high levels of participation. To meet their needs and expectations will require strengthening the quality and frequency of both training and recognition programs. The recruitment and retention of volunteers could also be encouraged by arranging for certificate or degree credit for skills developed through volunteer work and by encouraging legislation providing benefits for volunteers.

Many states and counties conduct training courses for 4-H volunteers. Such courses often prepare volunteers for increased involvement in management roles. Others train in high-technology skills. The National 4-H Center provides leadership training for many youth and adults each year.

Some 4-H professionals are exploring innovative methods for finding and recruiting new volunteer leaders. Extension in Ramsey County, Minnesota, for example, is recruiting such leaders from among child-care providers. Child-care providers are increasing rapidly in number and they all have in common responsibility for large numbers of children for long periods of time. They share a need for high-interest, attention-keeping activities for youngsters. The Ramsey County 4-H staff began its program for interested licensed child-care providers with a six-part correspondence series on nutritious snacks. At the end of the series, children who participated received a 4-H certificate. Subsequent series included such 4-H projects as the use of small appliances, beginning consumer awareness, natural science, creative arts, drama and writing, and first aid and safety.

PROFESSIONAL STAFF.   If volunteers are the heart of 4-H, then the professional staff must be its soul. The annals of 4-H abound with stories of dedicated persons who devoted their lives to 4-H and to the young people they served.

Some of that same dedication is required of today's professional staff, but it must be complemented by a high degree of professionalism. The National Association of Extension 4-H Agents has stimulated such professionalism by providing training development workshops. New curricula in the universities have done the same. Human development workshops, with their emphasis on training in the social sciences, began at the University of Maryland and at Cornell University and then spread throughout the nation. In the 1970s several universities including Kansas State, Maryland, Purdue, Rutgers, and Wisconsin developed curricula for educating future Extension agents. Most state Extension services now require an appropriate master's degree for appointment as a 4-H agent.

The National 4-H Center has been a major resource for training professional 4-H agents. With support from the W. K. Kellogg Foundation and other private groups, the center conducts a continuing series of seminars, workshops, and training programs for agents from all over the United States and abroad.

The ECOP Subcommittee on 4-H suggests several steps for 4-H staff development in the future. Midcareer professional training opportunities contribute to the maintenance of a competent and articulate staff. Clarifying the cooperative roles of 4-H and Extension subject-matter specialists is a continuing responsibility. Strengthening orientation training and increasing training opportunities for the development of management skills creates a stronger staff, concerned more with middle management than with direct work with youth. Additional encouragement of professional university-level youth development degree programs increases professionalism. In general, the development and support of policies that maintain high levels of competence and performance for the professional staff benefits 4-H.

FUTURE ORGANIZATION.   An important part of the Cooperative Extension System, 4-H has ambitious goals spelled out for the future. Nevertheless, there are questions as to how 4-H will meet these goals. By 1988 4-H and home economics had been combined in several states. This was done, at least in part, to cut costs.

As 4-H is broadening its clientele and addressing issues as well as projects, it must relate to many departments in the university. The suggestion has been made that 4-H be taken out of the college of agriculture and relocated in the university. Similarly, 4-H could possibly benefit by drawing upon the resources of all the federal departments, and not just the Department of Agriculture. One way to bring this about would be to make 4-H a key part of an overall National Commission on Youth.

Still another idea, one that has limited support, is to make 4-H independent of all government, as are many other youth organizations. However, 4-H today cuts across many lines in carrying out its mission and gaining support, and this is one of its greatest strengths. It works through local, state, and federal governments. It has support from private concerns, foundations, and the public, and it owes much of its effectiveness to volunteers. In light of its need to reach more of today's youth, it must have greater support rather than less. Even more important, an effective nationwide structure is in place for reaching today's youth, including many who are not reached by any other youth programs. The nation's needs can best be met, according to most authorities, by strengthening and refining the present structure, rather than by risking weakening it by some radical reorganization.

Russell G. Mawby of the W. K. Kellogg Foundation has put the problem in perspective: "The government cannot meet these challenges alone, nor can the private sector hope to provide the unity and the resources to do the job by itself. The solution certainly lies in this kind of a joint partnership of government, private business, committed individuals and the unequaled educational and communications resources of this great network of land-grant universities across the country." Mawby was speaking of "Project: Youth for America," a major 4-H youth development initiative designed to address the challenging problems facing young people. It seeks to combine the resources of federal, state, and county governments with the private sector to expand the youth outreach effectiveness of each state land-grant university.

Meeting Today's Issues.   Today 4-H is in a period of dynamic change. It is committed, so far as its resources will permit, to dealing with issues it is qualified to handle wherever they may arise. Staff training and retraining programs and new curricula in the universities have prepared county staff and state specialists to undertake educational programs relating to most youth issues.

Some changes have evolved over the years, while others have come quickly. In some instances Congress has brought about rapid change by earmarking funds for specific programs, although all such programs had at least some previous status in 4-H.

NEW EDUCATIONAL TOOLS.   As 4-H has changed directions to meet today's needs, added new participants, and served new audiences, it has adopted new educational tools. Television, videotapes, and computers have found a place in today's 4-H programs.

Television, when it first entered American homes, seemed to offer an unusual opportunity for 4-H to reach a wide audience. As early as 1957 Michigan State University Extension was producing half-hour shows designed for nine- to eleven-year-olds. Other states followed. However, the technical problems involved in producing quality programs that would be widely accepted, as well as the costs involved, limited the use of television even though a number of well-received programs were developed. The most successful was "Mulligan Stew," a series of six half-hour films accompanied by leaders guides and a comic book/workbook. The series, financed by EFNEP and developed by the federal Extension Service in cooperation with several state Extension services, aimed at promoting better nutrition among young people. Shown and reshown through the 1970s and into the 1980s, the series reached six million youngsters.

In spite of the success of "Mulligan Stew," 4-H and Extension have turned from television films to videotapes, usually circulated as cassettes. The video cassettes are versatile. They can be targeted to particular audiences and can be made available for club, family, or individual use. While requiring careful planning and skillful production, excellent videotapes can be written and produced by Extension staff. The cost is considerably less than a comparable film for television, and the videotapes can also be used for television.

Computers and related electronic information devices have been called the new methodology of Extension. They have been widely accepted in 4-H, since young people find them intriguing as well as useful. "Computer camps" are attended by numbers of 4-H'ers every summer. Indeed, many young people have received their first hands-on computer education through 4-H.

MEETING RURAL NEEDS.   About one-half of the 4.5 million young people participating in 4-H programs live on farms, in rural areas, or in small towns. Some 1.4 million projects involve animal and poultry production, while plant sciences and natural resources each account for more than one-half million. These projects reflect scientific advances and new technology and often have an impact on farming practices. Each fall 4-H'ers still show their best animals and crops at thousands of county and state fairs. At the same time, they are learning life skills that go beyond their specific projects. Essentially, their projects are a means to an end. For example, Oregon Extension found in a survey of 5,000 4-H'ers carrying out animal science projects, that a majority of the young people identified "life skills" as the most important things they learned from the projects. For many comparatively isolated rural youth, 4-H is an important force in their development as responsible citizens.

COMMUNITY DEVELOPMENT.   In 1973 Congress appropriated a $7.5 million increase in 4-H funding, of which $2.5 million was used for the involvement of 4-H in rural community development projects and $5 million was used for 4-H urban programs. The community development program that has evolved stresses the principle of learning by doing. The work carried out has ranged widely from participation in environmental protection campaigns to taking an active part in local government.

Workshops on recycling, energy, and ecology issues brought these matters to public attention and resulted in the establishment of a number of action programs. Florida 4-H members were appointed to boards and commissions in a number of counties. Ohio 4-H members conducted a campaign to register eighteen- to twenty-one-year-olds as voters. Benton County, Oregon, 4-H has a long-term program of citizenship education with work on such issues as juvenile justice and the role of communication skills in good citizenship. Utah 4-H began a juvenile justice program to give some youths a second chance instead of sending them to detention homes. Montana and other states held workshops at their state capitols while the legislature was in session, giving youth opportunity to see and, in some instances, to participate in government in action. The emphasis in all of these activities was to learn by doing—a continuing concept in 4-H.

Inadequate after-school child care of unacceptable quality is a growing problem in communities and in the nation. More and more youngsters between the ages of five and thirteen are left unsupervised to care for themselves for a part of each day. The Cooperative Extension Service in Placer County, California, has developed an after-school program that addresses this issue while extending the usefulness of 4-H. The program is financed primarily by a small fee paid by parents. It is conducted under the auspices of the county 4-H volunteer leaders council, through a volunteer board of directors, and is housed in school facilities. Each site has a teaching staff of one adult for every fourteen youngsters enrolled. In addition, volunteer 4-H leaders, both adults and teens, provide supplemental support. The program uses the proven 4-H methods of experimental activities and learn-by-doing projects. Each week a new theme based on 4-H project work is introduced. In 1987 the program was available to twelve sites in Placer County and was being expanded to Los Angeles County and San Diego.

URBAN 4-H.   Although Extension makes no marked distinction between rural and urban 4-H, much of the work in urban communities started after Congress began earmarking funds for that purpose in 1973. Nevertheless, there have been significant activities in urban areas ever since World War II. A survey of Extension work in the Northeast in 1949 showed that most states were carrying out 4-H programs in urban areas in gardening, nutrition and health, clothing, landscaping, and home grounds improvement. Programs in such cities as Paterson, New Jersey, and Providence, Rhode Island, were being undertaken at the request of local service organizations, often with funding from private and local sources. A 1950 study showed that all forty-eight states were doing some urban work.

During the 1950s Michigan 4-H under the leadership of Russell Mawby established programs in Detroit, Flint, Grand Rapids, and Kalamazoo. The first programs were funded by the Michigan 4-H Foundation. Mawby said later that his approach was to not ask too many questions before doing something and eventually to not distinguish between rural and urban 4-H. A major urban 4-H effort got under way in Chicago in 1957 with a grant from John B. Clark, head of a large manufacturing company. Private business leaders in Michigan and Illinois supported 4-H because they believed that rural values were badly needed in the cities and they saw 4-H as the best vehicle for inculcating such values in urban communities. Urban 4-H continues to grow, mainly with funding from private, state, and local sources. However, 4-H received more federal funding for basically urban programs in 1969, when $4.5 million of the Expanded Food and Nutrition Education Program (EFNEP) appropriation was earmarked for 4-H nutrition education. A 1973 appropriation of $5 million followed.

Urban 4-H today, like 4-H generally, is concerned primarily with human development. City young people acquire feelings of self-worth, acquire leadership abilities, learn skills that may start them on particular careers, and overcome some of the social problems threatening youth in today's world. Their aspiration levels are raised. The young people themselves determine what specific urban programs are to be. In Minnesota programs have included bicycle safety, landscape and mural painting, play production, studying the role of women in America, and community beautification. Kentucky taught urban youth the basics of animal nutrition and health by having them work with pets, including mice. An urban club in Massachusetts used Double Dutch, a fast-paced, acrobatic jump-rope game, to teach values associated with teamwork and commitment to a group, personal accomplishment, responsibility, and community pride. Other urban 4-H club members have learned skills in nutrition, fitness, health, clothing, maintaining and repairing mechanical devices and automobiles, and other traditional subjects—all useful in human development.

COOPERATIVE PROGRAMS.   Because 4-H reaches every part of the nation, it frequently is called upon to work with other agencies on particular youth programs. For example, in Arizona, a state experiencing heavy drug traffic, 4-H cooperated with VISTA, schools, and other agencies to combat substance abuse through parent education and support groups. New York 4-H, working with local business groups, established a program called the "Job Express" to develop job-finding skills and positive work attitudes in youth. The North Carolina Agricultural & Technical State University Extension program undertook a successful "4-H in Public Housing" project dealing with fitness and self-esteem and involving thousands of minority children. The program was conducted with staff assistance and financial help from the Department of Housing and Urban Development. Vermont 4-H, in close cooperation with local school and other groups, provided weekend retreats for preteens and their parents; parents and youngsters together studied human sexuality, decision making, and understanding values. These are only a few examples of the types of cooperative programs in which 4-H takes part.

INTERNATIONAL 4-H PROGRAMS. When it was established, the National 4-H Club Foundation, now National 4-H Council, was charged with sponsoring educational exchanges between American 4-H members and leaders and youth leaders of similar programs in other nations. Actually, there had been an early international contact. In 1923 the American Committee for Devastated Europe, a philanthropic group formed to help Europe recover from the effects of the war, sent 4-H teams and their state leaders from Iowa and Colorado to France. These teams had won a national canning contest at the first National 4-H Club Congress and then had the opportunity to give canning demonstrations in France. Over the years the council has supported exchanges and has trained many foreign youth leaders. That program continues today. The entire Cooperative Extension System has assisted with the program. A number of state Extension offices have given training and field experience to foreign visitors, in addition to working with the council to place exchange visitors with families.

The first 4-H exchange delegates from the United States, seventeen in number, spent the summer of 1948 with European farm families. The International Farm Youth Exchange (IFYE) organization, as it was named, grew steadily. By 1953 more than three hundred American farm youth had been IFYE delegates and more than two hundred foreign young people had come to the United States. While the first programs were exchanges with Western European nations, IFYE spread to Latin America and other parts of the world. In the early 1970s Idaho, Washington, and Utah 4-H began exchange programs with Japan. These program exchanges are now being carried on in a number of states. Exchange programs also were established with Poland, Russia, Hungary, and other Eastern European nations, giving young people from widely differing political systems an opportunity to learn how rural people live in markedly different societies.

The young people who take part in exchange programs return home to serve as leaders of international programs in their local clubs. In addition, many of them speak of their experiences before local community organizations and to the general public through media interviews. IFYE, renamed the International Four-H Youth Exchange in 1977, remains at the heart of 4-H international programs. It continues to make young people in many parts of the world aware of other cultures as it promotes international understanding.

A Look Ahead.   Helping young people achieve their greatest potential has been for seventy-five years one of the true accomplishments of the Cooperative Extension System. As the twentieth century draws to a close and the twenty-first nears, 4-H is changing to meet the various transformations taking place in the world. It is meeting particular needs without regard to place of residence, family occupation, family income, or ethnic background.

Assisting young people to meet their needs with practical programs fosters development of their innate abilities, their management skills, and their leadership qualities. That is the true measure of the future — not just acquiring skills, important as that is, but developing abilities, life skills, and leadership. Youth today is at risk, and threats against young people achieving their full potential continue. 4-H and other institutions that give youth a feeling of self-worth and lead to new aspirations can counter these threats and reduce the risks.

The emphasis on volunteers in 4-H has given many Americans an opportunity to achieve their potentials while being of service to their fellow citizens. Numbers of outstanding Americans have said that their 4-H experiences as leaders and volunteers started them on the road to achievement.

Extension is in a period of dynamic change, restating its mission, developing new initiatives, and addressing issues. However, through 4-H and other programs, training for leadership and encouraging human development will remain key elements of future Extension programs. This is the future of 4-H and of the nation.

CHAPTER NINE

Building a Stronger Society:
Rural and Community Development

Introduction. As the Cooperative Extension System begins a new era, it faces a challenge in rural and community development, a challenge it is qualified to meet with the support of the American people and of local communities. Many rural communities and the services they provide are threatened; some even have disappeared. The farm population and the number of farms continue to decline. The resulting erosion of rural communities and of the services available in them means there are fewer rural schools, churches, farm-oriented businesses, and local services at the end of the 1980s than there were in the 1970s. The needs are still there and new ways must be found to meet them. Local units of government, some of which might not be necessary, are losing tax bases essential for survival. Extension is working with communities on these problems, but much remains to be done.

Four fundamental elements have been the strength of successful rural and community development programs: Providing a perspective on local development issues; increasing the knowledge base for individual and community decision making; developing the skills necessary to achieve individual and community goals; and helping strengthen the environment for decision making. These elements have been provided through traditional Extension approaches: Help people and communities identify their problems; help them to evaluate choices; and help people and communities gain access to resources that will solve the problems.

Extension knows what can be done to revitalize rural communities and improve rural life. The problem, however, is that the United States has no widely accepted national goals for community and rural development. Some political leaders have spoken in favor of such programs and some national legislation has been passed, but the programs never have been funded consistently. Several states, including Wisconsin, Iowa, Missouri, and others, have maintained long-term programs with state and local support, but they are the exceptions. These exceptional programs, say leaders concerned with revitalizing rural America, should serve as models reaching into every corner of the nation. Otherwise, the nation is in danger of losing its family farms, its rural communities, and its rural heritage.

Extension leaders have used a number of titles for rural and community development. The term "rural development" is widely used but may be too broad, in the sense that practically all Extension programs can be called rural development. "Community resource development (CRD)" is also widely used. Others write of "community and rural development." All of these terms are used in the following discussion. In general, the chapter deals with problems and opportunities that require group or community decisions and actions.

Is rural and community development primarily a process or is it concerned with content? Those arguing that it is a process hold that if the Extension agent can get the right group of people together in a community, that group can work together to make the right kind of decisions. Others contend that the responsibility of the Extension agent is to analyze problems, describing the relevant alternatives and enumerating the consequences of each so that local leaders can make informed decisions. In either case, more university research in rural and community development is needed so that the county Extension staff can bring research-based knowledge to bear on local needs.

While Extension always has carried on some rural and community development work, it began the type of programs we see today after World War II. County agricultural and home economics agents became involved when they concluded a community had limited opportunities in agriculture and something more was needed; they were the best source of information on state and federal programs; they were among the best-trained persons in the county and had university sources to turn to for advice and counsel; and they had the trust of the local community. In some states, notably in Wisconsin, county staff work in CRD was encouraged by the state Extension leadership's commitment to the program.

This chapter begins with a brief review of rural and community development programs through World War II, continues with a discussion of legislation, planning, and organization from 1945 to the 1980s, emphasizes successful development work, reviews some of the problems still to be overcome, and concludes with a look ahead.

Background

COUNTRY LIFE COMMISSION.   In 1908 the Country Life Commission, the true progenitor of rural and community development programs in the United States, stated that the ultimate need of the open country was the development "of community effort and of social resources." The commission made a number of recommendations for improving rural life. Those enacted into law included: The Extension Service, a parcel post system to give rural families better access to consumer goods, a postal savings system, and a land bank credit system. The recommendations also led to more development of rural or farm-to-market roads.

From its very beginning, the Extension Service had an opportunity to work in communities. The House Committee on Agriculture, in its report on the Smith-Lever bill, stated that the trained demonstrator contemplated for each agricultural county "must give leadership and direction along all lines of rural activity—social, economic and financial." Several relevant steps were taken, mainly by state Extension services. A 1915 publication, *Community Development: Making the Small Town a Better Place to Live and a Better Place in Which to Do Business,* was one of the first. The West Virginia Agricultural Extension Service published bulletins in 1918 and 1919 on resources for community improvement. Community improvement clubs were started in several parts of the South in the 1920s. They had a considerable degree of success.

THE NEW DEAL.   Congress and USDA took the next major steps in rural development during the New Deal of the 1930s. The many legislative acts relating to agriculture that were passed between 1933 and 1938 touched upon virtually every aspect of the issue. In the late 1930s the Extension Service joined the Bureau of Agricultural Economics in a broad program of land-use planning. County Extension offices organized discussion groups and made background materials available. While land-use policies were the starting point, local groups also studied taxation, foreign trade, farm prices, cooperatives, and farm credit.

Developing Today's Program

THE FIRST STEPS.   The Country Life Commission and the New Deal were forerunners of today's rural development programs. These began in 1954, in answer to the persistence of rural poverty in the midst of agricultural abundance and national prosperity. Attention focused at first on finding solutions to the problems of low-income farmers, but a study requested by President Eisenhower, *Development of Agriculture's Human Resources,* strongly implied that human and other resources should be moved out of agriculture. The study concluded that special funds should be provided to set up pilot Extension programs, with an individualized approach to farm problems.

Within the USDA rural development programs, administered by Under Secretary True D. Morse, were largely decentralized, with emphasis upon state and county action in fifty designated pilot counties and areas. The Cooperative Extension Service took the lead in program development, with the programs themselves carried out by a number of federal, state, and local agencies.

LEGISLATION.   The Smith-Lever Act was modified in 1955 by the addition of a new Section 8. It provided that if certain agricultural areas were at a disadvantage in agricultural development, funds could be appropriated to encourage change. Extension was to give "assistance and counseling to local groups in appraising resources for capability of improvements in agriculture or introduction of industry designed to supplement farm income (and) cooperation with other agencies and groups in furnishing all possible information as to existing employment opportunities. . . . "

Congress authorized a rural renewal program in 1962. Under it, USDA provided technical and financial assistance for locally initiated and sponsored programs aimed at eliminating chronic underemployment and fostering a sound rural economy. Loans were made to local groups to establish recreation areas, to build hospitals, to establish small manufacturing plants, and to carry out similar developmental activities. An unstated major goal behind this and other legislation and programs was to stem the tide of rural poor emigrating to the cities. Thus the emphasis was upon providing jobs in local areas and upon using existing public facilities and housing. Extension was responsible for organizational and educational leadership in the Rural Areas Development (RAD) program established under this authority. The Agriculture Act of 1970 included a section on rural development; it began with the statement that "the Congress commits itself to a sound balance between rural and urban America." Two years later, after nationwide hearings, Congress passed the Rural Development Act of 1972, which ever since has been the charter for the work. Extension responsibilities were defined by Title V of the act. Rural development Extension programs, consisting of the collection, interpretation, and dissemination of useful information, were to be made available to multistate and multicounty agencies, other units of government, Indian tribes, industries that employed people in rural areas, and others. The programs, conducted in cooperation with colleges and universities, were to include technical services and educational activities. Research useful in achieving increased rural development was authorized. Extension was to carry out research and development programs for small farms. Of the appropriations authorized under Title V, 4 percent was for federal work, 10 percent for work serving two or more states, 20 percent for allocation equally among the states, and 66 percent for the states. One-half of the state appropriation was to be determined by the rural population of each state and one-half by the farm population. These allocations were made in accordance with traditional funding patterns, except for the 10 percent going to universities working on projects serving two or more states. The authority to make appropriations under Title V was extended by the Rural Development Policy Act of 1980 and the Agriculture and Food Act of 1981. After 1985 earmarked appropriations for community and rural development were limited to small sums for regional rural development.

Most of this legislation authorized Congress to appropriate funds of up to certain specified amounts for carrying out the programs. However, Congress never appropriated the full amounts authorized and appropriations were often inconsistent from one year to another. State Extension Services wishing to maintain community and rural development programs often had to draw upon state and local funding or regular Smith-Lever Act appropriations.

PLANNING.   Since 1954 many studies of the place of rural and community development have been published. A few, written by leaders in Extension and CRD, have influenced the planning and conduct of programs.

In 1958 the Extension Committee on Organization and Policy (ECOP) of the National Association of State Universities and Land-Grant Colleges (NASULGC) issued a report entitled *A Statement of Scope and Responsibility.* It emphasized that Extension must become aware of and then address the needs of the broader rural community. Ten years later the study *A People and a Spirit* recommended a major expansion in program resources for rural community development.

In 1983 a Joint USDA-NASULGC Committee on the Future of Cooperative Extension in its report, *Extension in the '80s,* listed community and small business development as a major program area. Its goals were the development of vigorous communities and community leadership, profitable businesses, a prosperous agriculture, and vital organizational leadership. Audiences who should benefit included public officials, organization leaders and persons engaged in small businesses, and the tourist-recreation industry. Late in 1986 in the publication *Revitalizing Rural America* Extension stated that the survival of rural America, both in farms and smaller communities, was dependent upon the expansion of income and employment possibilities. Revitalizing rural America is in the best interest not only of the 64 million people who live there but also the entire nation. Extension could be a key because of its federal/state/local partnership, its relationships and collaboration with many other institutions, and its long-standing commitment to rural Americans.

The major concept of the study was the involvement of all Extension programs working together to insure the survival of rural America. A national Revitalizing Rural America Task Force, representing several states and the Washington office with members from all program areas, was established in 1987 to review what had been done and what could be done. In 1988 the task force issued a *Resource Book* containing program ideas for dealing with the six major issues it had identified: Economic competitiveness, diversification of sources of income, strengthening local government, adjustment to changes in rural life, developing skilled leadership, and maintaining the quality of the natural resource base. The program ideas are essentially issue oriented.

It is clear that the research community must provide the research-based information essential for a successful revitalization program. During the 1980s the state experiment stations began to give more attention to rural development. Agricultural economists, rural sociologists, water quality specialists, and many others became involved. The Economic Research Service (USDA) maintains an active research program in community and rural development, publishing its research findings in a quarterly journal and in bulletins.

Access to research-based information is being made available by the Rural Information Center, which opened in September 1987. Developed by Extension, it is housed in the National Agricultural Library (NAL) located in Beltsville, Maryland, and functions as an NAL activity. State and local officials have access to the computerized, national rural information and referral system through cooperative Extension Service offices. The center gives priority to economic development and local government.

ORGANIZATION AT THE NATIONAL LEVEL.   Even though there has been program planning, there never has been a clearly delineated organization of community and rural development work in the USDA. Every new administration has abolished what had gone before and established another office and a complex committee structure to coordinate the work of the different agencies that had some responsibility for CRD. The federal Extension Service organized a separate CRD unit in 1970 and has since maintained a small CRD staff, which varied in size as appropriations waxed and waned and as the responsibilities assigned to Extension increased and decreased. While Extension always has been assigned educational responsibilities and at times administrative duties, it never has been directly responsible to the office of the under secretary charged with the overall responsibility for rural development. The closest tie came during the early and mid-1970s, when Extension's assistant administrator for Rural Development chaired the USDA Rural Development Staff Group, which reported directly to the under secretary for rural development.

REGIONAL RURAL DEVELOPMENT CENTERS.   The regional rural development centers in the late 1980s are the last rural development projects being funded in part by earmarked appropriations first authorized by Congress in Title V of the Rural Development Act of 1972. They have provided some continuity for Extension's CRD programs in the 1970s and 1980s.

Initially, the Cooperative State Research Service made funds available and solicited proposals for a regional rural development center. This led to the first Regional Rural Development Center, established for the North Central region in 1971 at Iowa State University. The Extension Service, USDA, soon joined in the funding and the center became a joint research and Extension effort. Subsequently, with encouragement from the Farm Foundation, centers were established for the Northeast region at Cornell University, for the Western region at Oregon State University, and for the Southern region at Mississippi State University.

In addition to Extension funds, which Congress specifically earmarks for the purpose, the centers receive support from the Cooperative State Research Service, private foundations, and the states in the regions. In fiscal year 1986 federal funding was $172,000 per center. The state Extension Services contributed in faculty time more than double the value of the federal contribution.

The general purpose of the regional centers is to encourage and conduct programs to improve the social and economic well-being of nonmetropolitan communities in their respective regions. Usually they work on projects crossing state lines. They are under the general supervision of the state directors of Extension and of the agricultural experiment stations and are governed by a board made up of Extension and experiment station personnel from the universities in the region.

STATE OFFICES.   State Extension Services have been of great importance in community and rural development work. All have made some effort, and a few have been outstanding. Wisconsin is an example. In 1961 Gale L. VandeBerg was appointed assistant director for Extension programs in Wisconsin, with the charge to maintain Extension's strong educational work in agriculture and to bring about a more comprehensive total Extension program for Wisconsin's rural people and their communities. Two years later, Extension issued a manual by VandeBerg entitled *Total Resource Development in Wisconsin: A Citizens Guide to Plans and Action*. Citizen committees throughout the state and nation used the step-by-step plan to execute successful community development programs.

In 1963 the university's Board of Regents merged the Cooperative Extension Service, the Division of General Extension, and Radio-Television into University of Wisconsin-Extension. Within a short time, county boards of supervisors were redirecting the work of some personnel employed jointly with the university towards community resource development. In 1988 fifty-seven of Wisconsin's seventy-two counties had a community resource development specialist in the county Extension office. They were backed by eight area business agents and thirty-eight full-time campus specialists, ranging from agricultural economists to wildlife ecologists.

The Wisconsin CRD programs receiving particular emphasis include recreation-tourism, local government, water resources, waste management, environmental education, economic development, small business, cultural arts, and rural leadership. During the 1980s Wisconsin Extension developed a community economic analysis program that has become a model for a number of other states. In 1985 the business development program reported improved sales of $13.1 million, an increase of 3,102 jobs, and an increase in state tax collections of $4.5 million. It also developed 1,698 new enterprises and 1,301 expanded enterprises. Its community revitalization program led to improved downtown and community appearance in fourteen communities and improved facilities and services in seventeen others.

Some states have limited CRD programs. Alaska, for example, maintains a small, rather specialized program. The state began rural development work in 1933, when it trained a group of colonists from Michigan, Minnesota, and Wisconsin, who were being settled in the Matanuska Valley, in agriculture and in living in a new environment.

The effort, extending over a period of years, was reasonably successful. Presently, Alaska Extension emphasizes fisheries and its Native Human Resources Development Program. Essentially, the major goal of the second program is to make all resources of the University of Alaska more readily available to the state's native community and to develop leaders among the younger natives.

CRD Pilot Projects.   The 1950s and 1960s were an experimental period in community and rural development. Most of the pilot projects were developed and carried out by state and county staffs in agriculture, home economics, and 4-H, since the status of rural and community development as a well-staffed field was still in the future. For example, in the 1950s home economists in Florida, working with a CRD program developed at Florida A. & M. University, emphasized improving health conditions as one of the most important of many projects undertaken. However, it was more usual to emphasize improving community facilities through county assistance and self-help. Projects to increase library facilities, to establish school lunch programs, to improve recreational facilities, to obtain paved roads, to install water systems, and to improve other aspects of community life frequently were undertaken.

A PILOT PROJECT IN WISCONSIN.   Price County, Wisconsin, was one of the counties selected for an experimental pilot program in rural resource development. A development committee, divided into working committees, began planning in late 1955. With the county Extension staff at the core of the work, the committee involved all elements of the community, including farm, village, and city residents. Rural sociologists, agricultural economists, foresters, and others from the University of Wisconsin contributed to the undertaking. The intensive educational program had its effect on community leadership, small businesses, and the tourist industry. The two-year project set the pattern for total involvement, with all county agents and personnel working toward the goal of overall community improvement and progress.

A PILOT PROGRAM IN NORTH CAROLINA.   Under Extension
leadership a pilot program began in Watauga County, North Carolina,
in the early 1960s. Three small factories employing 625 people were
established. A new bank came into operation, and a small college was
established in the county. Emphasis on tourism led to the construction
of golf courses that soon were crowded with tourists and to the development of tourist service industries. Finally, a high-quality housing
program appealing to persons interested in purchasing summer homes
successfully added to the income of the county. The development process continues today.

PILOT MANPOWER PROGRAMS.   Because it has a successful program reaching into every county in the nation, Extension has been
asked to participate in a number of interagency projects. The Con-
certed Service on Training and Education (CSTE) was such an effort.
CSTE demonstration projects were established in Arkansas, Minnesota, and New Mexico in 1965, under the joint administration of the
Cooperative Extension Service, the State Employment Service, and the
State Vocational Agency. Within four years, training opportunities had
become available where none had existed before, the public employment service was being more fully used, and additional job opportunities had been developed. Over the next five years fourteen additional
projects were established. However, passage of the Comprehensive Employment and Training Act of 1974 led to elimination of federal funding for CSTE and the program came to an end, even though the pilot
programs generally were successful.

"Operation Hitchhike" was another pilot program for delivering
manpower services to rural areas. The idea proposed that the Employment Service "hitch a ride" with Extension to deliver manpower services to unserved rural areas. In the early 1970s Extension carried out
the program in seventeen states through a contractual arrangement
with the State Employment Services. Programs varied widely among
the states, but all were to provide rural areas access to the full range of
manpower services through an efficient and inexpensive system of delivery. In general, the pilot programs were successful. However, with
the end of federal funding, Extension involvement in the program disappeared over time. Nevertheless, these pilot manpower programs

demonstrated both that Extension, given the proper support, could manage programs for other agencies and that it had the potential for handling manpower programs.

Rural and Community Development Today.   An increasing interest in rural and community development may indicate the days of pilot projects and of ups-and-downs in support are at an end. The new interest has arisen, at least in part, because of the depression of the 1980s in the key rural industries of agriculture, mining, and energy. This depression adversely affected jobs, incomes, and government revenues in rural America. Rural employment grew only 4 percent between 1979 and 1986, compared with 13 percent for urban areas.

Extension's rural and community development educational projects are making it possible for at least some rural communities and their residents to overcome major economic and social problems. CRD staffs usually have called upon agricultural agents, home economists, 4-H agents, and university specialists to assist in meeting particular needs.

ECONOMIC COMPETITIVENESS.   Extension's CRD programs are enhancing the profitability of rural business in a number of states and communities. The Alabama Cooperative Extension Service, with financial support from the U.S. Department of Housing and Urban Development and the Alabama Department of Economic and Community Affairs, operates a statewide "small business rural incubator" network. The goal of the network's involvement with selected communities is to provide a physical environment and an educational background that will permit new small businesses to develop, grow, and become competitive. The Extension Service in coordination with the College of Business provides educational programs that teach technical, managerial, and administrative skills to these small business operators to assist their survival during the critical early stages of development.

The successful marketing of forest products, or of any farm commodity, is important both for landowners and for industries dependent upon those products. The Extension Services of New Hampshire, Maine, and Vermont have joined in a computerized forest products marketing program to improve marketing efficiency for all forest products and to expand marketing and increase returns for the community involved in the forest industry. Computerized data banks listing known buyers of forest products have been compiled. Sellers of such products can identify buyers, using an interactive retrieval process through a network of access points at county Extension offices.

Mississippi Extension is encouraging expansion of forest industries in northern Mississippi. Its objectives are to improve timber markets, promote the expansion of wood-based industries, regenerate harvested stands, manage existing stands, and create a positive relationship between landowners and the forest industry. Since the program began, four major wood-using industries have installed plants in Granada, a forest landowner association has been formed, and a positive public attitude toward forest industry expansion has developed.

A community in New Mexico faced a difficult problem when a major employer shut down and the unemployment rate rose to nearly 19 percent. An Extension specialist conducted a business analysis of the community and led workshops in which the community's problems were addressed. The program was assisted by a Western Rural Development Center grant and supported by a regional group of researchers and Extension specialists. The results were improved awareness of how to address the community's problems and a change in the practices of business people.

DIVERSIFICATION OF THE RURAL ECONOMIC BASE.   Maintaining and enhancing the profitability of existing rural businesses and agriculture is important. It is also productive to find alternative uses for rural resources and to diversify existing economic bases. Some examples have been discussed in previous chapters, but there are many others. Missouri Extension is searching for opportunities, in cooperation with the University of Missouri-Columbia and Lincoln University, for rural communities to develop new sources of income. One successful and unique project was the publication of two catalogs — *Best of Missouri's Hands* and *Best of Missouri's Farms*. The catalogs offered the work of some 180 rural Missouri artisans and the products of a number of Missouri farms. These catalogs opened up significant new sources of income for rural residents.

Iowa Extension offers community economic development workshops. The workshops are conducted by specialists from Iowa State University Extension for representatives of leadership groups in the community. Participants in the workshops develop a ranked list of actions the community can take to enhance prospects for growth and prepare plans for accomplishing the projects. Following the workshop in Oskaloosa, the community opened a new shopping center, garnered two new industries, achieved improvements in attitude and community self-image, undertook programs to control litter and plant flowers, and initiated a Main Street renewal.

Main Street renewal or downtown revitalization programs are being conducted by CRD staffs, often with the assistance of university specialists, in a number of states. The emphasis is upon business development, but projects may include work in architectural design, beautification, and historic preservation. Among the state Extension services carrying out such projects are New York, Wisconsin, Minnesota, Texas, Mississippi, Utah, Georgia, South Carolina, and Illinois.

Rhode Island Extension has added another dimension to economic diversification with its home-based business project. It is reaching individuals with skills in particular subject matters but without business knowledge. CRD begins with an eight-hour course on what is needed to start a home-based business and follows up with individual consultations, a newsletter, and advanced courses. Tennessee Extension undertook another approach when it assisted local craftworkers in Coffee County to identify their marketing problems and organize an association to deal with them. Within the association, instruction is provided to craft producers in improving their work and in basic business management. More than four hundred people belong to the association. Sales are approximately $40,000 a year and are growing.

Historic farms and villages add still another dimension to economic diversification. Extension has been active in this area. Old Sturbridge Village in Massachusetts, the National Colonial Farm in Maryland, Iowa Living History Farms, and Old Bedford Village in Pennsylvania, for example, create jobs and new sources of income for area residents. In addition, each of these facilities, with the exception of the National Colonial Farm that is located in a national park site, has created substantial economic growth in its community in the form of new service facilities. Extension is working with each institution to make materials available and providing consultation on plans for the farm and craft operations.

LOCAL GOVERNMENT.   Service demands on local governments and community organizations are growing while resources are diminishing. Extension's rural and community development staffs in a number of states make educational programs available to local officials, many of whom are inexperienced in government. They provide similar assistance to local groups concerned with new ways to develop and deliver community facilities and services. For a number of years the Cornell Cooperative Extension Service has provided local officials with educational courses aimed at specific needs. In addition, it is working with the New York State Supervisors and County Legislators Association, giving one- and two-day workshops to acquaint local government officials with microcomputer technology and its applications for local government. Judging from both enrollments and evaluations, the effort is meeting a high-priority demand.

The high turnover rate among local officials leads to a continuing demand for courses such as those given by Cornell. For example, Michigan's 722 county commissioners are elected for two-year terms, with about 30 percent changing each two years. Since 1968 Michigan Extension, in cooperation with the Michigan Association of Counties, has sponsored "new county commissioner" workshops each January following a general election. The workshops acquaint newly elected officials with the roles and responsibilities of their offices. The January workshops are followed in midsummer by a series of regional workshops on budgeting and financial management. Thirty-five percent of the state's county commissioners attend the workshops.

In some states and territories a sparse population and difficulties in reaching local officials makes the problem more complex. Under the leadership of the Western Rural Development Center, Montana, New Mexico, Alaska, Guam, Washington, Utah, and Wyoming have joined in a program to pool limited Extension resources to produce local government education programs and materials, to team faculty from several states to present regional workshops, and to adapt the programs and materials for use with indigenous populations.

In other parts of the nation states are joining together to deal with specific problems. The CRD staff in Illinois saw that local townships faced a difficult problem in maintaining rural roads and bridges. The staff began work on the problem and was joined by Extension CRD in Wisconsin, Ohio, and Minnesota. The program documents details on the condition of rural road systems and the fiscal health of townships responsible for their maintenance. It identifies and presents policy alternatives for consideration at the local and state level and seeks to improve the governance capacity of elected township road officials so they can manage limited resources more effectively.

LEADERSHIP PROGRAMS.   Over the years Extension has given many people an opportunity to acquire knowledge and skills and to develop leadership abilities. This was recognized early in the history of Extension. Martin Mosher, a pioneer in Illinois Extension, commented in 1922: "I believe that one of the most valuable functions of the Extension Service in the future will be to develop local leaders and give them work to do." At about the same time Kansas agent Ellen Batchelor was becoming aware, as she later concluded: "The real history of home demonstration work is in the lives of our local leaders, our organization committees and advisory committees. . . . " Since then virtually every study of Extension has stressed the importance of the development of local leadership.

A number of states have undertaken leadership development programs. Oklahoma, for example, has an Agricultural Leadership Program for young adults actively engaged in farming, ranching, or affiliated agribusiness. Its goal is to provide for a select group the training and experience that will enable them to assume leadership roles in the state of Oklahoma. The intensive two-year study program includes leadership development, communications, economics and policy, international trade, institutions and agencies that serve Oklahoma agriculture, family strength, urban understanding, state and national government, water, energy, and other major issues affecting Oklahoma agriculture.

The Kellogg Foundation has made grants to a number of state Extension services for a rural leadership project called the Kellogg Extension Education Program. During the 1970s more than 1,000 Montanans were involved in the program. In 1979 they established the Montana Leadership Association to hold forums and workshops each year. Wisconsin undertook a similar program in the early 1980s.

A similar Minnesota program called "Emerging Leadership" improves leadership skills and encourages participation in the public decision-making process. The Michigan Agricultural Leadership Program began in 1965 as the Kellogg Farmers' Study Program, developed in

Michigan State University's Department of Agricultural Economics, with a grant from the Kellogg Foundation. Currently, the program provides in-depth leadership development experiences to expand the pool of rural persons able to assume leadership in agriculture and in the rural communities of Michigan.

Purdue University Extension holds a junior leader conference and a state fair leadership school each year. The junior leader conference, lasting four days, is planned and conducted jointly with teens. Its objectives are to develop leadership skills and abilities, increase self-concept and self-confidence, and to develop skills in working in small groups. The conference, held in a camp setting, reaches some 500 members annually. The state fair leadership program, conducted during the Indiana State Fair, is designed to develop leadership through activities related to state government and the legislative process. Some 250 teen leaders between the ages of sixteen and nineteen take part each year.

NATURAL RESOURCES. The quality of the natural resource base is critical to revitalizing rural communities. While individual farmers and landowners are responsible for the efficient management of the natural resources under their direct control, actions by communities, states and the nation have effects on both publicly and privately controlled natural resources. Extension specialists in rural and community development are building educational programs with a dual purpose. They foster an understanding of the role of natural resources in the quality of both urban and rural life, and they encourage affected parties to cooperate in making assessments and developing public policy.

California's program to increase wildlife and its habitat illustrates the benefits of obtaining group as well as individual action. Wildlife habitat on mostly privately owned hardwood rangeland was being lost. Extension provided advice to agencies and legislative staff regarding the impact of proposed legislation on private-land wildlife management and to landowners regarding sound wildlife management. It also stimulated trade associations of hunting club owners. The program is bringing more land into wildlife management programs, is giving ranchers income from hunting access fees, and is making legislators aware of the importance of sound wildlife management.

North Carolina Extension, with the cooperation of the North Carolina Wildlife Resources Commission, is bringing landowners and the citizens who use wildlife resources together to set up demonstration areas. Each area combines farming operations typical of the region in which it is located with forest and wildlife management practices. Similarly, Vermont and Connecticut, with the cosponsorship of the Ruffled Grouse Society, are bringing owners of private woodlands together with hunters to establish in each state demonstration sites featuring good forest and wildlife management practices.

The successful use of natural resources for community development requires planning by the community, whether the program establishes a dude-ranchers association in Montana or develops a ski-resort complex in West Virginia. For example, development of a state park was scheduled for a small, rural Kentucky county of five thousand people; the facility would attract up to one million visitors per year. Local communities needed assistance in planning for waste disposal, transportation, crime control and prevention, and other potential problems. The Extension Service brought local government officials, citizens groups, and business people together to tour similar developments in other locations. The citizens group held community meetings to identify problems and develop solutions. The park facility was constructed and the county gained improved county access roads, tourist-related small business developments, commercial developments, and increased employment opportunities.

Many communities in the western states are dependent upon public lands for their ranching, logging, and mining enterprises. This is true of Nevada, but the proliferation of environmental interests and subsequent legislation has swamped many Nevada communities in a quagmire of litigation, threatening local economies. Extension has brought local public land users such as livestock producers and those representing recreational interests together with the district-level staff responsible for land management and local environmental interest groups. The goal is to provide public land resource planning in which local users and interest groups could participate effectively. In many instances, rather than accepting unilateral, down-from-the-top decisions, the groups, using consensus rules of order, have forged land-use decisions acceptable to all interested parties.

Water quality protection and management is the responsibility in part of individuals and in part of large organizations and communities. Contamination of water resources by both individuals and communities is a crucial issue in the state of Washington. Groundwater supplies drinking water to three-fourths of the people of the state, while one-fifth of the population relies on rural well systems. There are groundwater contamination sites in thirty-eight of the state's thirty-nine counties. Dryland, irrigated, and dairy agriculture are significant causes of surface-water pollution. Extension is conducting educational programs to control such pollution. Extension is also developing educational programs to encourage the control of pollution from industrial, human, and animal wastes; agribusiness; and on-site and municipal sewage treatment. These programs have made communities, industries, and individuals aware of the problem; many have adopted practices to reduce pollution.

A Look Ahead.　　Rural America is home to one in every four Americans and three out of every four units of government; it is responsible for nearly 90 percent of the nation's natural resources. It includes the families living in the nation's fourteen thousand small towns and cities; the commercial farmer who is making a living from agriculture or who has supplemented the family income with off-farm income; the people whose homes are clustered about highway intersections or strung along a county road; the individuals living in villages where fishing, mining, or timber are the major sources of income; the part-time farmers who derive the major share of their income from off-farm work; and the people who have chosen the life-style advantages of living in the country. Over the years rural America has provided many of the people and a large portion of the capital needed for the development of urban America. Yet today much of rural America is faced with continuing deterioration in its economic and social structure. Rural Americans in general have lower incomes, fewer job opportunities, and higher unemployment rates, and they are more likely to be in poverty or to live in substandard housing than their metropolitan counterparts.

　　Rural revitalization is essential to the preservation of rural America and of the nation. Not every rural family is in economic difficulty and not every rural community is deteriorating, but many of these more fortunate citizens also would benefit from a revitalized rural America. Education is at the heart of the revitalization effort.

　　The Cooperative Extension System as a whole, particularly in its rural and community development programs, is a key in revitalizing many rural communities. It is working with state departments of development, regional and local economic development associations, other government agencies, chambers of commerce, businesses, commodity and trade associations, educational institutions, and individuals to develop reasonable, achievable programs. Yet Extension must have consistent national support for the work if it is to reach its full potential.

The support both within and outside the Cooperative Extension System for rural revitalization may mean a new national upswing in rural and community development throughout the nation. At the same time, Extension and rural communities must do more to make the nation as a whole aware of the importance of rural and community development to the national welfare.

4-H'ers marched in the Bicentennial parade in Washington, D.C., in 1976. (Extension Service, USDA, Ovid Bay photo)   *Right:* 4-H members in Brazil pose at a bus stop they built as a project. (Extension Service, USDA photo)

Guilford County, North Carolina home economics agent works with residents of a facility for older Americans on a nutrition education program. (Photo North Carolina A&T University Agricultural Extension Program)

Right: A Nutrition Diet Assessment exhibit developed by the Georgia Extension staff in the 1980s attracted 1,700 participants during three days at a farm show. Participants obtained a blood pressure check, diabetes check, height-weight measurement, cholesterol reading, diet assessment, and individual nutrition counseling. (University of Georgia photo)

Above: Approximately 600 rural residents of Idaho have attended Extension's Rural Education Adult Development program in sixteen locations in two years. Computer literacy can be an important resource to rural communities. (University of Idaho photo)

Left: An Extension agricultural economist, University of Nebraska, explains to a dairy farmer how to use the videodisc in the "Managing for Tomorrow" program for financially stressed farmers. (University of Nebraska Extension Service photo)

Below: County agents take calculators and programs for dairymen to the field to disseminate research information.

Desktop publishing is becoming increasingly popular as a supporting technology for Extension education. The Telecommunications Development Center, University of Minnesota, provides training in this technology.

Missouri dairy farm wife uses an Extension microcomputer program to assist in financial planning for the family farm. (University of Missouri, Duane Dailey photo)

Virginia dairyman, who milks 110 cows, works with the Extension dairy specialist and says computer management is limited only by what he can produce in a management chart. (William Carnahan photo)

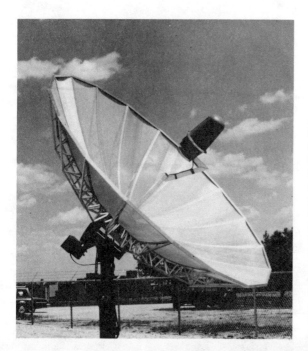

Left: Ohio Extension Service staff interviews Extension specialists and research scientists to link information programs to clientele by using the university satellite equipment. (Ohio State University photo)   *Below:* People who can benefit from financial and family stress counseling have to take the first step of calling their county Extension offices. An Extension communications specialist, University of Florida, uses radio spot announcements to urge farm families to ask for help. (University of Florida photo)

Above: This urban garden on a vacant lot in New York City is an example of the Extension program that started in 1977 in six cities and expanded to sixteen cities. Besides contributing to family food supplies, urban gardens have beautified the environment and fostered a spirit of neighborhood purpose. (Cornell University photo)

Left: The Consumer and Homemaking Education Program, operated by Illinois Cooperative Extension Service for the State Board of Education, teaches low-income families their rights and responsibilities as consumers. (Illinois Cooperative Extension Service photo)

A 4-H Extension Agent on a Peace Corps assignment promotes improved gardening techniques among natives in Cambodia. (Peace Corps photo)

Above: Approximately three hundred women attended farrowing schools initiated in the mid-1970s by Extension specialists in Missouri for women who take care of sows farrowing while the husband works off the farm. The private sector is now sponsoring the schools. *Left:* A University of Alaska livestock specialist uses ultrasonics to aid producers in the selection of superior breeding stock. The painless sound waves measure body parts to determine optimum fat to lean ratios in breeding animals for the production of top quality meat. (Cooperative Extension Service, Alaska, Kecia K. Siah photo)

Right: An Extension turfgrass specialist and a plant scientist study water consumption of six varieties of turfgrasses at the University of Arizona. A Flagstaff ranch is growing turfgrass as an alternative cash crop, using varieties tested and recommended by Extension. (University of Arizona photo) *Below:* Rain simulator used by Nebraska Cooperative Extension Service to demonstrate value of leaving residue on fields as a conservation practice. (Photo Department of Agricultural Communications, University of Nebraska)

Mississippi Extension has been a leader in the development of farm-raised catfish in that state. Some 410 farmers produce more than 300 million pounds annually valued at $250 million, about 80 percent of total U.S. production. (Mississippi Cooperative Extension Service photo)

A California couple makes a substantial income from a 20-acre farm raising speciality crops such as baby turnips, exotic greens, Asian pears, melons, and tomatoes, with advice from California Extension's small farms and sustainable agriculture programs. (California Cooperative Extension Service photo)

Extension specialists and county agents in Arkansas demonstrate soybean planting in wheat stubble in a double cropping system. (Arkansas Extension Service photo)

4-H'ers enrolled in the Citizenship-Washington Focus program visit the Lincoln Memorial.

CHAPTER TEN

Beginning the Next Seventy-Five Years

Extension for Today and Tomorrow: An Overview.   Extension has completed seventy-five years of service to the American people. It has carried the results of research from the land-grant universities directly to broad segments of the population. It has taught these people how to use this knowledge to improve their lives. Because of its accomplishments this public service institution has the support of a majority of citizens, both rural and urban. The development of Extension over the years has been called a paradox of success — its problems have arisen not from its failures but from its achievements.

Extension has carried the results of research from the land-grant universities, the Department of Agriculture, and private agencies to commercial farmers, with the county agricultural agent traditionally the link between the researcher and the farmer. Today, American agriculture is the most productive the world has ever seen, with each American farmer providing farm products for ninety-three people. Fewer workers are needed in farming, thus providing manpower for other occupations. Extension leaders agree that Extension agriculture agents, whatever may be their title or wherever they may be stationed, will continue to convey the results of research to farmers.

Today's 4-H agents and home economists are assisting people, particularly youngsters and families, build more satisfying lives. For more than seventy-five years 4-H clubs and homemaker's clubs have brought research-based information and taught leadership skills to members and, perhaps just as important, have helped end rural isolation. Education in the field of nutrition, especially as it affects health, is improving the quality of life for many families. It is reaching into urban areas in a number of ways, including the Expanded Food and Nutrition Education Program (EFNEP) through which Extension reaches low-income people in both rural and urban areas.

Extension's rural and community development programs are helping transform life in many states and counties. Rural development has been something of a political football on the national scene, with much talk and little action. However, it has been supported and developed into a significant educational program by a number of state directors of Extension. Extension's educational programs for county officials are helping improve the levels of local government in a number of states. Its leadership in encouraging residents of local communities to identify their problems, determine how they can be overcome, and find the resources to implement the solutions is strengthening many communities and improving the quality of life for their residents. Helping communities develop new industries and retain existing ones, while developing other sources of income and employment, is especially important in times of farm depression. However, obtaining a true national commitment to and continuing national and state funding for rural and community development continues to be a major problem.

Educating people, especially young people, to become better citizens is a task Extension has proven it can perform. Sometimes called developing human potential, sometimes building human capital, it is of special importance at a time when the nation faces major social and economic problems. Extension is particularly successful in developing human potential through programs that recruit and train volunteer leaders; provide educational forums to help farm and rural people understand and act on the issues facing them and the nation; encourage international exchange programs for youth; and give young people, notably through 4-H, an opportunity to develop skills and a feeling of self-worth along with the ability to apply the knowledge they have acquired.

The accomplishments of the Cooperative Extension System over its first seventy-five years were possible because certain fundamental principles were developed. These include helping people help themselves, identifying and meeting the needs of the people served, developing new methods of education, undertaking programs based upon research, making needs known to research institutions, and maintaining Extension as a cooperative program carried on by the local, state, and federal governments. As Extension develops a vision for the future and formulates plans to achieve desired and essential changes, it should keep in mind the principles that brought it success in the past.

The following pages look at some of the proposals made by Extension and other leaders regarding the future of the Cooperative Extension System, particularly those made in 1987 by the Futures Task Force of the Extension Committee on Organization and Policy (ECOP) and the National Initiatives Coordinating Committee of the Cooperative Extension System. The Futures Task Force held hearings in each region of the United States before making its report. These proposals concern in particular the future mission of Extension, identification of the people whom it should serve, the roles of the federal, state, and local parts of the system, and programs that might or should be undertaken.

Extension's Mission.   The first sentence of the Smith-Lever Act of 1914 contained a statement of mission: "to aid in diffusing among the people of the United States useful and practical information on subjects relating to agriculture and home economics, and to encourage the application of the same." Additional subjects were added so that the phrase read in part: "agriculture, uses of solar energy with respect to agriculture, home economics, and rural energy." This statement was widely accepted during Extension's first seventy-five years, but both agriculture and the social and economic structure of the nation changed to the extent that a new one was needed.

In 1988 the Cooperative Extension System, as noted earlier, adopted the following mission statement: "The Cooperative Extension System helps people improve their lives through an educational process which uses scientific knowledge focused on issues and needs." The statement emphasizes the philosophy of helping people help themselves, the research base of Extension programs, and the basing of programs on issues unbounded by discipline, audience, or geography.

Who Should Extension Serve?   The mission of Extension, the determination of programs, and decisions on how programs should be delivered all depend on who Extension serves—its clientele. It has become a truism that Extension cannot be all things to all people. In the beginning it was charged with serving "the people of the United States," but since the context in which it was established was in improving farming and farm life, it did not, with some exceptions, attempt to reach beyond people on farms and in rural areas. This was true especially of large urban areas, even though home economics and 4-H were relevant to urban residents. At that time the rural population was nearly one-half the total population; in recent years it is one-quarter of the total. During its first seventy-five years, Extension's primary clientele was farm and rural people.

URBAN SERVICES.   Today Extension is serving many suburban and urban residents through horticultural, urban gardening, family economics, nutrition, and 4-H programs. Many of the noncommercial horticultural programs are financed with county funds; they often are carried out by volunteers. Urban 4-H programs usually result from citizen demand and are, for the most part, financed by state and local funds, with much of the work being carried out by volunteers. However, some of the 4-H, urban gardening, and urban nutrition programs, including EFNEP, are carried out at the direction of Congress and are financed by appropriations earmarked for those programs. Many farm organizations oppose the urban programs or at least suggest that agricultural production and rural problems be given almost exclusive priority. But since the work is funded by all of the public, it will not be workable in the future to treat rural and urban populations unequally.

CRITICAL ISSUES AS AN ANSWER.   One way of looking at this problem is to identify clientele through a process that selects the most critical issues the expert knowledge available to the system has the capacity to address. Many critical issues that Extension may address are of importance to people regardless of where they live. This means that rural and urban audiences do not necessarily have mutually exclusive needs. If it focuses on issues and leaves some flexibility to states and regions, Extension need not make a national decision regarding the priority or importance of clientele on the basis of residence.

Nutrition education is one critical issue in which the place of residence is irrelevant to need and in which states and communities may decide how far to go in meeting urban needs. Too, some programs such as suburban horticulture may become so popular that local communities will insist upon having them and will finance them. In some instances, of course, as in the EFNEP program, Congress may decide that a particular critical issue is so important that it deserves Extension's nationwide attention. Similarly, congressional leaders concerned with agriculture may place some programs on a nationwide basis with earmarked funds appropriated in order to get support for Extension from legislators who have urban constituencies. EFNEP and urban gardening funds are recent examples.

Managing the Cooperative System.   The strength of Extension traditionally has been in its cooperative nature. Federal, state, and local governments each have had influence over the system, but none has been completely dominant. The system has been flexible and, most important, responsive to local needs. This is evident when one looks at some Extension systems in other nations that are established on a straight-line basis, with complete control coming from a national government. Such systems have fallen far short of the success of America's Cooperative Extension System. Today, however, there are some questions being raised about the system. Is the federal office necessary? Should state and county services primarily be drawing upon the research and programs of the colleges of agriculture or should they be the conduit for the entire range of research conducted by the land-grant universities? With good roads, automobiles, and better communication through radio and television and computer networks, is it necessary to have an Extension agent in every county?

THE FEDERAL OFFICE.   A state director of Extension has said that if the federal office is abolished and federal appropriations discontinued, Extension would continue in many states but would disappear in the states that most need it. There can be little doubt that if the federal office were to be discontinued, federal appropriations also would end.

The Futures Task Force saw anticipatory planning as the most critical function of the federal office. That office should undertake an annual assessment of possible alternative futures and should take the lead in identifying major national issues. In doing so, it should de-emphasize its traditional permanent disciplinary positions in favor of limited-term, issue-oriented interdisciplinary teams. The federal office should be responsible for program planning for subjects of national importance. It should identify the need for and help to coordinate multistate efforts to devise basic programs common to several states; guard against duplication of effort; take leadership in guaranteeing that the educational content in state programming is research-based and meets high standards; take responsibility for relations with Congress; provide a national data base for educational programs and a source of national data essential to work in high priority subject areas; and take substantial responsibility for the successful functioning of the required coordinated partnership between 1862 and 1890 institutions within their individual states. The federal office also would continue to account for the states' use of federal funds.

THE STATE EXTENSION OFFICE.   State Extension services should meet the basic needs of their states. State organizations should continue to serve in the future as the focal point of organizational discipline within the system, since most of its personnel changes take place at this level. Some county leaders and agents argue for greater autonomy, but this does not appear to be in the picture. Other recommendations — and these relate to the land-grant universities as well as to Extension — include: Planning programs and conducting anticipatory, innovative planning on state issues and needs; identifying and helping to coordinate multicounty efforts to meet program needs common to several counties; ensuring that state-level cooperative research can meet adequately Extension's future needs for applied research; ensuring a functioning and constructive partnership between the 1862 and 1890 institutions; and cooperating with the private sector to conduct educational programs on priority issues.

If these roles are to be carried out as the system moves toward a new century, it will require a structure and organization that can call upon a broader range of resources than is now available. Total university involvement, as well as cooperation with other universities and with the private sector, is needed to meet multidisciplinary applied research and educational programming requirements. There must be a stronger innovation and planning focus in Extension management at the state level. One of the truly major problems, according to several state Extension directors, is determining how far the land-grant universities will go in directing research to needs perceived by Extension, and, on the other hand, how far Extension can go in representing the entire university at the county level.

THE COUNTY OFFICE.   If much of the system's authority is concentrated in the state office, the county office is the cutting edge. Through it the results of research are brought to bear upon the problems of people. The county staff is responsible for meeting those local needs that Extension is capable of satisfying. The county office should insist that the state office provide quality educational programs and should make the state office aware of those local needs to which research can respond. It should initiate local anticipatory planning for local needs and issues and cooperate with local organizations and agencies in the conduct of programs. The county-level organization of the future will require greater planning and communication skills than it has in the past.

So far as communications are concerned, Extension agents traditionally worked directly with their clientele; in addition, they presented material through meetings, radio, television, newspapers, and farm journals. Publications containing research-based information were the national symbol of Extension from its beginning through World War II. In its early decades Extension really was the library of rural America. Publications were free; they were widely distributed by mail; and they covered a great range of topics. Today, though, the agent has a new battery of communications devices — computers tied into the land-grant universities and the farm, satellite broadcasting, videotapes, and electronic mail. More innovations are on the way.

One of the difficult questions facing Extension is whether or not every county should continue to have a county Extension office, and if so, how it should be staffed. Funding problems, better communication tools, and the availability of automobiles and good roads are cited as reasons for consolidating offices. A number of states have experimented with consolidated offices, regional offices, and different staffing plans. In some areas county offices are staffed by program or commodity specialists who are responsible for their specialties in two or three counties. In other areas the county office has a nonprofessional who handles many of the routine requests for information and refers other questions to the agent who serves two or three counties. Many state Extension directors say that it is essential to have Extension represented one way or another in every county if the Cooperative Extension program is to continue to enjoy local support. Without such local representation, local support, and local direction, Extension could become another state-administered program that would lose touch with local conditions and local people.

The Futures Task Force recommended that in each county one or more Extension staff positions be continued at the local level. These staff members should represent a blend of subject matter and applied research skills, programming skills and skills in communications, group process and team building. Each staff member should have at least one technical skill appropriate to the locality. It is unrealistic to expect county-level personnel to serve as technical experts dealing with the entire range of needs of today's clientele. Rather, the staff of the future should concentrate on accomplishing the mission of Extension, have increased multicounty responsibilities, and cooperate with state specialists in conducting local educational programs and providing the opportunity to apply research. Staffing of this type would encourage some of the variations in staffing patterns required by tomorrow's high-technology society.

INNOVATIVE APPROACHES.   Extension leaders agree that the organization must be capable of responding quickly and effectively to a broad set of issues and to a changing clientele. As Brice Ratchford, former president of the University of Missouri, has argued: "Extension must move away from its inability or unwillingness to modify structure and must give up what sometimes appears to be its objective of maintaining its present structure." This is not a simple task. Many diverse interests, including Congress, the Department of Agriculture, state legislators, university administrators, county supervisors, agricultural organizations, Extension clientele, and others may not want changes or may insist that changes be of a particular type. Greater flexibility could be brought into the organization at federal, state, and county levels by the appointment of limited-term, issue-oriented interdisciplinary teams in place of some permanent disciplinary positions currently in staffing plans.

Users of Extension want to obtain current, unbiased knowledgeable information in a timely manner. They are not concerned about its source. Extension should provide its clientele access to specialized staff assistance through the effective use of multicounty, area, or state specialists. Many states have this type of organization in place, but it should be extended more widely and substituted for more traditional patterns of organization.

FUNDING.   Funding became a more important question in the 1980s than it had been for many years. A short national depression and a farm depression that continued through most of the decade led to calls for cuts in expenditures for public services. This occurred just as the demand for Extension's services increased. However, when the president's Office of Management and Budget proposed sharp cuts in Extension's funding, a flood of protests from all parts of the United States led Congress to reject major cuts. Nevertheless, the lack of funding increases took its toll during the 1980s. The net effect after inflation has been a decrease of fully 25 percent in real federal funding during this period.

State funding has increased during the last ten years in proportion to both federal and local support. At the same time, energy- and natural resource-dependent states, as well as a number of rural states hard hit by the farm depression have reduced their financial support. For example, one thinly populated western state had eight commodity specialists in the early 1980s but was forced to cut back to four by 1986. Few states have escaped significant staff cuts during this period.

Extension directors in several states successfully have sought alternative sources of funding—a number of examples are found in earlier chapters. Such funding has included grants, primarily from foundations; subcontracts with other agencies, mostly federal; contributions from the private sector, especially in 4-H; and, in limited instances, users' fees. There can be problems with certain types of funding. Grants carry the risk that the grant source rather than an assessment of issues and needs will control program content. Extension must ensure that it does not seek or accept grants that fail to relate directly to the needs of its clientele. Subcontracting can put Extension in the position of working for the contracting agency rather than addressing the needs of the clientele it should serve. Again, Extension can exercise the option of subcontracting only when the work being done will benefit its clientele and its ongoing programs. Users' fees, if imposed, might adversely affect those who are in greatest need but are least able to pay for fee-based services. Extension could fall into a trap that plagued its early years in some states—providing services only to those who paid membership fees in a particular organization. Perhaps some of these problems could be avoided by establishing fees only for those services that are unique or that demand an unusual amount of time on the part of the Extension staff.

If the Cooperative Extension System is to remain a cooperative system, and that is one of its greatest strengths, then it must continue to be funded from federal, state, and local sources. In any case, nothing is really free and services must be financed either privately or publicly. Historically, public funding has been the pattern. All three of the cooperating levels of government have distinct program priorities that should be supported by that level of government. None of the three should dictate programs and their delivery, but each should recognize that it has an interest both in effective programs and in their efficient delivery. Furthermore, the dropping of funding by any one of the three sources could mean the end of the cooperative program as it has developed over the years. Obviously, any of the three levels of government that did not contribute to the funding of the programs would have little influence over their determination or their delivery.

The best source of funding over the long run lies in the development and delivery of programs that will meet the critical needs of many Americans. Those users, in turn, will fully support the funding of the Cooperative Extension system at each level of government.

Issues and Programs.   As Extension moves toward the twenty-first century, it is reevaluating its effectiveness in reaching various groups—including agriculture, families, and youth—and communities with programs that address the most important issues. It is also reviewing its use of appropriate methods of program delivery, particularly electronic technologies. Extension should adopt program delivery systems that will enable it to act as the resource base for disseminating applied research, reaching a wide range of new and present audiences, and extending its educational programs beyond traditional spheres. Extension must act decisively to maintain its role as the arm of the land-grant university providing research-based knowledge and educational programs having a positive impact on issues affecting agriculture, communities, families, and youth. It must move beyond service to the traditional agricultural producers, homemakers clubs, and 4-H clubs to become a recognized program developer and valued educational resource for organizations, agencies, and localities as well as for its traditional clientele.

NATIONAL PRIORITY INITIATIVES.   The relevance of issues and programs and the manner in which they are delivered will determine the future of Extension. The Cooperative Extension System has selected nine critical areas as national priority initiatives as the 1990s approach. They are: (1) competitiveness and profitability in American agriculture; (2) alternative agricultural opportunities; (3) conservation and management of natural resources; (4) water quality; (5) revitalizing rural America; (6) improving nutrition, diet, and health; (7) family and economic well-being; (8) building human capital; and (9) youth at risk. Critical issues, goals for Extension, and roles for Extension are identified for each initiative. Of course, no initiative is necessarily permanent. The initiatives provide a focus for programs developed at the local level to meet local needs. They indicate in this age of a communications revolution that many of the same problems affect virtually every American. As Myron D. Johnsrud, administrator of the Extension Service, said in 1987, the initiatives represented "a redirection toward issue-oriented, action-teamwork to help people resolve critical issues of public concern."

ISSUES AND PROGRAMS IN AGRICULTURE.   Extension's ability to respond to the needs of agriculture is essential to a successful future. The current technology delivery system must be adapted into a new model reflecting the concerns of commercial agriculture while it serves the small and noncommercial agricultural clientele. The Futures Task

Force proposed establishment of a nationwide network to serve high-technology agriculture. The network would improve the integration of research and Extension while giving innovative farmers ready access to current knowledge through high-technology centers. These centers would be a cooperative effort among the federal, state, and local partners in the Extension services. They would concentrate on problem solving, and interested producers would have direct access to them. They would provide multicounty, statewide, or multistate continuing education programs on high-technology issues. The centers would also train professionals and consultants in emerging technologies. Emphasis would be on educating for problem solving rather than on knowledge transfer for its own sake.

Extension will be dealing with a number of agriculture's critical issues, especially those affecting domestic and international competitiveness. Work is underway on such major issues as improving the economic efficiency and integration of the total agricultural system from producer to consumer and balancing human wellness, nutrition, and environmental concerns with goals concerning competitiveness and profitability. At the same time, Extension will be strengthening business and community support systems, developing long-term agricultural policies that meet the needs of the nation, and enhancing the number of competent human beings in the agricultural system.

The majority of our farms are small and part-time and their number is increasing. The farmers who operate them, according to some economists, are those whose need for assistance from Extension is greatest, even though the total value of their farm production is small. One state director has proposed that the problem is social rather than economic, but added that Extension should deal with social as well as economic questions affecting farmers and rural residents. Another director observed that as Extension turns more to issues and away from discipline-oriented problem solving, while at the same time adopting high-technology information delivery systems, it should not lose sight of the small and part-time farmers. Any delivery system should ensure that they are reached with the education they need to solve their problems. This alone is a strong reason for maintaining some professional staff in county offices.

Just where Extension should commit its limited resources is a problem. The very large commercial farms are increasing in size but staying about the same in number; small and part-time farms are increasing in number; and the midlevel family farms are decreasing in number. In a 1987 discussion of agricultural institutions, James B. Kendrick, Jr., formerly vice-president for agriculture of the University of California, observed: "The most significant change required for the future involves Cooperative Extension. For a substantial number of the moderate-size farming units to survive, Extension will need to direct its primary attention to this group. If this isn't done, an important feature of our rural environment will disappear and rural America will be damaged." It may be possible to meet the needs of large-scale agriculture through the centers of high technology recommended by the Futures Task Force, with the needs of the moderate-size farmer being met by more traditional Extension services in conjunction with the centers. Help for the part-time and small farmer would come from the traditional county staff and through special programs administered by volunteers or financed locally.

CONSERVATION AND MANAGEMENT OF NATURAL RESOURCES.
Extension has a long record of encouraging soil conservation and since World War II has been active in the conservation and management of natural resources. Critical issues in the conservation and management of natural resources include: Sustaining the natural resource base; managing soil resources and, in particular, reducing soil erosion; effectively managing and marketing renewable natural resources; formulating natural resource policy; and increasing natural resource productivity. Every state Extension service has a program for soil conservation and protection. A number have forestry programs, and others are encouraging the production of fish for market. Such projects provide alternative agricultural opportunities while helping the nation both conserve and use wisely its natural resources.

The 1985 Food Security Act required agricultural producers to carry out significant conservation practices if they were to be eligible for farm price support. Historically, the Cooperative Extension System has focused mainly on production activities. Soil and water conservation has been viewed as peripheral, except where it might increase agricultural production or productivity. In contrast, the major conservation agencies traditionally have focused on receptive landowners or producers who benefit financially by participating in conservation practices.

Resource conservation must be made an integral part of agricultural production processes. Accomplishing this requires modifications in current production practices. Extension's information and educational resources should focus on this area. Producers and other land users need to understand the economic and agronomic consequences of conservation and production alternatives. With traditional agricultural practices encountering the need for adaptation to take into account complicated conservation and environmental factors, Extension faces a difficult educational task.

WATER QUALITY AND MANAGEMENT.   Water is essential to human life and to agricultural production. More than half of the nation's population depends on groundwater for drinking water and more than 95 percent of rural residents drink groundwater, most of which is neither tested nor treated.

Extension over the next few years is in a position to take decisive action to assure our water supply. Extension can develop and implement educational programs that: Help people understand the importance of water supplies, sources of contamination, the need for testing, and potential treatment methods; make farmers and resource managers sensitive to water issues and management practices, especially as they affect their families, neighbors, and communities; create consumer awareness of water quality and conservation issues and their role in shaping water policies; and help local government officials develop effective and equitable water policies.

REVITALIZING RURAL AMERICA.   Although Extension in a number of states has been carrying out substantial rural and community development programs for several decades, federal support has been inconsistent, with programs shifting as one administration succeeds another. But as Richard Fenwick of the Central Bank of Cooperatives, Denver, has explained: "Educational needs, particularly in rural America, shift with changing economic and social environments. Today, needs relating to rural economic development are once again apparent as rural America adjusts to the changing structure of agriculture." Like other Extension programs, those delivered to communities should be research-based and designed to assist communities cope with issues that emerge from the changing socioeconomic environment. Extension should work with all departments of the land-grant universities to provide specialized information and research findings from different disciplines to communities. It should integrate resources to address the common needs of agriculture, community, family, and youth. At the local level Extension should deliver relevant programs to local governments and improvement associations. Extension's task is to build a community network of agencies and individuals to coordinate efforts to use effectively available resources in addressing community problems and concerns.

With the end of federal revenue sharing in the 1980s, 80 percent of all localities no longer had any direct financial relationship with Washington. Communities large and small are left with unfunded mandates and reporting requirements by both federal and state governments. Extension workers, from the agent to the university staff, realize that they are in the forefront of a significant change in rural America. Rural America will be revitalized, preferably and most effectively with Extension's leadership, but with or without, it will be revitalized.

FAMILY AND ECONOMIC WELL-BEING.   The well-being of the family is essential to national strength and economic stability. According to several recent studies, Extension should continue to address the critical issues and needs of families through educational programs that improve the overall quality of life and contribute to human growth and development. To do so, Extension should use analyses anticipating future economic, political, environmental, technical, and social trends in developing active programs that address real problems. Programs must be research-based and directed to clearly defined audiences, and they must have behavioral change as their objective. They also should be related to programs of other federal agencies and to the total land-grant university system.

Extension could expand its outreach by using appropriate technology and by using volunteers more effectively in their delivery of research results. Volunteers represent the greatest potential for extending or multiplying programs for families, as many home economics agents have found in the past. Experience has shown that professionals, paraprofessionals, and volunteers working together make good delivery teams. Volunteer management of other volunteers also has been effective, freeing professionals for other essential tasks. Additional educational programs can be initiated through cooperation with volunteer service organizations that assume responsibility for organizational development and management. Over the years both homemakers and 4-H clubs have been important avenues for making programs available to families and to youth. This record of success should be remembered as new methods for delivering programs are developed.

Over the next several years Extension will be dealing with a number of critical issues concerning family and economic well-being. It will be essential to provide research-based educational programs to deal with such problems as these: Family disruption and dislocation through loss of the farm or job, or through divorce or death; escalating costs of health care and housing; alcohol and drug abuse; inadequate parental care and guidance; responsibility for dependent elderly; and family financial stability.

IMPROVING NUTRITION, DIET, AND HEALTH.   One of the most substantial contributions Extension has made historically to family and economic well-being and to the welfare of the nation is to educate Americans on how to improve their nutrition and diet, and hence their health. It is a contribution Extension can continue to make. In recent years advances in science and technology have increased greatly knowledge about the relationship between food and nutrition and physical and emotional health. Americans increasingly have become aware of the role that diet and nutrition play in preventing disease and promoting good health. Today's consumers need reliable information to help them make informed decisions about food choices, consumption, preparation, and preservation. Many consumers want to change their eating habits to decrease health risks, but they are confused by conflicting recommendations, health fads, and new theories not based on sound research findings.

Attention should be focused on the interrelationships within the food system, from production through consumption to issues related to the health and safety of the food supply. Food producer groups should be better informed and more responsive to consumers concerns about diet and health. These are issues Extension is competent to handle.

DEVELOPING HUMAN POTENTIAL. The term "building human capital" is used interchangeably with "developing human potential" in some of the discussions about the future of Extension. Another term, "leadership development," is sometimes used, particularly in connection with increasing the skills and abilities of volunteers to provide leadership in education and community services. Whatever the term may be in any particular discussion, these programs have been of signal importance throughout the history of Extension, particularly as they applied to youth. There is every reason to believe that they will continue that key importance into the future. As Grant Shrum, president of National 4-H Council, has said: "While Extension contributes positively to the economic goals, and that is very important, the primary focus should be to provide a practical, educational experience for the development of productive, responsible citizens and to develop and train tomorrow's leaders." This suggests that the leadership development emphasis in Extension should include and go beyond the traditional 4-H club and activity groups to include older people as well.

As is true in other areas, those responsible for youth should undertake anticipatory planning and should stress research-based programs. Extension youth programs have the capacity to—and should—explore the possibility of contracting with other agencies within federal, state, and local governments to provide issue-oriented educational programs. Some have already done so very successfully in such areas as adolescent health, nutrition, pregnancy, suicide, drugs, and crime. A "youth at risk" initiative has been developed within Extension as a national critical issue.

Training programs for volunteers enable them to assume an expanded role in the delivery and implementation of educational programs. This is a field in which 4-H and home economics have been particularly successful over the years and one that is part of the national initiatives. Others, too, need the advantages of youth education and adult re-education to handle technological innovations and for lifelong use in solving problems relating to personal, family, social, economic, and political issues. They will better understand the changing role of the United States in the world and will be able to handle the questions of public policy and leadership facing communities, states, and the nation. It is imperative that these educational opportunities for involvement and interaction with others be expanded to include those youth and adults who currently are isolated from the mainstream of American society.

Communications Technology as the New Methodology.

Recent advances in electronic technology as they have affected communications in Extension foreshadow a new methodology in Extension education. Its significance, although the term "methodology" was not used, was pointed out in some detail in 1985 in a report issued by an Electronic Technology Task Force of the Extension Service and the Extension Committee on Organization and Policy.

The report showed the relationship of media technologies to the three functions of Extension and to audience size and type. The traditional delivery methods used by Extension were not discarded, but were related to the electronic methods, both those in place and those in prospect. Indeed, the task force stated forthrightly that new methods would not replace specialists and agents in the future.

The task force listed information delivery, educational delivery, and problem solving as the three functions of Extension, and then related the methods of delivery to audience size and selectivity. Information delivery to large, general audiences could best be accomplished by electronic publishing, computer networks, and broadcast television, along with the traditional newspapers and radio. Smaller and more select audiences would benefit from telephone access and publications. The methods listed as important for one function usually overlapped others. However, educational delivery could make particular use of teleconferencing, computer networks, personal computers, video tapes, and meetings and demonstrations. Problem-solving needs could be met by use of personal computers, call-in radio, video tapes, telephone access, meetings, and personal contact.

New technologies or methodologies emphasize the differences, which have always been there, between the Cooperative Extension System and traditional straight-line agencies. Rather than telling an audience what it should know, Extension educates its clientele, using the methods best suited to help that clientele meet its needs. At the same time, county Extension people advise state staff what needs exist which should be addressed by research, and which require Extension to provide problem-solving information. The state office then gets research started at the experiment station and the university.

In the future, program delivery as well as the transmission of information from the county to the state level will have even newer electronic technologies. Some such technologies are being evaluated and tested to determine their appropriate role in supporting the mission of Extension.

Videotapes have become a valuable educational tool, in part because their use is already a popular media trend. They are especially useful for programs that require demonstrations of complex techniques or of newer technologies. But the production of quality videotapes is costly. For this reason, Extension might consider establishing a program through which successful video presentations developed in each state would be shared with others.

Satellite broadcasting will play an important part in getting informational and educational programs to rural residents. However, regular programming, like that for radio and television, may be necessary if Extension is to reach audiences consistently. Because most broadcasts can be received beyond state boundaries, states might well cooperate in the production, scheduling, and transmission of issue-focused materials.

Computers and computer networks have proven their value. They are an important resource if they promptly deliver useful material and if potential users are familiar with this medium. Computer-controlled, laser-read discs have great potential as educational tools, but their usefulness to Extension is still to be determined.

Newer electronic tools for rapid communication are continually in prospect. However, Extension might keep in mind the perspective stated by Earl Manning of *Progressive Farmer* magazine:

> Rapid transmission of data via computer as well as by radio and television must be rapidly adopted as Extension adjusts to future technology. Videotapes on how-to methodology will become commonplace, as more and more clients own and use VCRs and video equipment. However, electronic tools will never fully replace personal contact and printed material with easy referability features. These tools can and must be used to deliver information rapidly with emotion and motivational power.

The Land-grant Concept Revisited.   The Morrill Land-Grant College Act of 1862 brought a new concept of education to American life. The purpose of the law was "to promote the liberal and practical education of the industrial classes in the several pursuits and professions in life" by establishing colleges to teach "such branches of learning as are related to agriculture and the mechanic arts," without excluding other scientific and classical studies. Over the next half century the colleges, now universities, were strengthened by the Hatch Experiment Station Act of 1887, the Second Morrill Land-Grant College Act of 1890, and the Smith-Lever Act of 1914. This legislation put into place a system of education that has transformed the nation.

Many of the system's contributions have been discussed in earlier chapters. But there also were broad contributions flowing out of the charge to promote "liberal and practical education of the industrial classes."

The first colleges in America were established to train the sons of the well-to-do and the elite for governing and leadership roles as ministers of the gospel, lawyers, physicians, and classicists. The new land-grant institutions were for the education of the "industrial classes," or in today's words, for the workers. Today the land-grant universities still offer an opportunity for a four-year college education to young people of limited circumstances with ordinary backgrounds. Without such an opportunity, many potential leaders of the nation might never develop their capabilities to the fullest.

The new land-grant universities were directed to teach agriculture and the mechanical arts, a purpose almost unique in higher education. At the same time the word "practical" was used, a word that still distinguishes the land-grant universities from most others. In the terminology of today and tomorrow, "practical" can be defined as "problem solving." Problem solving becomes possible through research directed to meeting needs. This concept is one of the major building blocks of the land-grant system. Currently, more than 10 percent of the nation's undergraduate college students are enrolled in land-grant institutions, while some 40 percent of the Ph.D. degrees earned each year are granted by these universities.

Another idea was added to the overall concept by the Smith-Lever Act — education can and should reach beyond the classroom to continue throughout life. Extension went even farther when it moved from the simple transfer of knowledge to the idea of helping people identify their problems and find the tools with which to solve them. This approach remains a capstone of the land-grant concept.

The land-grant concept lives. Its basic ideas are as valid and useful today as they were when they first were developed. Together, they provide an integrated concept by which America can live. Simply, the land-grant concept is to provide research-based education, continued throughout life, that is devoted to helping people solve problems.

The Future Is Now.   Extension must anticipate the major changes taking place in the United States as it moves from an industrial to an information society. Extension can continue to broaden its leadership in continuing education and in educational methodology made possible by the new electronic technology. Extension will change to deal with change, but Extension must carry out change within the framework of helping people help themselves through research-based educational programs—the basic concept with which Extension has so well served the American nation.

Can and will the necessary changes take place? The answer is a resounding "Yes!" The Cooperative Extension System, in spite of, or perhaps because of, its lack of central control, is outstanding among the nation's institutions for information delivery, educational delivery, and problem solving. Its uniqueness has served the nation well and will continue to do so.

But the major reason why the Cooperative Extension System will perceive and meet the nation's needs in the future lies in the character of its people. Extension is an educational organization, but its staff members, from top-level administrators and directors to the people in the county offices, are dedicated to service. They have devoted their lives to solving other people's problems and they can solve Extension's. That is why, as a new era begins, Extension will continue to serve the American people and to make the United States a better place in which to work and live.

Administrators
of the Extension Service, USDA

Alfred Charles True (1914–1923). Dr. True received his Ph.D. degree at Erskine College after doing graduate work at Harvard. He joined the staff at Wesleyan University where he was associated with the famous chemist W. O. Atwater. While Atwater was director of the federal Office of Experiment Stations, True joined him to prepare special reports. True stayed on as editor and advanced to director of the Office of Experiment Stations from 1893–1914. As the first director of the States Relations Service of the Department of Agriculture, True exerted significant influence on research in agriculture and home economics. His wise counsel and guidance were invaluable during the formative period in continuing education for rural people. This period saw the beginning of the concept of education in which federal, state, and county workers cooperated with local people to develop the Cooperative Extension System in the United States.

Charles W. Pugsley (1923). Pugsley received two degrees from the University of Nebraska and stayed on as an instructor in animal husbandry, agronomy, and farm management. In Nebraska, he served as state statistical agent, leader of boys' and girls' club work, and director of Extension. He then entered the field of agricultural journalism and was editor of the *Nebraska Farmer* when he was appointed assistant secretary of agriculture in 1921. Pugsley served as acting director of the Extension Service when it first became a separate agency on July 1, 1923. He held this position until September 14, 1923, when he became president of South Dakota State College.

Clyde W. Warburton (1923–1940).   Warburton received his Doctor of Science degree from Iowa State College and spent many years as an agronomist in the Bureau of Plant Industry, U.S. Department of Agriculture. He served as president of the American Society of Agronomy in 1925. He was associate editor of the *Farmer* magazine, book editor for the Webb Publishing Company, and editor of the *Journal of the American Society of Agronomy.* He served sixteen years as director of the Extension Service—the longest period of any of its directors or administrators. Under his leadership the Extension Service matured as an independent agency, survived the Depression of the early thirties, and became well established in the rural communities as "the educational arm of the U.S. Department of Agriculture."

Milburn Lincoln Wilson (1940–1953).   "M. L." grew up on an Iowa farm, was a tenant farmer in Nebraska, and homesteaded in Montana. He had degrees from Iowa State College and the University of Wisconsin, and a Doctor of Science degree from Montana State College. In 1912 he became one of the first county agents in Montana and was state Extension leader in Montana from 1914–1922. He was an outstanding leader throughout his career. For example, he organized the wheat program of the Agricultural Adjustment Administration in 1933, and he headed the Subsistence Homesteads Division in the U.S. Department of the Interior. He served as Assistant Secretary of Agriculture from 1934 to 1937, as Under Secretary from 1937 to 1940, and as director of the Extension Service from 1940 to 1953. He was also responsible for the nutrition programs of the World War II Food Administration. Wilson, recognized for his leadership in agricultural economics, was one of the five recipients in 1947 of the first "Distinguished Service Awards" to be granted by the U.S. Department of Agriculture.

Clarence M. Ferguson (1953–1960).   "Fergie" was born on a farm in Ontario, Canada. After graduating from the Ontario Agricultural College, he spent most of his professional career in the Extension Service. He served as poultry specialist, and director of the Extension Service in Ohio before becoming director of the Federal Extension Service in January 1953. Under a reorganization, his title was changed to "administrator" in December 1953. In 1956, he received the USDA Distinguished Service Award "For strengthening Cooperative Extension Service relations with Land-Grant colleges and promoting effective agricultural programs and Extension work with farm people." Under Fergie's leadership, Extension demonstrated that it could cooperate nationwide in many program areas and, at the same time, leave responsibility for final fulfillment in the hands of states. Such programming strengthened Extension as a great educational force in this country and throughout the world. Ferguson's leadership in Extension was recognized by his promotion to Assistant Secretary of Agriculture in 1960.

Paul K. Kepner (1960–1961).   Hoosier farm boy, teacher, farmer, Extension specialist, and administrator provide a quick sketch of Kepner. He graduated from Purdue University with distinguished honors and did graduate work at Cornell University while serving part time on the state Extension staff in agricultural economics. In 1935 Kepner joined the federal Extension Service staff as senior economist and in 1942 he moved into administration. During World War II and after, he helped guide emergency programs in which Extension Service had leadership responsibility. He headed a committee to study Extension programming, which later provided the "Scope Report." In his twenty-five years on the federal staff, Kepner worked to strengthen the federal-state-county partnership and in 1958 he was recognized for his efforts by receiving the USDA Distinguished Service Award.

E. Travis York, Jr. (1961–1963).   "E. T." at age thirty-seven was the youngest administrator of the federal Extension Service. A native of Alabama, he has two degrees from Auburn University and a Ph.D. degree from Cornell University. York headed the agronomy department at North Carolina State University before serving as eastern director of the American Potash Institute. York was director of the Alabama Extension Service when he was appointed administrator of the federal Extension Service. He left this position to become provost for agriculture at the University of Florida and, later, chancellor of the State University System of Florida. As chancellor emeritus, he is now at Gainesville, Florida, doing international work in agriculture. York has served as vice-chairman and chairman of the board for International Food and Agricultural Development. At the request of President Ronald Reagan, he served as chairman of three presidential missions on agricultural development to Central America and the Caribbean, Egypt, and Liberia. Honors include being the first recipient of the E. T. York, Jr., Distinguished Service Award from the Institute of Food and Agricultural Sciences, University of Florida, in recognition of outstanding contributions to agriculture and to the people of Florida.

Lloyd H. Davis (1963–1970).   Dr. Davis has three degrees from Cornell University. His state Extension experience includes assistant county agent and specialist in New York and associate director in Massachusetts. He was a member of the federal Extension Service staff in marketing and served as deputy administrator before becoming administrator in 1963. Seven years later, Davis became director of Science and Education Coordination Staff, USDA. In 1975, he became executive director of the National Advisory Council on Extension and Continuing Education. He has also served as executive director of the National University Continuing Education Association, and as interim executive director of the Adult Education Association of the U.S.A. from 1981 until he retired in November 1982. His home is in Great Falls, Virginia.

Edwin L. Kirby (1970–1977).   Kirby became administrator of the federal Extension Service on January 15, 1970, after serving as associate administrator for one year. In March 1970 the agency returned to its earlier name, "Extension Service," dropping the word "Federal." Kirby came from the Ohio Cooperative Extension Service, where he was associate director, administratively responsible for the Ohio CES. He has a B.S. degree from Ohio State University and a Master of Education degree from Cornell University. He received the USDA Distinguished Service Award for his leadership. Kirby returned to Columbus, Ohio, where he was environmental science administrator, Ohio Department of Agriculture, responsible for environmental quality, agriculture, finance, and rural affairs issues. He retired in 1983.

W. Neill Schaller (1977–1979).   Schaller came to the Extension Service after serving seven years as associate managing director of the Farm Foundation, Chicago. His tenure coincided with implementation of the USDA reorganization, which merged Extension Service, Agricultural Research Service, Cooperative State Research Service, and National Agricultural Library into one agency—the Science and Education Administration (SEA). He received a B.A. degree from Princeton University and a Ph.D. degree in agricultural economics from the University of California, Berkeley. He is now on the staff of the Economic Research Service, USDA.

Mary Nell Greenwood (1979–1986).   Serving first as an associate administrator, Dr. Greenwood became the first female administrator of the Extension Service in 1979. Her tenure was marked with another reorganization—this time to reestablish the four agencies as separate agencies under an assistant secretary for science and education. Her accomplishments include the writing of the monograph *Blueprint for the Future—Extension Service, USDA.* A native Missourian, she received her first degree from Central Missouri State University and earned two advanced degrees from the University of Wisconsin. Prior to joining Extension Service, USDA, Greenwood served as director of

Extension programs, University of Missouri, involving four campuses and twenty off-campus program planning units. In recognition of her leadership she was named honorary alumnus by the University of Missouri College of Home Economics. Dr. Greenwood stepped down from her position as administrator in July 1986 and became assistant to the administrator until her untimely death in November 1986.

Myron D. Johnsrud (1986–   ).   Dr. Johnsrud is a native of North Dakota where he farmed for seven years before beginning his career in Extension as an assistant county agent. He was selected administrator of the Extension Service, USDA, on February 27, 1987, after serving as interim administrator since July 14, 1986. He came to the national office of the Extension Service from North Dakota State University where he served as director of the Cooperative Extension Service for twelve years. His experience includes two years as director of staff development, Extension Service, USDA; state leader, staff development; and associate director of Extension at North Dakota State University. As a state director, Johnsrud served as a member of the Extension Committee on Organization and Policy and chaired its budget subcommittee. He provides leadership for the development and implementation of the national priority initiatives during a period of changing program development within the Extension System. He received his B.S. degree from North Dakota State University and two advanced degrees from the University of Wisconsin. Johnsrud is a former U.S. Air Force and Air National Guard pilot.

Distinguished Service Ruby Awards

In 1927, Epsilon Sigma Phi, national honorary fraternity for Extension Service, established the Distinguished Service Ruby Award. This is the highest award of recognition by ESP. The following awards have been made:

1927	A. C. True, Federal Extension Service
1929	W. D. Bently, Oklahoma
1930	J. A. Evans, Federal Extension Service
1931	William B. Mercier, Louisiana
1932	None Awarded
1933	W. A. Lloyd, Federal Extension Service
1934	C. B. Smith, Federal Extension Service
	M. L. Wilson, Assistant Secretary of Agriculture
1935	None Awarded
1936	C. W. Warburton, Federal Extension Service
	Jane S. McKimmon, North Carolina
1937	Liberty Hyde Bailey, New York, Honorary Member
1938	Cecil W. Creel, Nevada
1939	A. Frank Lever, South Carolina, Honorary Member
1940	I. O. Schaub, North Carolina
1941	William Peterson, Utah
1942	H. J. C. Umberger, Kansas
1943	Arthur L. Deering, Maine
1944	Albert E. Bowman, Wyoming

1945	F. A. Anderson, Colorado
1946	J. E. Carrigan, Vermont
1947	John C. Taylor, Montana
1948	William H. Browkaw, Nebraska
1949	Harry G. Ramsower, Ohio
1950	Willard A. Munson, Massachusetts
1951	Madge J. Reese, Federal Extension Service
1952	Henry P. Rush, Illinois
1953	Theodore A. Erickson, Minnesota
1954	Frank L. Ballard, Oregon
1955	Meredith C. Wilson, Federal Extension Service
1956	Ralph Kenneth Bliss, Iowa
1957	J. W. Burch, Missouri
1958	None Awarded
1959	Harry C. Sanders, Louisiana
	Gladys Gallup, Federal Extension Service
1960	Paul V. Kepner, Federal Extension Service
1961	Leroy E. Hoffman, Indiana
1962	Clarence M. Ferguson, Ohio
1963	William Abner Sutton, Georgia
1964	Charles Austin Vines, Arkansas
1965	Mary Louise Collings, Federal Extension Service
1966	Charles Brice Ratchford, Missouri
1967	Luke M. Schruben, Federal Extension Service
1968	Roland H. Abraham, Minnesota
1969	Harriette E. Cushman, Montana
1970	William E. Skelton, Virginia
1971	Lowell H. Watts, Colorado
1972	Edward W. Aiton, Maryland
1973	Henry Lawrence Ahlgren, Wisconsin
1974	Paul Brinton Crooks, Indiana
1975	Dorothy Emerson, Maryland
1976	George Hyatt, Jr., North Carolina
1977	John E. Hutchinson, Texas
1978	Marvin Anderson, Iowa
1979	Ann Thompson, Virginia
1980	George R. Gist, Jr., Ohio
1981	Mary Nell Greenwood, Science and Education Administration

1982   Gale L. VandeBerg, Wisconsin
1983   T. Carlton Blalock, North Carolina
1984   Tal C. DuVall, Georgia
1985   Charles W. McDougall, Federal Extension Service
1986   Robert C. Clark, Wisconsin
1987   Anne H. Rideout, Connecticut
1988   Myron D. Johnsrud, North Dakota and USDA

APPENDIX C

Amount and Percent of Cooperative Extension Funds Available, by Source, from Fiscal Year Beginning July 1, 1914 (Thousands of dollars)

Fiscal year	Grand total	Federal		State Appropriation		County Appropriation		Private	
		Dollars	Percent	Dollars	Percent	Dollars	Percent	Dollars	Percent
1915	$ 3,597	1,486	41	1,044	29	780	22	287	8
1916	4,864	2,143	44	1,471	30	973	20	277	6
1917	6,150	2,719	44	1,928	31	1,258	21	245	4
1918	11,303	6,476	57	2,469	22	1,864	17	494	4
1919	14,662	9,039	62	2,961	20	2,291	16	371	2
1920	14,658	5,891	40	5,229	36	2,866	20	672	4
1921	16,792	6,434	38	6,044	36	3,294	20	1,021	6
1922	17,182	6,727	39	6,528	38	2,973	17	954	6
1923	18,485	7,101	38	7,054	38	3,420	19	910	5
1924	18,879	6,924	37	7,040	37	4,259	23	656	3
1925	19,250	6,862	36	7,203	37	3,858	20	1,326	7
1926	19,417	6,891	35	7,327	38	4,055	21	1,144	6
1927	19,748	6,916	35	7,423	38	4,363	22	1,046	5
1928	20,398	6,929	34	7,767	38	4,673	23	1,029	5
1929	22,513	8,573	38	6,406	28	6,282	28	1,252	6
1930	23,804	8,798	37	6,865	29	7,036	30	1,105	4
1931	25,581	9,705	38	7,243	28	7,523	30	1,110	4
1932	25,399	9,716	38	7,189	28	7,365	29	1,129	5
1933	23,405	9,653	41	6,390	27	6,394	28	967	4
1934	19,896	9,376	47	4,889	25	4,844	24	787	4
1935	20,042	9,000	45	5,045	25	5,152	26	844	4
1936	28,780	16,936	59	5,465	19	5,569	19	811	3
1937	29,764	17,256	58	5,795	19	5,888	20	825	3
1938	31,037	17,541	57	6,467	21	6,241	20	778	3

Year									
1941	33,194	18,591	56	6,707	20	6,807	21	1,089	3
1942	34,111	18,956	56	7,141	20	6,960	21	1,054	3
1943	34,865	18,957	54	7,312	21	7,442	22	1,154	3
1944	36,740	18,997	52	8,466	23	8,168	22	1,110	3
1945	37,836	18,997	50	9,158	24	8,480	23	1,201	3
1946	44,548	23,407	53	10,738	24	9,059	20	1,345	3
1947	52,993	27,323	52	12,855	24	11,076	21	1,739	3
1948	58,463	27,457	47	17,174	29	12,268	21	1,564	3
1949	65,733	30,531	46	18,867	29	14,214	22	2,121	3
1950	73,394	32,160	44	23,464	32	15,528	21	2,242	3
1951	75,983	32,174	42	24,942	33	16,534	22	2,333	2
1952	79,999	32,091	40	27,693	35	17,859	22	2,356	2
1953	84,593	32,150	38	30,544	36	19,644	23	2,255	2
1954	89,531	32,163	36	33,875	38	21,166	24	2,327	1
1955	100,617	39,675	39	35,998	36	22,403	22	2,541	1
1956	109,912	45,475	41	37,840	35	24,282	22	2,315	2
1957	119,195	49,865	42	40,516	34	26,502	22	2,312	2
1958	128,060	50,715	40	46,993	37	28,358	22	1,994	2
1959	134,836	53,715	40	49,517	37	30,102	22	1,502	2
1960	140,071	53,715	38	53,583	38	31,231	23	1,542	2
1961	150,098	56,715	38	57,895	38	32,782	22	2,706	2
1962	159,227	59,590	37	62,226	39	34,530	22	2,881	2
1963	168,621	63,430	38	65,704	39	36,402	22	3,085	2
1964	177,920	67,108	38	69,907	39	37,804	21	3,101	2
1965	188,884	71,684	38	74,341	39	39,776	21	3,083	2
1966	201,223	75,184	37	80,345	40	41,941	21	3,753	2
1967	213,669	78,256	37	87,461	41	44,096	20	3,856	2
1968	225,477	77,882	35	96,752	43	46,600	20	4,243	2
1969	241,952	80,762	33	106,326	44	50,288	21	4,576	2
1970	290,688	112,719	39	119,115	41	53,485	18	5,369	1
1971	331,897	138,191	42	129,562	39	58,613	18	5,531	2
1972	354,359	148,520	42	136,090	38	63,582	18	6,167	2
1973	385,091	163,104	42	148,218	39	66,387	17	7,382	2
1974	407,452	165,605	41	161,897	40	71,744	18	8,206	2
1975	448,334	178,821	40	181,848	41	79,126	18	8,539	2
1976	498,452	190,954	38	206,854	42	91,805	18	8,839	2
1977	525,362	199,232	38	220,906	42	93,612	18	11,612	2
1978	586,744	215,300	37	245,638	42	111,019	19	14,787	2
1979	624,923	221,076	35	270,047	43	119,193	19	14,607	3
1980	682,698	230,820	34	304,883	45	130,630	19	16,365	3
1981	746,515	248,935	33	335,723	45	142,390	19	19,467	3
1982	853,908	302,920	36	368,846	43	157,671	18	24,471	3
1983	897,303	316,197	35	389,423	44	164,706	18	26,977	3
1984	937,823	322,219	34	415,521	45	171,335	18	28,748	3
1985	996,629	330,939	33	452,866	46	182,253	19	30,571	3
1986	1,039,029	316,460	30	489,424	47	200,912	20	32,233	3
1987	1,052,026	322,309	31	500,601	48	194,693	18	34,423	3
1988	1,144,996	343,179	30	553,311	48	210,111	18	38,395	4

Basic Legislation Authorizing Cooperative Agriculture Extension Work

Smith-Lever Act, 1914

Be it enacted by the Senate and House of Representatives of the United States of America in Congress assembled, That in order to aid in diffusing among the people of the United States useful and practical information on subjects relating to agriculture and home economics, and to encourage the application of the same, there may be inaugurated in connection with the college or colleges in each State now receiving, or which may hereafter receive, the benefits of the Act of Congress approved July second, eighteen hundred and sixty-two, entitled "An Act donating public lands to the several States and Territories which may provide colleges for the benefit of agriculture and the mechanic arts" (Twelfth Statutes at Large, page five hundred and three), and of the Act of Congress approved August thirtieth, eighteen hundred and ninety (Twenty-sixth Statutes at Large, page four hundred and seventeen and chapter eight hundred and forty-one), agricultural extension work which shall be carried on in cooperation with the United States Department of Agriculture: Provided, That in any State in which two or more such colleges have been or hereafter may be established the appropriations hereinafter made to such State shall be administered by such college or colleges as the legislature of such State may direct: Proved further, That, pending the inauguration and development of the cooperative extension work herein authorized, nothing in this Act shall be construed to discontinue either the farm management work or the farmers' cooperative demonstration work as now conducted by the Bureau of Plant Industry of the Department of Agriculture.

Sec. 2. That cooperative agricultural extension work shall consist of the giving of instruction and practical demonstrations in agriculture and home economics to persons not attending or resident in said colleges in the several communities, and imparting to such persons information on said subjects through field demonstrations, publications, and otherwise; and this work shall be carried on in such manner as may be mutually agreed upon by the Secretary of Agriculture and the State agricultural college or colleges receiving the benefits of this Act.

Sec. 3. That for the purpose of paying the expenses of said cooperative agricultural extension work and the necessary printing and distributing of information in connection with the same, there is permanently appropriated, out of any money in the Treasury not otherwise appropriated, the sum of $480,000 for each year, $10,000 of which shall be paid annually, in the manner hereinafter provided, to each State which shall by action of its legislature assent to the provisions of this Act: Provided, That payment of such installments of the appropriation hereinbefore made as shall become due to any State before the adjournment of the regular session of the legislature meeting next after the passage of this Act may, in the absence of prior legislative assent, be made upon the assent of the governor thereof duly certified to the Secretary of the Treasury: Provided further, That there is also appropriated an additional sum of $600,000 for the fiscal year following that in which the foregoing appropriation first becomes available, and for each year thereafter for seven years a sum exceeding by $500,000 the sum appropriated for each preceding year, and for each year thereafter there is permanently appropriated for each year the sum of $4,100,000 in addition to the sum of $480,000 hereinbefore provided: Provided further, That before the funds herein appropriated shall become available to any college for any fiscal year plans for the work to be carried on under this Act shall be submitted by the proper officials of each college and approved by the Secretary of Agriculture. Such additional sums shall be used only for the purposes hereinbefore stated, and shall be allotted annually to each State by the Secretary of Agriculture and paid in the manner hereinbefore provided, in the proportion which the rural population of each State bears to the total rural population of all the States as determined by the next preceding Federal census: Provided further, That no payment out of the additional appropriations herein provided shall be made in any year to any State until an equal sum has been appropriated for that year by the legislature of such State, or provided by State, county, college, local authority, or individual contributions from within the State, for the maintenance of the cooperative agricultural extension work provided for in this Act.

Sec. 4. That the sums hereby appropriated for extension work shall be paid in equal semiannual payments on the first day of January and July of each year by the Secretary of the Treasury upon the warrant of the Secretary of Agriculture, out of the Treasury of the United States, to the treasurer or other officer of the State duly authorized by the laws of the State to receive the same; and such officer shall be required to report to the Secretary of Agriculture, on or before the first day of September of each year, a detailed statement of the amount so received during the previous fiscal year, and of its disbursement, on forms prescribed by the Secretary of Agriculture.

Sec. 5. That if any portion of the moneys received by the designated officer of any State for the support and maintenance of cooperative agricultural extension work, as provided in this Act, shall by any action or contingency be diminished or lost, or be misapplied, it shall be replaced by said State to which it belongs, and until so replaced no subsequent appropriation shall be apportioned or paid to said State, and no portion of said moneys shall be applied, directly or indirectly, to the purchase, erection, preservation, or repair of any building or buildings, or the purchase or rental of land, or in college-course teaching, lectures in colleges, promoting agricultural trains, or any other purpose not specified in this Act, and not more than five per centum of each annual appropriation shall be applied to the printing and distribution of publications. It shall be the duty of each of said colleges annually, on or before the first day of January, to make to the governor of the State in which it is located a full and detailed report of its operations in the direction of extension work as defined in this Act, including a detailed statement of receipts and expenditures from all sources for this purpose, a copy of which report shall be sent to the Secretary of Agriculture and to the Secretary of the Treasury of the United States.

Sec. 6. That on or before the first day of July in each year after the passage of this Act the Secretary of Agriculture shall ascertain and certify to the Secretary of the Treasury as to each State whether it is entitled to receive its share of the annual appropriation for cooperative agricultural extension work under this Act, and the amount which it is entitled to receive. If the Secretary of Agriculture shall withhold a certificate from any State of its appropriation, the facts and reasons therefor shall be reported to the President, and the amount involved shall be kept separate in the Treasury until the expiration of the Congress next succeeding a session of the legislature of any State from which a certificate has been withheld, in order that the State may, if it should so desire, appeal to Congress from the determination of the Secretary of Agriculture. If the next Congress shall not direct such sum to be paid, it shall be covered into the Treasury.

Sec. 7. That the Secretary of Agriculture shall make an annual report to Congress of the receipts, expenditures, and results of the cooperative agricultural extension work in all of the States receiving the benefits of this Act, and also whether the appropriation of any State has been withheld; and if so, the reasons therefor.

Sec. 8. That Congress may at any time alter, amend, or repeal any or all of the provisions of this Act.

Approved, May 8, 1914. (38 Stat. 372)

Smith-Lever Act As Amended through 1985

An Act to provide for cooperative agricultural extension work between the agricultural colleges in the several States receiving the benefits of an Act of Congress approved July second, eighteen hundred and sixty-two, and of Acts supplementary thereto, and the United States Department of Agriculture

Sec. 1. In order to aid in diffusing among the people of the United States useful and practical information on subjects relating to agriculture, uses of solar energy with respect to agriculture, home economics, and rural energy, and to encourage the application of the same, there may be continued or inaugurated in connection with the college or colleges in each State, Territory, or possession, now receiving, or which may hereafter receive, the benefits of the Act of Congress approved July second, eighteen hundred and sixty-two, entitled "An Act donating public lands to the several States and Territories which may provide colleges for the benefit of agriculture and the mechanic arts" (Twelfth Statutes at Large, page five hundred and three) and of the Act of Congress approved August thirtieth, eighteen hundred and ninety (Twenty-sixth Statutes at Large, page four hundred and seventeen and chapter eight hundred and forty-one), agricultural extension work which shall be carried on in cooperation with the United States Department of Agriculture: Provided, That in any State, Territory, or possession in which two or more such colleges have been or hereafter may be established, the appropriations hereinafter made to such State, Territory, or possession shall be administered by such college or colleges as the legislature of such State, Territory, or possession may direct. For the purposes of this Act, the term "solar energy" means energy derived from sources (other than fossil fuels) and technologies included in the Federal Non-Nuclear Energy Research and Development Act of 1974, as amended.

Sec. 2. Cooperative agricultural extension work shall consist of the development of practical applications of research knowledge and giving of instruction and practical demonstrations of existing or improved practices or technologies in agriculture, uses of solar energy with respect to agriculture, home economics, and rural energy, and subjects relating thereto to persons not attending or resident in said colleges in the several communities, and imparting information on said subjects through demonstrations, publications, and otherwise and for the necessary printing and distribution of information in connection with the foregoing; and this work shall be carried on in such manner as may be mutually agreed upon by the Secretary of Agriculture and the State agricultural college or colleges or Territory or possession receiving the benefits of this Act.

Sec. 3. (*a*) There are hereby authorized to be appropriated for the purposes of this Act such sums as Congress may from time to time determine to be necessary.

(*b*)(*1*) Out of such sums, each State and the Federal Extension Service shall be entitled to receive annually a sum of money equal to the sums available from Federal cooperative extension funds for the fiscal year 1962, and subject to the same requirements as to furnishing of equivalent sums by the State, except that amounts heretofore made available to the Secretary for allotment on the basis of special needs shall continue available for use on the same basis.

(2) There is authorized to be appropriated for the fiscal year ending June 30, 1971, and for each fiscal year thereafter, for payment to the Virgin Islands and Guam, $100,000 each, which sums shall be in addition to the sums appropriated for the several States of the United States and Puerto Rico under the provisions of this section. The amount paid by the Federal Government to the Virgin Islands and Guam pursuant to this paragraph shall not exceed during any fiscal year, except the fiscal years ending June 30, 1971, and June 30, 1972, when such amount may be used to pay the total cost of providing services pursuant to this Act, the amount available and budgeted for expenditure by the Virgin Islands and Guam for the purposes of this Act.

(c) Any sums made available by the Congress for further development of cooperative extension work in addition to those referred to in subsection (b) hereof shall be distributed as follows:

1. Four per centum of the sum so appropriated for each fiscal year shall be allotted to the Federal Extension Service for administrative, technical, and other services, and for coordinating the extension work of the Department and the several States, Territories and possessions.

2. Of the remainder so appropriated for each fiscal year 20 per centum shall be paid to the several States in equal proportions, 40 per centum shall be paid to the several States in the proportion that the rural population of each bears to the total rural population of the several States as determined by the census, and the balance shall be paid to the several States in the proportion that the farm population of each bears to the total farm population of the several States as determined by the census: Provided, That payments out of the additional appropriations for further development of extension work authorized herein may be made subject to the making available of such sums of public funds by the States from non-Federal funds for the maintenance of cooperative agricultural extension work provided for in this Act, as may be provided by the Congress at the time such additional appropriations are made: Provided further, That any appropriation made hereunder shall be allotted in the first and succeeding years on the basis of the decennial census current at the time such appropriation is first made, and as to any increase, on the basis of decennial census current at the time such increase is first appropriated.

(d) The Federal Extension Service shall receive such amounts as Congress shall determine for administration, technical, and other services and for coordinating the extension work of the Department and the several States, Territories, and possessions.

(e) Insofar as the provisions of subsections (b) and (c) of this section, which require or permit Congress to require matching of Federal funds, apply to the Virgin Islands of the United States and Guam, such provisions shall be deemed to have been satisfied, for the fiscal years ending September 30, 1978, and September 30, 1979, only, if the amounts budgeted and available for expenditure by the Virgin Islands of the United States and Guam in such years equal the amounts budgeted and available for expenditure by the Virgin Islands of the United States and Guam in the fiscal year ending September 30, 1977.

(*f*)(*1*) The Secretary of Agriculture may conduct educational, instructional, demonstration, and publication distribution programs through the Federal Extension Service and enter into cooperative agreements with private nonprofit and profit organizations and individuals to share the cost of such programs through contributions from private sources as provided in this subsection.

(*2*) The Secretary may receive contributions under this subsection from private sources for the purposes described in paragraph (1) and provide matching funds in an amount not greater than 50 percent of such contributions.

Sec. 4. On or about the first day of October in each year after the passage of this Act, the Secretary of Agriculture shall ascertain as to each State whether it is entitled to receive its share of the annual appropriation for cooperative agricultural extension work under this Act and the amount which it is entitled to receive. Before the funds herein provided shall become available to any college for any fiscal year, plans for the work to be carried on under this Act shall be submitted by the proper officials of each college and approved by the Secretary of Agriculture. Such sums shall be paid in equal quarterly payments in or about July, October, January, and April of each year to the treasurer or other officer of the State duly authorized by the laws of the State to receive the same, and such officer shall be required to report to the Secretary of Agriculture on or about the first day of April of each year, a detailed statement of the amount so received during the previous fiscal year and its disbursement, on forms prescribed by the Secretary of Agriculture.

Sec. 5. If any portion of the moneys received by the designated officer of any State, for the support and maintenance of cooperative agricultural extension work, as provided in this Act, shall by any action or contingency be diminished or lost or be misapplied, it shall be replaced by said State, and until so replaced no subsequent appropriation shall be apportioned or paid to said State. No portion of said moneys shall be applied, directly or indirectly, to the purchase, erection, preservation, or repair of any building or buildings, or the purchase or rental of land, or in college-course teaching, lectures in college, or any other purpose not specified in this Act. It shall be the duty of said colleges, annually, on or about the first day of January, to make to the Governor of the State in which it is located a full and detailed report of its operations in extension work as defined in this Act, including a detailed statement of receipts and expenditures from all sources for this purpose, a copy of which report shall be sent to the Secretary of Agriculture.

Sec. 6. If the Secretary of Agriculture finds that a State is not entitled to receive its share of the annual appropriation, the facts and reasons therefore shall be reported to the President, and the amount involved shall be kept separate in the Treasury until the expiration of the Congress next succeeding a session of the legislature of the State from which funds have been withheld in order that the State may, if it should so desire, appeal to Congress from the determination of the Secretary of Agriculture. If the next Congress shall not direct such sum to be paid, it shall be covered into the Treasury.

Sec. 7 (Repealed)

Sec. 8. (*a*) The Congress finds that there exists special circumstances in certain agricultural areas which cause such areas to be at a disadvantage insofar as agricultural development is concerned, which circumstances include the following: (1) There is concentration of farm families on farms either too small or too unproductive or both; (2) such farm operators because of limited productivity are unable to make adjustments and investments required to establish profitable operations; (3) the productive capacity of the existing farm unit does not permit profitable employment of available labor; (4) because of limited resources, many of these farm families are not able to make full use of current extension programs designed for families operating economic units nor are extension facilities adequate to provide the assistance needed to produce desirable results.

(*b*) In order to further the purposes of section 2 in such areas and to encourage complementary development essential to the welfare of such areas, there are hereby authorized to be appropriated such sums as the Congress from time to time shall determine to be necessary for payments to the States on the basis of special needs in such areas as determined by the Secretary of Agriculture.

(*c*) In determining that the area has such special need, the Secretary shall find that it has a substantial number of disadvantaged farms or farm families for one or more of the reasons heretofore enumerated. The Secretary shall make provisions for the assistance to be extended to include one or more of the following: (1) Intensive on-the-farm educational assistance to the farm family in appraising and resolving its problems; (2) assistance and counseling to local groups in appraising resources for capability of improvement in agriculture or introduction of industry designed to supplement farm income; (3) cooperation with other agencies and groups in furnishing all possible information as to existing employment opportunities, particularly to farm families having underemployed workers; and (4) in cases where the farm family, after analysis of its opportunities and existing resources, finds it advisable to seek a new farming venture, the providing of information, advice, and counsel in connection with making such change.

(*d*) No more than 10 per centum of the sums available under this section shall be allotted to any one State. The Secretary shall use project proposals and plans of work submitted by the State Extension directors as a basis for determining the allocation of funds appropriated pursuant to this section.

(*e*) Sums appropriated pursuant to this section shall be in addition to, and not in substitution for, appropriations otherwise available under this Act. The amounts authorized to be appropriated pursuant to this section shall not exceed a sum in any year equal to 10 per centum of sums otherwise appropriated pursuant to this Act.

Sec. 9. The Secretary of Agriculture is authorized to make such rules and regulations as may be necessary for carrying out the provisions of this Act.

Sec. 10. The term "State" means the States of the Union, Puerto Rico, the Virgin Islands, and Guam.

Memoranda of Understanding and Project Agreements between the Land-Grant Institutions and the United States Department of Agriculture in Effect in 1988

Memorandum of Understanding Between (1862 Land-Grant Institutions) and the United States Department of Agriculture on Extension Work

Whereas (1862 Land-Grant Institution) has under its control Federal and State funds for extension work in agriculture and home economics which are and may be supplemented by funds contributed for similar purposes by counties and other organizations and individuals within said State, and the United States Department of Agriculture (USDA) has funds appropriated directly to it by Congress which can be spent for extension work in the State of _____;

Therefore, with a view of securing economy and efficiency in the conduct of extension work in the State of _____, the President of the (1862 Land-Grant Institution) acting subject to the approval of the Board of _____ of the said (1862 Land-Grant Institution) and the Secretary of Agriculture of the United States, hereby execute the following memorandum of understanding with reference to cooperative relations between said (1862 Land-Grant Institution) and the United States Department of Agriculture for the organization and conduct of extension work in agriculture and home economics in the State of _____.

I. The (1862 Land-Grant Institution) agrees:
   (a) To organize and maintain at said institution a definite and distinct

administrative division for the management and conduct of all cooperative extension work in agriculture and home economics, with a director selected by the institution and satisfactory to the Department;

(b) To administer through such division thus organized, known as the (State Cooperative Extension Service), any and all funds it has or may hereafter receive for such work from appropriations made by Congress or the State Legislature, by allotment from its Board of _____, or from any other sources;

(c) To accept the responsibility for conducting all educational work in the fields of agriculture, uses of solar energy with respect to agriculture, home economics and subjects related thereto, as authorized by the Smith-Lever Act, as amended, and other Acts supporting cooperative extension work, and such phases of other programs of the USDA as are primarily educational, which the Department has been authorized to carry on within the State.

II. The United States Department of Agriculture agrees:

(a) To maintain in the Department an Extension Service which, under the direction of the Secretary, (1) shall be charged with the administration of the Smith-Lever Act, as amended, and other Acts supporting cooperative extension work insofar as such administration is vested in the Department; (2) shall have primary responsibility for and leadership in all educational programs under the jurisdiction of the Department, except the graduate school; (3) shall be responsible for coordination of all educational phases of other programs of the Department, except the graduate school; and (4) shall act as the liason between the USDA and officials of the Land-Grant Colleges and Universities on all matters relating to cooperative extension work in agriculture and home economics and educational activities relating thereto.

(b) To conduct through (1862 Land-Grant Institution) all extension work in agriculture, uses of solar energy with respect to agriculture, home economics and subjects relating thereto authorized by Congress to be carried on within the State except those activities which by mutual agreement it is determined can most appropriately and effectively be carried out directly by the Department.

III. The (1862 Land-Grant Institution) and the United States Department of Agriculture mutually agree:

(a) That, subject to the approval of the President of the (1862 Land-Grant Institution) and the Secretary of Agriculture, or their duly appointed representatives, all cooperative extension work in agriculture and home economics in the State of _____, involving the use of Federal funds shall be planned under the joint supervision of the Director of (State Cooperative Extension Service) of _____, and the Administrator of the Extension Service;

and that approved plans for such cooperative extension work in the State of _____ shall be carried out through the (State Cooperative Extension Service) of _____ in accordance with the terms of the single project agreement.

(b) That all State and county personnel appointed by the Department as cooperative agents for extension work in agriculture and home economics in the State of _____ shall be joint representatives of the (1862 Land-Grant Institution) and the Department unless otherwise expressly provided in the project agreement.

(c) That the cooperation between the (1862 Land-Grant Institution) and the USDA shall be plainly set forth in all publications or other printed matter issued and used in connection with said cooperative extension work by either the (1862 Land-Grant Institution) or the Department.

(d) That plans of work for the use of Smith-Lever and other Federal funds in support of cooperative extension work shall be made by the Cooperative Extension Service of the State of _____ and shall be subject to the approval of the Secretary of Agriculture in accordance with the terms of the Smith-Lever Act, as amended, or other applicable laws, and when so approved shall be carried out by the (State Cooperative Extension Service) of the said State of _____.

IV. The (1862 Land-Grant Institution) and the United States Department of Agriculture further mutually agree:

(a) That the Department shall make final determination on any proposed supplementary memoranda of understanding or similar documents, including those with other agencies, affecting the conduct of cooperative extension work only after consultation with appropriate designated representatives of the Land-Grant Colleges and Universities.

(b) That the (1862 Land-Grant Institution) will make arrangements affecting the conduct of cooperative extension work with agencies of the Department, or with other Federal agencies, only through the Administrator of the Extension Service, or in accordance with an existing general agreement which has been approved by the Administrator.

(c) That all memoranda and similar documents hereafter executed affecting cooperative extension work, whether between agencies of the Department or between State Cooperative Extension Services and other agencies or departments of the Federal Government, shall be within the framework of, and consistent with the intent and purpose of, this Memorandum of Understanding.

(d) That all memoranda and agreements affecting policies in cooperative extension work shall be reviewed periodically by appropriately designated representatives of the Land-Grant Colleges and Universities and the Secretary of Agriculture for the purpose of determining whether modification is necessary or desirable to meet more effectively current developments and program needs.

V. This memorandum shall effect when it is approved by the
_____ of the _____ (1862 Land-Grant Institu-
tion) and the Secretary of Agriculture of the United States, and shall
remain in force until it is expressly abrogated in writing by either one of
the signers or his successor in office. The agreement executed
_____, shall be deemed abrogated upon the effective date
hereof.

(LAND-GRANT INSTITUTION)
_____

_____   By
_____
Date

                                    UNITED STATES DEPARTMENT
                                    OF AGRICULTURE

_____   By
_____
Date   Secretary

Memorandum of Understanding Between (1890 Institution or Tuskegee University) and the United States Department of Agriculture on Extension Work in Agriculture, Natural Resources, and 4-H Youth Development

Whereas, Section 1444 of Public Law 95-113, Food and Agriculture Act of 1977 (hereinafter referred to as Section 1444), authorizes appropriations to the U.S. Department of Agriculture (USDA) to support continuing agricultural and forestry extension at the colleges eligible to receive funds under the Act of August 30, 1890 (7 U.S.C. 321 through 326 and 328), including the Tuskegee University (hereinafter referred to as eligible institutions); and

Whereas, Section 1444 requires that a single, comprehensive program of Extension be developed for each State where an eligible institution is located;

Now, therefore, in order to provide for the effective administration of a single, comprehensive State Extension Program to meet the needs of the citizens of the State of _____, the President of the (eligible institution) acting subject to the approval of the Board of _____ of the said Institution (hereinafter referred to as Institution) and the Secretary of Agriculture of the United States hereby agree as follows:

I. The Institution agrees:
   (a) To maintain a definite and distinct administrative office for the management and conduct of all Extension work, which shall be under the direction of the Administrative Head of Extension whose selection is subject to the approval of USDA;
   (b) To administer through such office any and all funds the institution now has or may hereinafter receive for Extension work regardless of whether such funds are from appropriations made by Congress or from other sources;
   (c) To work with the (1862 Land-Grant Institution) to mutually develop a single, comprehensive Extension program for the State of _____ that, among other things, outlines the division of responsibilities and areas of cooperation between the Institutions;
   (d) To work with the (1862 Land-Grant Institution) to mutually develop detailed plans of work for the conduct of Extension activities in the State of _____; and
   (e) To conduct Extension activities and account for the use of Federal funds in accordance with such policy guidelines and conditions as may be promulgated by USDA.

II. The United States Department of Agriculture agrees:
   (a) To maintain an administrative unit within the Department which, under the direction of the Secretary, shall:
      1. Administer all Extension programs under the jurisdiction of USDA;
      2. Coordinate the Extension phases of all other programs under the jurisdiction of USDA; and
      3. Act as liaison between USDA and the eligible institutions on all matters relating to Extension work in Agriculture, Natural Resources, Food and Nutrition, Family Education, Rural Development, and 4-H Youth Development.

III. The Institution and USDA mutually agree:
   (a) That all Extension work involving the use of Federal funds shall be a part of a single, comprehensive State program of Extension and a plan of work, which shall be jointly planned by the Administrative Head for Extension of the Institution and the State Director of Extension at (1862 Institution) subject to the coordination and approval of the Administrator of Extension Service and that the approved program shall be carried out by the Institution in accordance with the terms of any agreement between the Institution and USDA setting forth project work areas and administrative requirements.
   (b) That the Institution shall be primarily responsible for the selection and performance of the Extension projects to be carried out by the Institution with Section 1444 funds as a part of the approved Extension program of the State.
   (c) That the cooperation between the Institution and USDA shall be plainly set forth in all publications or other printed matter issued in connection with the conduct of Extension work by the Institution or USDA.
   (d) That USDA shall not enter into any agreements with other parties affecting the conduct of Extension work by the Institution without first consulting with the Administrative Head for Extension of the Institution.
   (e) That all State and county personnel appointed by the Department as cooperative staff members for Extension work in the State shall be joint representatives of the Institution and USDA, unless otherwise expressly provided in writing.
   (f) That the Institution will make arrangements with Federal agencies affecting the conduct of Extension work only through the Administrator of Extension Service or in accordance with an existing agreement approved by the Administrator.
   (g) That all agreements hereafter executed by either party, which affect the conduct of Extension work, shall be within the framework of and consistent with the intent and purpose of this Memorandum of Understanding.

(h) That all memoranda and agreements affecting policies in Extension work shall be reviewed periodically by appropriately designated representatives of the eligible institutions and the Secretary of Agriculture for the purpose of determining whether modification is necessary or desirable to meet current developments and program needs more effectively.

(i) This Memorandum of Understanding shall take effect when it is signed by the President of the Institution and the Secretary of Agriculture, and shall remain in force until it is expressly abrogated in writing by either one of the signers or his or her successor in office.

(LAND-GRANT INSTITUTION)

_____

By _____

Date

UNITED STATES DEPARTMENT OF AGRICULTURE

_____

By _____

Date   Secretary

Project Agreement Between Extension Service— USDA and Cooperative Extension Service, State of

I. AUTHORITY

Include reference to Smith-Lever Act, as amended, Public Law 95-113, memorandum of understanding; also, State enabling laws and county-State agreements.

II. ORGANIZATION

Describes how the State Cooperative Extension Service is organized to meet its program objectives including organizational relationships with State and county governments. Include description of Cooperative Extension's position within the University including relationships with departments within the College of Agriculture and all other colleges, the unit responsible for general Extension activities, and others.

III. PROJECT WORK AREAS

Set forth the established areas of work such as:
- Agriculture and Natural Resources
- Community Resource Development
- 4-H and Youth Development
- Home Economics and Human Nutrition

IV. ADMINISTRATIVE PROCEDURES (The following are suggested standard provisions)
  a. The State Cooperative Extension Director will provide the Administrator, ES
    (1) A statistical plan of work and statistical report of work accomplished.
    (2) An annual budget and revision thereof if necessary showing the total financial support to carry out the Cooperative Extension program in the State.
    (3) Prior to December 1 (for 1890 Land-Grant Institutions) or April 1 (for 1862 Land-Grant Institutions) of each year a financial report of all expenditures incurred in the support of the State Cooperative Extension program for the previous fiscal year on forms provided by the Administrator, Extension Service.
  b. Equipment acquired, as well as the products resulting from expenditures of Federal and offset funds, or proceeds from the disposition of such equipment or products, will remain the property of the State Extension Service for use in furtherance of Cooperative Extension Work.

   c. Personnel employed under this agreement will be –

     (1) Administratively responsible to the Director of Cooperative Extension or his designated representative.

     (2) Subject to the leave regulations of the State Cooperative Extension Service.

     (3) Subject to Equal Employment Opportunity programs as required by 7 CFR 18 which prohibit discrimination on the basis of race, color, national origin, sex, or religion.

   d. Programs under this agreement will be carried out in compliance with Title VI of the Civil Rights Act of 1964 which prohibits exclusion of persons from participation because of race, color or national origin.

   e. When information, responsibility and other services are shared with research, teaching, or other divisions of the University, cost will be shared consistent with services performed for the Cooperative Extension Service. The Director of Extension shall be responsible for conducting periodic appraisals of operations to determine whether costs paid from Extension appropriations are adequate or excessive in relation to services and materials provided the Extension Service.

   f. This agreement will be reviewed at least every five years and revised whenever all or any part of the provisions become inoperative, or when a change in program or operations requires additional provisions or changes in existing programs.

Effective Date _____

APPROVED   _____   _____
                     Director   Date

APPROVED   _____   _____
                     Administrator, Extension   Date
                     Service, USDA

Selected References

This list of suggested material for additional reading is a very small part of the extensive literature by and relating to the Cooperative Extension System. Its emphasis is on policy studies and histories published in the past twenty years, on references used in the preparation of this volume, and on writings by early leaders reflecting their thinking on the development of Extension. Insofar as possible, the actual authors of entries are listed, while other works are listed under the institutions sponsoring them.

General

Araji, A. A., R. J. Sim, and R. L. Gardner. "Returns to Agricultural Research and Extension Programs: An 'Ex-Ante' Approach." *American Journal of Agricultural Economics* 60 (December 1978): 964–68.

Arnold, Eleanor, ed. *Voices of American Homemakers.* National Extension Homemakers Council, 1985, 295 pp.

Baker, Gladys L. *The County Agent.* Chicago: University of Chicago Press, 1939, 226 pp.

_____. "The County Agent Revisited." In *Southwestern Agriculture: Pre-Columbian to Modern,* ed. Henry C. Dethloff and Irvin M. May, Jr., 126–44. College Station: Texas A & M Univ. Press, 1982.

Baker, Gladys L., Wayne D. Rasmussen, Vivian Wiser, and Jane M. Porter. *Century of Service: The First 100 Years of the United States Department of Agriculture.* Washington: USDA, 1963, 560 pp.

Bay, Edwin. *The History of the National Association of County Agricultural Agents, 1915–1960.* Springfield, Mo.: National Association of County Agricultural Agents. 1961, 184 pp.

Bay, Ovid. "Cooperative Extension Service: Born from a Need of People." *Extension Service Review* 47 (May-June 1976): 3–27.

Bennett, Claude. "Improving Coordination of Extension and Research Through Use of Interdependency Models." In *Foundations and Changing Practices in Extension,* ed. Donald J. Blackburn, Chap. 14. Ontario: Univ. of Guelph, 1988.

Benoir, Daniel, James Q. Harriman, and Michael Baxter. *Agricultural Extension: The Training and Visit System.* 3d ed. Washington: World Bank, 1984, 85 pp.

Bliss, R. K., ed. *The Spirit and Philosophy of Extension Work.* Washington: USDA Graduate School, 1952, 393 pp.

Block, William J. *The Separation of the Farm Bureau and the Extension Service.* Urbana: Univ. of Illinois Press, 1960, 304 pp.

Bonnen, James T. "Improving Information on Agriculture and Rural Life." *American Journal of Agricultural Economics* 57 (December 1975): 753–64.

Brown, Thomas G. "Changing Delivery Systems for Agricultural Extension: The Extension Teacher—Changing Roles and Competencies." *American Journal of Agricultural Economics* 63 (December 1981): 859–62.

Brunner, Edmund deS., and E. Hsin Pao Yang. *Rural America and the Extension Service.* New York: Teachers College, Columbia Univ., 1949, 210 pp.

Brunner, Edmund deS., Irwin T. Sanders, and Douglas Ensminger, eds. *Farmers of the World: The Development of Agricultural Extension.* New York: Columbia Univ. Press, 1945, 208 pp.

Campbell, J. Phil. "Action Programs in Education." *Agricultural History* 15 (April 1941): 68–71.

Campbell, Thomas M. *The Movable School Goes to the Negro Farmer.* Tuskegee: Tuskegee Institute Press, 1936, 170 pp.

Cole, Jacquelyn M., and Maurice F. Cole. *Advisory Councils: A Theoretical and Practical Guide for Program Planners.* Englewood Cliffs: Prentice-Hall, 1983, 207 pp.

Cooperative Extension System. *Revitalizing Rural America.* Madison: University of Wisconsin Extension, 1986, 28 pp.

Cooperative Extension System, National 4-H Panel. *4-H Future Focus: 1986–1996.* Columbus: Ohio Cooperative Extension Service, 1986, 12 pp.

Crosby, Earl W. "Limited Success Against Long Odds: The Black County Agent." *Agricultural History* 57 (July 1983): 277–88.

———. "The Roots of Black Agricultural Extension Work." *Historian* 39 (February 1977): 228–47.

———. "The Struggle for Existence: The Institutionalization of the Black County Agent System." *Agricultural History* 60 (Spring 1986): 123–36.

Diesslin, Howard G. "The Computer: Extension's Delivery System of the Future." *American Journal of Agricultural Economics* 63 (December 1981): 863–67.

Dillman, Don A. "Cooperative Extension at the Beginning of the 21st Century." *Rural Sociologist* 6 (April 1986): 102–19.

Eddy, Edward Danforth. *Colleges for Our Land and Time: The Land-Grant Idea in American Education.* New York: Harper & Row, 1957, 328 pp.

Ellsworth, Clayton S. "Theodore Roosevelt's Country Life Commission." *Agri-*

cultural History 34 (October 1960): 155–72.

Extension Committee on Organization and Policy, 4-H - Youth Subcommittee. *4-H in the 70's.* Washington: Extension Service, USDA, 1971, n.p.

Extension Committee on Organization and Policy, Futures Task Force. *Extension in Transition: Bridging the Gap Between Vision and Reality.* Blacksburg: Virginia Cooperative Extension Service, 1987, 38 pp.

Extension Committee on Organization and Policy, Task Force on 4-H in Century III. *4-H in Century III.* East Lansing: Michigan State Univ., 1976, 12 pp.

Feller, Irwin, et al. *Agricultural Technology Delivery System.* 5 vols. University Park: Pennsylvania State Univ., 1984.

Fisher, Dennis U., ed. *Manpower Programs, A Survey of Theory and Extension Opportunities.* Washington: Extension Committee on Organization and Policy, 1983, 111 pp.

Graham, A. B. "Boys' and Girls' Agricultural Clubs." *Agricultural History* 15 (April 1941): 65–68.

Headley, J. C. "Soil Conservation and Cooperative Extension." *Agricultural History* 59 (April 1985): 290–306.

Hightower, Jim. *Hard Tomatoes, Hard Times.* Washington: Agribusiness Accountability Project, 1972, 308 pp.

Hildebrand, Peter E., ed. *Perspectives on Farming Systems Research and Extension.* Boulder, Colo.: L. Reinner, 1986, 167 pp.

Hildreth, R. J., and Walter J. Armbruster. "Extension Program Delivery— Past, Present, and Future: An Overview." *American Journal of Agricultural Economics* 63 (December 1981): 853–58.

Huffman, Wallace E. "Assessing Returns to Agricultural Extension." *American Journal of Agricultural Economics* 60 (December 1978): 969–75.

Huffman, Wallace E., and Mark McNulty. "Endogenous Local Public Extension Policy," *American Journal of Agricultural Economics* 67 (November 1985): 761–68.

Hussey, G. Art. *Electronic Technology: Impact on Extension Delivery Systems.* University Park: Pennsylvania State Univ., 1985, 31 pp.

Infanger, Craig L., Lynn W. Robbins, and David L. Debertin. "Interfacing Research and Extension in Information Delivery Systems." *American Journal of Agricultural Economics* 63 (December 1978): 915–20.

Jensen, Joan M. "Crossing Ethnic Barriers in the Southwest: Women's Agricultural Extension Education, 1914–1940." *Agricultural History* 60 (Spring 1986): 169–81.

Johnson, Glenn L. "Agro-Ethics-Extension, Research and Teaching." *Southern Journal of Agricultural Economics* 14 (July 1982): 1–10.

Jones, C. Clyde. "The Burlington Railroad and Agricultural Policy in the 1920's." *Agricultural History* (October 1957): 67–74.

Jones, Gwyn E., ed. *Investing in Rural Extension: Strategies and Goals.* London: Elsevier Applied Science Publishers, 1986, 297 pp.

Journal of Extension. Madison: Extension Journal. 1963–present.

Kammlade, W. G. "Fifty Years of Progress in Livestock Extension Teaching." *Journal of Animal Science* 17 (November 1958): 1088–1100.

Kelsey, Lincoln David. *Cooperative Extension Work.* 3d ed. Ithaca: Comstock, 1963, 490 pp.

Knapp, Seaman A. "The Farmers' Cooperative Demonstration Work." In USDA *Yearbook of Agriculture,* 1909, pp. 153–70. Washington: Government Printing Office. 1909.

Korshing, Peter F., and Judith Gildner, eds. *Interdependencies of Agriculture and Rural Communities in the Twenty-first Century: The North Central Region.* Ames: North Central Regional Center for Rural Development, Iowa State Univ., 1986, 237 pp.

Lacy, William B., Kenneth E. Pigg, and Lawrence Busch. "Clients, Colleagues, and Colleges: Perceived Influences on Extension Agents." *Rural Sociology* 45 (October 1980): 469–82.

Ladewig, Howard, and John K. Thomas. *Assessing the Impact of 4-H on Former Members.* College Station: Texas A & M Univ. System, 1987, 145 pp.

Lenzi, Raymond C., and Bruce H. Murray, eds. *Downtown Revitalization and Small City Development.* Ames: North Central Regional Center for Rural Development, Iowa State Univ., 1987, 280 pp.

Lifer, Charles W., and Gary W. Gerhard. *A Taxonomy of the Knowledge Base for 4-H Youth Development.* Columbus: Ohio Cooperative Extension Service, 1987, 228 pp.

Lifer, Charles W., and Roger A. Rennekamp. *Strengthening the 4-H Professional Knowledge Base.* Columbus: Ohio Cooperative Extension Service, 1987, n.p.

Lipman-Blumen, Jean, and Susan Schram. *The Paradox of Success: The Impact of Priority Setting in Agricultural Research and Extension.* Washington: USDA, Science and Education, 1984, n.p.

Loomis, Charles P., and G. A. Beegle, eds. *Rural Social Systems and Adult Education.* East Lansing: Michigan State College Press, 1953, 392 pp.

Lord, Russell. *The Agrarian Revival: A Study of Agricultural Extension.* New York: American Association for Adult Education, 1939, 236 pp.

McDowell, George R. "The Political Economy of Extension Program Design: Institutional Maintenance Issues in the Organization and Delivery of Extension Programs." *American Journal of Agricultural Economics* 67 (November 1985): 717–25.

Miller, Paul A. *The Cooperative Extension Service: Paradoxical Servant.* Syracuse: Syracuse Univ., 1973, 28 pp.

———. *Cooperative Extension: An Historical Perspective.* Rochester: Rochester Institute of Technology, 1976, 21 pp.

Mumford, Frederick B. *The Land Grant College Movement.* Columbia: Missouri Agricultural Experiment Station Bulletin 419, 1940, 140 pp.

Nelson, Donald L. *Silver Threads Among the Gold: The First 25 Years of Community and Rural Development Programs.* Washington: USDA, Science and Education, 1980, 34 pp.

North Carolina Cooperative Extension Service. *Extension's 4-H: Toward the '90s.* Washington: USDA Extension Service, n.d., 15 pp.

Office of Technology Assessment. *Technology, Public Policy, and the Changing Structure of American Agriculture.* Washington: Government Printing Office, 1986, 374 pp.

Ordon, David, and Steven T. Buccola. "An Evaluation of Cooperative Extension Small Farm Programs in the Southern United States." *American*

Journal of Agricultural Economics 62 (May 1980): 218–23.

Peterson, Willis L. "The Allocation of Research, Teaching, and Extension Personnel in U. S. Colleges of Agriculture." *American Journal of Agricultural Economics* 51 (February 1969): 41–56.

Prawl, Warren, Roger Medlin, and John Gross. *Adult and Continuing Education Through the Cooperative Extension Service*. Columbia: Univ. of Missouri, 1984, 279 pp.

Rasmussen, Wayne D. "90 Years of Rural Development Programs." *Rural Development Perspectives* 2 (October 1985): 2–9.

Rasmussen, Wayne D., ed. *Agriculture in the United States: A Documentary History*. 4 vols. New York: Random House, 1975.

Rasmussen, Wayne D., and Gladys L. Baker. *The Department of Agriculture*. New York: Praeger, 1972, 257 pp.

Raudabaugh, J. Neil. *Extension Service USDA Interaction from 1914 to 1977 with National Issues and with State Extension Services*. Washington: USDA Extension Service, 1978, n.p.

Raudabaugh, J. Neil, and Torlief S. Aasheim. *Extension Program Development*. Washington: USDA Extension Service, 1979, n.p.

Reeder, R. L. *The People and the Profession*. Epsilon Sigma Phi, 1979, 128 pp.

Rodgers, Ava D., and Bonnie Tanner, eds. *National Extension Homemakers Study*. Washington: USDA, Extension Service, 1981, 60 pp.

Sanders, H. C., ed. *Cooperative Extension Service*. Englewood Cliffs: Prentice-Hall, 1966, 436 pp.

Schaub, I. O. *Agricultural Extension Work: A Brief History*. Raleigh: North Carolina Agricultural Extension Service Circular 377, 1953, 39 pp.

Schor, Joel. "The Black Presence in the U. S. Cooperative Extension Service Since 1945: An American Quest for Service and Equity." *Agricultural History* 60 (Spring 1986): 137–53.

Scott, Roy V. "American Railroads and Agricultural Extension, 1900–1914: A Study in Railway Developmental Techniques." *Business History Review* 39 (January 1965): 74–98.

_____. *The Reluctant Farmer: The Rise of Agricultural Extension to 1914*. Urbana: Univ. of Illinois Press, 1970, 362 pp.

_____. *Railroad Development Programs in the Twentieth Century*. Ames: Iowa State Univ. Press, 1985, 231 pp.

Simons, Lloyd R. *Early Development of Cooperative Extension Work in Agriculture and Home Economics in the United States*. Ithaca: New York State College of Agriculture, 1962, 63 pp.

Smith, Clarence B., and Meredith C. Wilson. *The Agricultural Extension System of the United States*. New York: Wiley, 1930, 402 pp.

True, Alfred C. *A History of Extension Work in the United States, 1785–1923*. Washington: USDA Miscellaneous Publication 15, 1928, 220 pp.

United States Congress. House of Representatives. Committee on Agriculture. Subcommittee on Department Operations, Research, and Foreign Agriculture. *Review of the Report "Extension in the Eighties."* 98th Cong., 1st sess., June 1983. 85 pp.

_____. Committee on Appropriations. *Department of Agriculture Appropriations . . . Hearings. . . .* 1921–1988. Washington: Government Printing Office, 1921–1988.

United States Department of Agriculture, Extension Service. *Challenge and Change: A Blueprint for the Future—Extension Service, USDA.* Washington: USDA Extension Service, 1983, 35 pp.

————. *Community and Rural Development: A Report on the National Extension Community and Rural Development Program Evaluation.* Washington: USDA Extension Service, 1980, 91 pp.

————. West Virginia Cooperative Extension Service and Missouri Cooperative Extension Service. *Strengthening the Research Base for Extension Programs: A National Study of Attitudes and Perceptions, Final Report.* Washington: USDA Extension Service, 1985, 217 pp.

United States Department of Agriculture, Science and Education Administration. *A Comprehensive National Plan for New Initiatives in Home Economics Research, Extension, and Higher Education.* Washington: USDA Miscellaneous Publication 1405, 1981, 180 pp.

United States Department of Agriculture and Association of Land-Grant Colleges and Universities. *Joint Committee Report on Extension Programs, Policies and Goals.* Washington: U. S. Government Printing Office, 1948, 72 pp.

United States Department of Agriculture and National Association of State Universities and Land Grant Colleges Committee on the Future of Cooperative Extension. *Extension in the '80s.* Madison: Cooperative Extension Service, Univ. of Wisconsin, 1983, 28 pp.

United States Department of Agriculture and National Association of State Universities and Land Grant Colleges Study Committee on Cooperative Extension. *A People and a Spirit.* Fort Collins: Colorado State Univ., 1968, 95 pp.

VandeBerg, Gale L. *The Cooperative Extension Service in Transition: A Report of the National Extension Committee on Organization and Policy.* Madison: Univ. of Wisconsin-Extension, 1979, 60 pp.

Veeder, James T. *From A Dream to Reality: A History of the National 4-H Service Committee, 1921–1971.* Chicago: National 4-H Service Committee, 1972, 56 pp.

Vines, C. Austin, and Marvin A. Anderson, eds. *Heritage Horizons: Extension's Commitment to People.* Madison: Journal of Extension, 1976, 236 pp.

Ward, Florence E. *Home Demonstration Work Under the Smith-Lever Act, 1914–1924.* Washington: USDA Circular 43, 1929, 35 pp.

Warner, Paul D., and James A. Christenson. *The Cooperative Extension Service: A National Assessment.* Boulder: Westview Press, 1984, 195 pp.

Wessel, Thomas, and Marilyn Wessel. *4-H: An American Idea 1900–1980.* Chevy Chase, Md.: National 4-H Council, 1982, 352 pp.

Wilkerson, Doxey A. *Agricultural Extension Services Among Negroes in the South.* Washington: Conference of Presidents of Negro Land Grant Colleges, 1942, 59 pp.

Williams, Donald B. "Production Economics, Farm Management, and Extension." *American Journal of Agricultural Economics* 51 (February 1969): 57–86.

Williams, Thomas T., ed. *Ushering in the Twenty-First Century: Emphasis on the Rural South.* Tuskegee: Tuskegee Univ., 1987, 184 pp.

Biographies

Bailey, Joseph C. *Seaman A. Knapp, Schoolmaster of American Agriculture.* New York: Columbia Univ. Press, 1945, 307 pp.

Cline, Rodney. *The Life and Work of Seaman A. Knapp.* Nashville: Peabody College for Teachers, 1936, 110 pp.

Ferguson, Clarence M. *Reflections of an Extension Executive.* Madison: National Agricultural Extension Center for Advanced Study, 1964, 132 pp.

Howard, Robert P. *James R. Howard and the Farm Bureau Federation.* Ames: Iowa State Univ. Press, 1983, 248 pp.

Jones, Allen W. "The South's First Black Farm Agents." *Agricultural History* 50 (October 1976): 636–44.

_____. "Thomas M. Campbell: Black Agricultural Leader of the New South." *Agricultural History* (January 1979): 42–59.

McCormick, Virginia E., and Robert W. McCormick. *A. B. Graham: Country Schoolmaster and Extension Pioneer.* Worthington, Ohio: Cottonwood, 1984, 216 pp.

Rodgers, Andrew Denny, III. *Liberty Hyde Bailey: A Story of American Plant Sciences.* Princeton: Princeton Univ. Press, 1949, 506 pp.

Thompson, D. O., and W. H. Glover. "A Pioneer Adventure in Agricultural Extension: A Contribution from the Wisconsin Cut-Over." *Agricultural History* 22 (April 1948): 124–28. [Fred Rietbrook]

Weinland, Henry A. *Now the Harvest: Memories of a County Agricultural Agent.* New York: Exposition Press, 1957, 96 pp.

State Histories

Abraham, Roland H. *Helping People Help Themselves: Agricultural Extension in Minnesota, 1879–1979.* Minneapolis: Minnesota Extension Service, 1986, 268 pp.

Alstad, George, and Jan Everly Friedson. *The Cooperative Extension Service in Hawaii, 1928 to 1981.* Manoa: Hawaii Institute of Tropical Agriculture and Human Resources, 1982, 28 pp.

Ballard, Frank L. *The Oregon State University Federal Cooperative Extension Service: 1911–1961.* Corvallis: Oregon State Univ. Extension Service, 1961, 543 pp.

Barrett, Irvy. *Seedtime and Harvest: The Story of Alabama Home Economics, 1911–1986.* Auburn: Alabama Cooperative Extension Service, 1986, 41 pp.

Bender, Lyle M. *The Rural Economy of South Dakota: An Area Analysis Aimed at Extension Program Development.* Brookings: South Dakota Extension Service, 1956, 464 pp.

Bliss, Ralph K. *History of Cooperative Agriculture and Home Economics Extension in Iowa: The First Fifty Years.* Ames: Iowa State Univ., 1960, 247 pp.

Bond, H. M. *Ham and Eggs: A History of the Fort Valley Ham and Egg Show.* Athens: Georgia Agricultural Extension Service Bulletin 513, 1944, 15 pp.

Boyd, George W., and Burton W. Marston. *The Wyoming Agricultural Extension Service and the People Who Made It.* Laramie: Wyoming Agricultural Extension Service, 1965, 225 pp.

Bryant, T. R. *Historical Sketch of Extension Work in Kentucky.* Lexington: Kentucky Cooperative Extension Service, 1939, 22 pp.

Burlingame, Merrill G., and Edward J. Bell, Jr. *The Montana Cooperative Extension Service: A History 1893–1974.* Bozeman: Montana State Univ., 1984, 365 pp.

Carpenter, William L. *Let the People Know: A History of Agricultural Information Activities and the Department of Agricultural Information at North Carolina State University, 1879–1978.* Raleigh: North Carolina Agricultural Extension Service, 1978, 171 pp.

Clark, James W., Jr. *Clover All Over: North Carolina 4-H in Action.* Raleigh: North Carolina State Univ., 1984, 299 pp.

Cooper, J. Francis, comp. *Dimensions in History: Recounting Florida Cooperative Extension Service Progress, 1909–76.* Gainesville: Epsilon Sigma Phi, Univ. of Florida, 1976, 224 pp.

Cotton, Barbara R. *The Lamplighters: Black Farm and Home Demonstration Agents in Florida, 1915–1965.* Tallahassee: Florida A & M Univ., 1982, 127 pp.

Davidson, Robert. *Highlights of the Vermont Extension Service from the Beginning.* Burlington: Villanti Press, 1982, 78 pp.

Davis, Charles S. "Early Agricultural Demonstration Work In Alabama." *Alabama Review* 2 (July 1949): 176–88.

Eastwood, Winifred. *60 Years of Cooperative Extension Service in Massachusetts.* Amherst: Massachusetts Cooperative Extension Service, 1973, 178 pp.

Georgia Cooperative Extension Service. *Meeting the Needs.* Athens: Georgia Cooperative Extension Service, 1983, 32 pp.

Gross, John, Warren Prawl, and Roger Medlin. *Adult Continuing Education Through the Cooperative Extension Service.* Columbia: Univ. of Missouri Press, 1984, 280 pp.

Hill, Kate Adele. *Home Demonstration Work in Texas.* San Antonio: Naylor, 1958, 208 pp.

Hutchinson, John E. "The Texas Agricultural Extension Service: A Historical Overview." In *Southwestern Agriculture: Pre-Columbian to Modern,* ed. Henry C. Dethloff and Irvin May, Jr., 123–35. College Station: Texas A & M Univ. Press, 1982.

Isern, Thomas D. "Between Science and Folklore: Images of Extension Work from the Flint Hills of Kansas." *Agricultural History* 60 (Spring 1986): 267–86.

James, Felix. "The Tuskegee Institute Movable School, 1906–1923." *Agricultural History* 45 (July 1971): 201–09.

Janey, Jane P., ed. *College of the Fields: Some Highlights of the Virginia Cooperative Extension Service, 1914–1980.* Blacksburg: Alpha Gamma Chapter of Epsilon Sigma Phi, 1987, 300 pp.

Kropp, Simon F. *That All May Learn: 1888–1964.* Las Cruces: New Mexico State Univ., 1972, 401 pp.

Larsen, R. Paul. *We're Working for You.* Logan: Utah State Univ., 1987, 24 pp.

Long, Howard Rusk. *Swat That Rooster.* Columbia: Univ. of Missouri Press, 1988, 75 pp.

McIntyre, E. R. *Fifty Years of Cooperative Extension in Wisconsin, 1912–1962.* Madison: Univ. of Wisconsin, 1962, 286 pp.

Morgan, Barton. *A History of the Extension Service of Iowa State College.* Ames: Collegiate Press, 1934, 107 pp.

Morgan, Thomas W. *The First 50 Years of Smith-Lever Extension.* Clemson: Clemson Univ., 1964, 24 pp.

Mosely, Lee H., et al. *History of Mississippi Cooperative Extension Service.* Nd. Mississippi State University: Mississippi Cooperative Extension Service, 231 pp. [draft]

Olstrom, Einar and Miller, Howard. *Plus Two Score: The Cooperative Extension Service in Michigan, 1940 to 1980.* East Lansing: Michigan State Univ. Cooperative Extension Service, 1984, 303 pp.

Prawl, Warren L., and Roger C. Medlin. *Kansans' Right to Know: 108 Years of Extension Education.* Manhattan: Cooperative Extension Service, Kansas State Univ., 1976, 29 pp.

Riggins, Dorothy P. *Ushering in the Eighties: Cooperative Extension Program, Tuskegee Institute, Alabama.* Tuskegee Institute, 1981, 49 pp.

Rogers, R. R. *Development of the University of Missouri Extension Division.* Columbia: Missouri Agricultural Experiment Station Special Report 29, 1963, 28 pp.

Rummell, Leo L. *One Hundred Years of Better Living through Education and Research in Agriculture and Home Economics.* Columbus: Ohio State Univ. Agricultural Extension Service Bulletin 422, 1962, 67 pp.

Scheuring, Ann Foley. *A Sustaining Comradeship: The Story of University of California Cooperative Extension, 1913–1988.* Berkeley: Univ. of California, 1988, 64 pp.

Schwieder, Dorothy. "Education and Change in the Lives of Iowa Farm Women, 1900–1940." *Agricultural History* 60 (Spring 1986): 200–215.

Scott, Roy V. "Railroads and Farmers: Educational Trains in Missouri, 1902–1914." *Agricultural History* 36 (January 1962): 3–15.

Simons, Lloyd R. *Wartime and Other Emergency Activities of the New York State Extension Service.* Ithaca: Cornell Extension Bulletin 1015, 1958, 100 pp.

Sims, Almon J. *A History of Extension Work in Tennessee: Twenty-five Years of Service to Rural Life, 1914–1939.* Knoxville: Tennessee Extension Service Publication 223, 1939, 44 pp.

Smith, Ruby Green. *The People's Colleges: A History of the New York State Extension Service in Cornell University and the State, 1876–1948.* Ithaca: Cornell Univ. Press, 1949, 593 pp.

Teagarden, Earl H., comp. *History of the Kansas Extension Service from 1868 to 1964.* 2 vols. Manhattan: Kansas State Univ., n.d.

Thompson, David O. *Fifty Years of Cooperative Extension Service in Indiana.* West Lafayette: Agricultural Extension Service, 1962, 159 pp.

Turner, Russell M. *The First 45 Years: A History of Cooperative Extension in Washington State.* Pullman: Washington Extension Miscellaneous Publication 55, 1961, 138 pp.

Vale, Stanley. *Hired Hands and Volunteers.* Fargo: North Dakota State Univ. Extension Service, 1988, 324 pp.

Vanlandingham, Eugenia P., et al. *Shared Ideals: The First Fifty Years of Epsilon Sigma Phi in North Carolina.* Raleigh: North Carolina Agricultural Extension Service, 1979, 84 pp.

Waller, Ingrid Nelson. *Where There Is Vision: 1880–1955.* New Brunswick: Rutgers Univ. Press, 1955, 284 pp.

Wheeler, John T. *Two Hundred Years of Agricultural Extension in Georgia.* Danville: Interstate, 1948, 397 pp.

White, Grace Witter. *Cooperative Extension in Wisconsin: 1962–1982.* Dubuque: Kendall Hunt, 1985, 396 pp.

Williamson, Frederick W. *Origin and Growth of Agricultural Extension in Louisiana, 1860–1948.* Baton Rouge: Louisiana Agricultural Extension Service, 1951, 345 pp.

Zettle, Frank. *Cooperative Extension: How It Began in Pennsylvania.* University Park: Pennsylvania State Univ., 1986, 149 pp.

Index